Understanding Interpersonal Communication

Making Choices in Changing Times

Enhanced Second Edition

Richard West
Emerson College

Lynn H. Turner
Marquette University

WADSWORTH
CENGAGE Learning

Australia • Brazil • Japan • Korea • Mexico • Singapore • Spain • United Kingdom • United States

WADSWORTH
CENGAGE Learning

Understanding Interpersonal Communication: Making Choices in Changing Times, Enhanced Second Edition
Richard West and Lynn H. Turner

Publisher: Lyn Uhl

Executive Editor: Monica Eckman

Senior Development Editor: Greer Lleuad

Assistant Editor: Rebekah Matthews

Editorial Assistant: Colin Solan

Media Editor: Jessica Badiner

Marketing Manager: Bryant Chrzan

Marketing Assistant: Mary Anne Payumo

Content Project Manager: Jessica Rasile

Art Director: Linda Helcher

Senior Print Buyer: Betsy Donaghey

Production Service/Compositor: Lachina Publishing Services, Inc.

Text Designer: KeDesign

Cover Illustration: Tim Zeltner/i2i Art

For product information and technology assistance, contact us at **Cengage Learning Customer & Sales Support, 1-800-354-9706**

For permission to use material from this text or product, submit all requests online at **www.cengage.com/permissions.**
Further permissions questions can be e-mailed to **permissionrequest@cengage.com.**

ISBN-13: 978-0-495-90875-3
ISBN-10: 0-495-90875-4

Wadsworth
20 Channel Center Street
Boston, MA 02210
USA

Cengage Learning is a leading provider of customized learning solutions with office locations around the globe, including Singapore, the United Kingdom, Australia, Mexico, Brazil and Japan. Locate your local office at **international.cengage.com/region**

Cengage Learning products are represented in Canada by Nelson Education, Ltd.

For your course and learning solutions, visit **www.cengage.com.**

Purchase any of our products at your local college store or at our preferred online store **www.ichapters.com.**

Printed in the United States of America
4 5 6 7 8 13 12 11

Brief Contents

Contents

8 Sharing Personal Information 252

9 Communicating Conflict 292

10 Communicating in Close Relationships 326

11 Technology and Interpersonal Communication 366

Preface

The 2nd edition of *Understanding Interpersonal Communication* underscores our ongoing commitment to make research and theory in interpersonal communication more accessible to students. We have been grateful for the many emails and calls we have received from those who used the 1st edition of this text, expressing support for this fundamental belief. We wrote this text because we believe students should have the knowledge, skills, and motivation to communicate in multiple circumstances with a variety of different people. Today, more than ever, students are confronted with choices in communication. For instance, emerging technologies continually expand our choices—whether via email, with a text messenger, through a MySpace page, or writing a blog. To be able to navigate this increasingly complex communication environment effectively, students need a well-developed knowledge base for making informed choices and improving their skills.

We contend that when students enter their interpersonal communication classrooms, they bring with them many habits and beliefs about effective communication that they have acquired from their own experiences observing friends, families, and coworkers. In addition, we cannot ignore the influence that popular culture and the media have played in students' understanding of communication and human relationships. Nonetheless, students lack an understanding of the theory and research that animate and clarify these practices and beliefs. In other words, students simply rely too much on what they have seen and heard, with little understanding of theoretical explanations for communication processes and outcomes. Consequently, students frequently make communication choices from an insufficient knowledge base. Such decisions limit their potential, leaving them frustrated and dissatisfied.

It is our belief that a fundamental approach to learning about an interpersonal communication skill is to ground it in adequate theory and current knowledge about the skill. Although knowledge cannot completely guarantee that students are going to be happy with the outcome of every communication transac-

tion, it does provide them with necessary and important analytical skills. In sum, we believe that theory informs skills and skills refine theory. As such, in *Understanding Interpersonal Communication* we intentionally integrate a theory-skill framework throughout each chapter. In this text, we move toward eliminating the false dichotomy between theory and skills. Additionally, we strive to demystify and clarify the intersection of theory and practice. In doing so, we hope to break down misguided and preconceived negative images of theory. Using a conversational tone, our text integrates research and theory in an inviting and engaging manner.

In addition, our approach to skill development provides a discussion of interpersonal skills and the behavioral choices students can make in order to become more effective communicators. We avoid "telling" students how to apply interpersonal skills to various situations. Instead, we provide a list of skills pertaining to the theory students read about in the chapter so that they will be able to draw upon a sort of toolbox, or set of skills, that are specific and workable.

And finally, we understand that students come to the interpersonal communication course from a variety of life experiences. We worked, therefore, to make our writing clear, to avoid clichés and to use technical terms only when necessary to make a point, explaining their meanings as needed. We also made a conscious effort to use examples that reflect the diversity of interpersonal encounters. Thus, we include examples of interpersonal communication between teacher-student, physician-patient, painter-client, landlord-renter, politician-voter, clergy-layperson, retail clerk-customer, husband-wife, and friend-friend, among others. We have never felt that a book of this nature should be a venue to express unfounded personal value systems. Simultaneously, we do not honor just one way of looking at relationships, but rather embrace an expansive view of human behavior and interpersonal communication.

Understanding Interpersonal Communication appeals to a diverse student population, presents scholarship and skills in a readable manner, and contains pedagogical features that will not only sustain interest, but also make a difference in students' lives. The result of our efforts—this text—reflects our commitment to ensuring that students understand the importance of interpersonal communication in their own lives and in the lives of others.

Features of the Book

Our experience teaching this course over many years has prompted us to offer the following pedagogical approach and features. These features are intended first to appeal to students, then to help them better understand the concepts in each chapter and apply them in their own lives.

A Bridge between Theory and Skills

With a clear, inviting presentation of the intersection of theory and practice, *Understanding Interpersonal Communication* will empower your students with the knowledge they need to be skillful communicators in today's society.

In addition to **chapter goals** that provide students with a basic roadmap of the theory and skills that will be discussed in the chapter, each chapter begins with a **Case in Point** case study pertaining to an issue or topic in interpersonal communication discussed in the chapter. These cases are drawn from real-life situations identified by students in past interpersonal communication courses we have taught. For example, in Chapter 3, "Communication, Culture, and Identity," we begin with an example of a U.S. student who learns more about Mexican culture. In Chapter 6, "Effective Listening," we present a director of volunteers for a local political campaign whose listening skills are called into question by a supervisor. These case studies include people of diverse ages, backgrounds, and educational levels. Videotaped versions of many of these case studies and accompanying critical thinking questions are featured in the book's online resources. Additionally, **Case in Point Revisited** review questions appear throughout each chapter, tying the Case in Point case study to the concepts discussed in that chapter.

So that students can assess their own communication behaviors and attitudes, each chapter features a **Communication Assessment Test (CAT)** inventory. This feature provides students with communication instruments, such as a measure of communication

apprehension or a quiz that will help students sharpen their vocabulary. For example, in Chapter 2, "Communication, Perception, and the Self," we include a "self-monitoring scale" quiz that asks students to consider the extent to which they actively think about and control their public behaviors and actions. These types of assessments allow students to evaluate their communication skills and take personal responsibility for skill development. We have found that students are also able to create their own assessments once they have read and understood material. The CATs, then, can be used as an effective way for students to become empowered in their classes.

Each chapter ends with **Questions for Understanding**, review and discussion questions that allow students to check their understanding of the chapter material. At least one question per chapter pertains to the chapter-opening Case in Point feature. This question allows students to reconsider how the concepts in the case study can be approached after learning the material in the chapter. Students can answer these questions by working in small groups or on their own.

A Wealth of Choices

Once students have a strong base in theory and skills, they are then able to make informed choices in their interpersonal communication. Many of the features of this book highlight the types of choices available to students in today's changing and technologically advanced world.

To encourage students to think about the material in a personal way, each chapter includes a prompt to an online **Your Turn** journal activity. With this feature, each student is asked to think about a particular topic and write about it in a journal. For example, in Chapter 1, "Introduction to Interpersonal Communication," we ask students to write about the primary influences shaping their interpersonal communication. Our experiences show that journals are excellent outlets for students to share their perceptions and reactions in a way that is personal, reflective, and informative. The Your Turn activities are also featured in the book's student companion workbook.

The **Ethics & Choice** boxed feature appears in each chapter, raising ethical questions and allowing students to consider ethical implications of the key topics or concepts in each chapter. These boxes include examples of ethical dilemmas and critical-thinking questions that challenge students to apply the ethical systems explained in Chapter 1. For instance, in Chapter 11, "Technology and Interpersonal Communication," students are asked to think about the ethical issues associated with presenting yourself in a false light on the Internet. The Ethics & Choice feature asks students to delve into how their ethical systems have been formed, influenced, and how they relate to communication choices. Online interactive activities about these ethical dilemmas are featured on the book's online resources. These activities allow students to choose possible responses to the dilemma, and then reflect on the consequences their choice brings about.

As appropriate to the content, select chapters feature discussions of the **dark and bright sides of interpersonal communication.** These discussions touch on topics such as domestic abuse, empathy, and forgiveness. For example, Chapter 7, "Communication and Emotion," discusses the notion of *schadenfreude,* or taking pleasure in another's misfortune. These discussions enable students to see that interpersonal communication can be both helpful and harmful.

Additionally, each chapter features a section that discusses interpersonal skills and the behavior choices students can make in order to become more effective communicators.

An Approach that Advocates the Wise Use of Technology

Technology has increased our options and choices in communication. Technology such as email and video-conferencing affects who we speak to and how we speak to them in ways that are continually evolving. *Understanding Interpersonal Communication* shows students how they are influenced by technology and how they can use it to become more effective communicators.

This book includes a full chapter on technology's impact on interpersonal communication, **Chapter 11, "Technology and Interpersonal Communication."** We live in a time of unprecedented technological change. One new technology quickly replaces another, affecting our interactions with others. For example, online relationships are now commonplace among people of various races, ages, and cultures. Chapter 11 addresses this relatively new area of interpersonal communication. The chapter identifies and explains characteristics of communication technology, discusses

the presentation of the self online, discusses the pervasiveness and importance of social networking, explains how relationships function online, and discusses skills that help improve electronic discussions and relationships. We are proud to be among the first to offer students the opportunity to explore the intersection of technology, communication, and human behavior in a chapter that is both interesting and timely.

In addition to emphasizing technology in the text, we also provide **thorough technology integration** and support for users of the text. **InfoTrac® College Edition exercises** found throughout the book make use of the InfoTrac College Edition database, a virtual library that can be accessed from student computers (see Resources for Students on p. xiii for more information). Web-based **Interactive Activities** that enrich and reinforce chapter content are integrated into every chapter, taking learning beyond the printed page. These brief exercises and activities, highlighted by icons, are easily accessed through the book's online resources.

New to This Edition

The 2nd edition of *Understanding Interpersonal Communication* features several new and updated features that enhance its usefulness.

- Chapter 7, "Communication and Emotion," and Chapter 11, "Technology and Interpersonal Communication," feature **new Case in Point case studies and videos.** The Case in Point for Chapter 7 explores how a young woman, Regina, handles telling good news to a friend who finds the news troubling. And the Case in Point for Chapter 11 explores a college student's realization that his online disclosures are influencing his life in ways he had never considered. In addition, the Case in Point for Chapter 8, "Sharing Personal Information," now features a video of Roberta and Philip's interaction.

- **Imagine Yourself** . . . boxed features in each chapter highlight interpersonal communication in various contexts. For example, the Imagine Yourself . . . box in Chapter 6, "Effective Listening," asks students to consider the consequences of their own faulty listening when confronted with a mechanic's bill that is much higher than expected. And in Chapter 3, "Communication, Culture, and Identity," two boxes address situations in which intersections of culture and gender affect interpersonal interactions.

- **IPC in the News** boxes in most chapters provide examples of coverage about interpersonal communication in the popular media. For instance, the IPC in the News box in Chapter 2, "Communication, Perception, and the Self," features an article in *The Oakland Tribune* about the "nocebo effect," which scientists from the Centers for Disease Control and Prevention explain is a form of self-fulfilling prophecy in which illness, and even death, result from a patient's expectation that a drug or illness will be harmful.

- **Interpersonal Explorer** boxes at the conclusion of each chapter provide students with the opportunity to review the theories and skills discussed in the chapter and consider the relationship between theories and skills. Each box also includes a prompt for students to complete an online activity related to the chapter content. Some of these activities are **interactive simulations** that ask students to consider the consequences of their choices in a hypothetical interpersonal situation, and others are critical thinking activities that incorporate **ABC News videos about interpersonal issues**.

- In response to reviewer feedback, the **table of contents has been reorganized** to better correspond to the order in which many instructors teach the chapters. "Chapter 4, Communicating Verbally," and Chapter 5, "Communicating Nonverbally," now precede Chapter 6, "Effective Listening," and Chapter 7, "Communication and Emotion."

- **Chapter 6, "Effective Listening,"** has been updated to include more listening research and more coverage of critical thinking.

- In addition to the coverage of interpersonal relationships in Chapter 10, "Communicating in Close Relationships," **increased discussion of relationship choices and contexts** has been integrated throughout the text.

- In addition to the **updated coverage of communication technologies** throughout the book, the **thoroughly revised Chapter 11, "Technology and Interpersonal Communication,"** includes updated coverage and examples of how new technologies influence interpersonal communication in various contexts. New discussions address topics such as the evolution of the World Wide Web from Web 1.0 to Web 2.0, social networking sites such as MySpace and Facebook, and the use of avatars as a means of self-presentation online.

Resources for Students

Understanding Interpersonal Communication features an outstanding array of supplements to assist in making this course as meaningful and effective as possible.

- The *Understanding Interpersonal Communication* **online textbook resources** are designed to meet the demands of today's visual, multimedia learners. These resources are rich with powerful learning resources that will broaden and test your students' critical understanding of each chapter's material. They include the Resource Center for *Understanding Interpersonal Communication*, chapter-by-chapter resources at the book companion website, interactive video activities, and InfoTrac College Edition. References to these resources are integrated throughout the chapters, highlighted with icons, and summarized at the ends of chapters. **Note to faculty:** If you want your students to have access to the online textbook resources, please be sure to order them for your course. The content in these resources can be bundled at no additional charge to your students with every new copy of the text. If you do not order them, your students will not have access to these online resources. *Contact your local Wadsworth Cengage Learning sales representative for more details.*

- The **Resource Center for *Understanding Interpersonal Communication*** offers a variety of rich learning resources designed to enhance the student experience. These resources include self-assessments, images, video, and Web resources such as the interactive simulations described in the Interpersonal Explorer boxes. All resources are mapped to key discipline learning-concepts, and users can browse or search for content in a variety of ways. More than just a collection of ancillary learning materials, the Resource Center also features important content and community tools that extend the education experience beyond a particular class or course semester.

- With the **Book Companion Website**, students have easy access to premium chapter-by-chapter content, including practice chapter quizzes, self-scoring Communication Assessment Test inventories, an interactive glossary that features games and flashcards, interactive Ethics & Choice activities, and InfoTrac College Edition and Internet activities that enrich and reinforce chapter content.

- The **Interactive Video Activities** include the Case in Point scenarios and the ABC News video activities described in the Interpersonal Explorer boxes. All the video activities are accompanied by interactive components that allow students to think critically about the interpersonal situations presented, and then compare their responses to the suggested responses of the authors.

- With **InfoTrac College Edition with InfoMarks**, your students will have access to this virtual library's more than 18 million reliable, full-length articles from 5,000 academic and popular periodicals and retrieve results almost instantly. They also have access to InfoMarks—stable URLs that can be linked to articles, journals, and searches to save valuable time when doing research—and to the InfoWrite online resource center, where students can access grammar help, critical-thinking guidelines, guides to writing research papers, and much more.

- The **iChapters.com** online store provides students with exactly what they've been asking for: choice, convenience, and savings. A 2005 research study by the National Association of College Stores indicates that as many as 60 percent of students do not purchase all required course material; however, those who do are more likely to succeed. This research also tells us that students want the ability to purchase "a la carte" course material in the format that suits them best. Accordingly, iChapters.com is the only online store that offers eBooks at up to 50 percent off, eChapters for as low as $1.99 each, and new textbooks at up to 25 percent off, plus up to 25 percent off print and digital supplements that can help improve student performance.

Resources for Instructors

Understanding Interpersonal Communication also features a full suite of resources for instructors. To evaluate any of these instructor or student resources, please contact your local Wadsworth Cengage Learning representative for an examination copy.

- **Instructor's Resource Manual** This helpful manual includes an overview of the book's features, syllabi and course outlines, chapter outlines, class-tested activities and exercises, transparency masters, and a test bank. The test items are also available electronically via ExamView® (see below).

- The **PowerLecture** CD-ROM contains an electronic version of the Instructor's Resource Manual, ExamView Computerized Testing, predesigned Microsoft® PowerPoint® presentations, and JoinIn™ classroom quizzing. The PowerPoint presentations contain text, images, and cued videos of the case studies and can be used as is or customized to suit your course needs.

- **JoinIn™ on TurningPoint®.** JoinIn content for Response Systems is tailored to *Understanding Interpersonal Communication*, allowing you to transform your classroom and assess your students' progress with instant in-class quizzes and polls. Turning-Point software lets you pose book-specific questions and display students' answers seamlessly within the Microsoft PowerPoint slides of your own lecture, in conjunction with the "clicker" hardware of your choice. The JoinIn content for each chapter includes two "conditional branching" scenarios that can be used as in-class group activities.

- **Communication Scenarios for Critique and Analysis Videos** Communication concepts previously presented in the abstract come to life in these videos. Each offers a variety of situations that allow students to watch, listen to, and critique model communication scenarios. Video policy is based on adoption size; contact your Wadsworth Cengage Learning representative for more information.

- **InfoTrac College Edition Student Activities Workbook for Interpersonal Communication** by Lori Halverson-Wente. This workbook features extensive individual and groups activities, focusing on specific course topics that make use of InfoTrac College Edition. Also included are guidelines for instructors and students that describe how to maximize the use of this resource.

- With the **TLC (Technology Learning Connects) Technology Training and Support**, you can get trained, get connected, and get the support you need for seamless integration of technology resources into your course. This technology service and training program provides online resources, peer-to-peer instruction, personalized training, and a customizable program. Visit **http://www. academic.cengage.com/tlc/** to sign up for online seminars, first days of class services, technical support, or personalized, face-to-face training. Our online or onsite trainings are frequently led by one of our Lead Teachers, faculty members who are experts in using Wadsworth Cengage Learning technology and can provide best practices and teaching tips.

- With Wadsworth's **Flex-Text Customization Program**, you can create a text as unique as

your course: quickly, simply, and affordably. As part of our flex-text program you can add your personal touch to Understanding Interpersonal Communication with a course-specific cover and up to 32 pages of your own content, at no additional cost.

Acknowledgments

The impetus for writing this book rests primarily with our students. We begin our acknowledgements, therefore, by thanking the thousands of students we have taught over a combined 40-plus years of teaching interpersonal communication. The insights, themes, and examples we've included in this book reflect those students who have provided us inspiration throughout our careers.

This text could not have existed without the generous time and talents afforded to us by the reviewers of the 1st edition and those who class-tested chapters for us. They numbered many, and their thoughts, examples, and critical observations prompted us to write a book that reflects their voices and the voices of their students.

In addition, we'd like to thank the reviewers and survey respondents for this 2nd edition for their insight and suggestions: Emelia Angeli, *Lackawanna College*; Martha Antolik, *Wright State University*; Tonya Blivens, *Tarrant County College*; Allison Carr, *Davidson County Community College*; Harold P. Donle, *Indiana University-Purdue University Indianapolis*; Diane Ferrero-Paluzzi, *Iona College*; Craig Fowler, *California State University, Fresno*; Lisa C. Hebert, *Louisiana State University*; Mark G. Henderson, *Jackson State University*; Mark Higgens, *Cleveland State Community College*; Krista Hoffmann-Longtin, *Indiana University-Purdue University Indianapolis*; Laura Janusik, *Rockhurst University*; Elaine B. Jenks, *West Chester University*; Leslie B. Henderson, *McLennan Community College*; Stan Malm, *Johns Hopkins University*; Tani McBeth, *Portland Community College*; M. Chad McBride, *Creighton University*; Virginia McDermott, *University of New Mexico*; Connie McKee, *West Texas A&M University*; David Moss, *Mt. San Jacinto College*; Keisha C. Paxton, *California State University, Dominguez Hills*; Nancy R. Pearson, *Minot State University*; Narissra Punyanunt-Carter, *Texas Tech University*; Michael Reiter, *Nova Southeastern University*; Curt

VanGeison, *St. Charles Community College*; Don Wallace, *Brewton-Parker College*; Emily Wilkinson Stallings, *Virginia Tech*; Janice Xu, *Western Connecticut State University*; and Christina Yoshimura, *University of Montana*.

We also gratefully acknowledge the excellent team at Wadsworth Cengage Learning, whose skills and thoughtfulness are unmatched. We never realized that writing a book with such a large company would result in lasting friendships. We first thank Holly Allen, former Publisher for Wadsworth's Communication Studies list, for "turning us on" to textbook writing in 1996. We have made many friends and cultivated close colleagues in publishing over these many years, but Holly will always remain a special confidant, and we are forever grateful to her for being the first to have faith in our ideas and writing. For this 2nd edition, the current Cengage Learning team has been nothing short of spectacular! First, we are indebted to Monica Eckman, our Acquisitions Editor, who provided those all-important "friendly nudges" throughout the writing of the book. Her sense of inclusiveness, steadfast support, and overall great persona made writing the 2nd edition a more exciting undertaking. Monica is an integral part of the soul of our writing. Greer Lleuad, our Developmental Editor, is the very *definition* of a perfect Developmental Editor. With Greer, we not only get a colleague with great instincts, but also a kind and generous person. Her sense of humor and persistent words of encouragement served as an important backdrop to the writing of this new edition. We also want to acknowledge the support and enthusiasm of Erin Mitchell, our Marketing Manager. Erin's grasp of our concept and her marketing skills provide a winning combination. Finally, we thank the others on the Cengage Learning team who contributed substantially to our text: Kim Gengler, Assistant Editor; Kim Apfelbaum, Editorial Assistant; Jessica Badiner, Associate Technology Project Manager; Linda Helcher, Art Director; Jessica Rasile, Content Project Manager; Katherine Wilson, Production Service Project Manager; and John Hill and Roberta Broyer, Permissions Account Managers.

We are also grateful to Larry Edmonds of Arizona State University for his expertise in updating the Instructor's Manual. He and Sally Vogl-Bauer, the author of this manual for the 1st edition of *Understanding Interpersonal Communication,* were able to take our text and provide superior teaching aids to supplement it, making it a more useful tool for classroom teachers. We appreciate their hard work. And many thanks to Bill Price of Georgia Perimeter College, Dunwoody Campus, for his dedication and expertise in the development of the InfoTrac College Edition exercises, Interactive Activities, and Ethics & Choice online activities for the book; to Cindy Kistenberg of Johnson C. Smith University, who created the online interpersonal simulations and ABC News video activities; to Christina Yoshimura of the University of Montana, who prepared the JoinIn questions; to Chad McBride of Creighton University, who wrote the quizzes for the companion website; and to Leslie Henderson of McLennan Community College, who prepared the PowerLecture slides and wrote important activities for the book's companion website.

In addition to all those just mentioned, we have a few personal comments. First, Rich thanks his co-author and close friend, Lynn, who, after working with him for more than 25 years, remains one of the most thoughtful and important people in his life. We encounter very few people who have a lasting and profound impact upon our lives. Lynn has been that person, and Rich continues to be honored with her friendship. Rich would also like to thank his mother, Beverly, for her ongoing presence in his life. Her genuineness, care, and sense of ethics are instrumental influences on his life. Rich would also like to thank his partner, Chris, who has helped to frame their relationship with humor, compassion, and ongoing moral support. Finally, Rich thanks his friends and colleagues at Emerson College. There is a wonderful spirit of support on the Emerson campus that has been unmatched in Rich's life. Lynn would also like to thank Rich. His insights, enthusiasm, and enduring friendship are what make writing a joy for her. Lynn also thanks Marquette University, especially Dean Pauly of the College of Communication, who provided enormous support during the writing of this book as well as at other times. Lynn thanks her husband, Ted, for being with her through thick and thin, cooking dinners, bringing coffee, and telling her to shut off the computer every once and a while!

About the Authors

Richard West is Professor and Chairperson of the Department of Communication Studies at Emerson College in Boston. Rich received his B.A. from Illinois State University in Speech Communication Education and his M.A from ISU in Communication Studies. His Ph.D. is from Ohio University in Interpersonal Communication. Rich's research interests span several areas, including family communication, classroom communication, and culture. Rich is the recipient of many teaching awards and has also been recognized with Outstanding Alumni Awards in Communication from both ISU and OU. Rich is co-author of several books and over 30 book chapters and articles with Lynn Turner. He is past President of the Eastern Communication Association (ECA), Director of the Educational Policies Board of the National Communication (NCA), and past Chair of the Instructional Communication Divisions for both ECA and NCA. Although Rich's passion remains in the classroom, he also enjoys gardening and updating his 100-year-old bungalow in Maine.

Lynn H. Turner is Professor in Communication Studies at Marquette University. Lynn received her B.A from University of Illinois, her M.A. from University of Iowa, and her Ph.D. from Northwestern University. At Marquette, she teaches interpersonal communication, among other courses, at both the undergraduate and graduate levels. Her research areas of emphasis include gender and communication, interpersonal and family communication. She is the co-author or co-editor of over ten books, as well as several articles and book chapters. Her articles have appeared in many journals, including *Management Communication Quarterly, Journal of Applied Communication Research, Women and Language,* and *Western Journal of Communication.* Her books include *From the Margins to the Center: Contemporary Women and Political Communication* (co-authored with Patricia Sullivan; recipient of the "Best Book" Award from the Organization for the Study of Communication, Language and Gender [OSCLG]), *Gender in Applied Communication Contexts* (co-edited with Patrice Buzzanell and Helen Sterk), *Introducing Communication Theory* and *Perspectives on Family Communication* (both co-authored with Richard West). In 2007, she was the recipient of the outstanding research award in the Diederich College of Communication. Lynn has served as Director of Graduate Studies for the Diederich College of Communication, President of OSCLG, President of Central States Communication Association, and Chairperson of the Family Communication Division for the National Communication Association.

We dedicate this book to the thousands of students who teach us what interpersonal communication means and to those others—our family, friends, and colleagues—whose interactions with us make these lessons come to life.

Chapter 1

Introduction to Interpersonal Communication

chapter ✚ goals

Explain three prevailing models of human communication

Describe the impersonal–interpersonal communication continuum

Define and interpret interpersonal communication

Understand the principles of interpersonal communication

Demystify stereotypes associated with interpersonal communication

Explain how ethical awareness relates to interpersonal encounters

CASEinPOINT:

Jackie Ellis stood in her driveway shoveling snow, she heard her neighbor, Scottie Perona, yell across the yard, "Hey, can't get any hired help for that?!"

Jackie yelled back, "Sure—show me the money! Like we needed to have another storm! Ever wonder why we even live here? I mean, don't you wonder why we're not in Arizona?! Of course, then we'd be complaining about the heat. . .but it's *dry* heat. . .we *have* to remember that!"

They both laughed. As Scottie approached Jackie's driveway, her cat rolled around on the ground. They began a casual conversation about the weather and the town's plows. Soon, however, the topic turned to something that was much more serious: Jackie's sister's death. Jackie told Scottie that it was exactly a year ago that her sister had died of skin cancer.

"I can't believe how fast time goes by, Scottie," Jackie said, sighing.

"Wow," he replied. "Incredible that it's been that long. It seems like we were just telling each other that everything would be fine. I mean where did the time go? I remember that day as if it happened a week ago. You were. . ." Scottie's voice began to trail as he looked at his neighbor's face.

As he spoke, tears welled up in Jackie's eyes. Jackie smiled ruefully and said, "Hey, we got by that one, and we're still here talking about it. And if we can survive that *and* this stupid winter, we'll make it through anything. Right?"

The two laughed awkwardly; both knew that the topic had to change quickly. They began to talk about Scottie's daughters and their holiday concert. As the minutes ticked by, they found themselves talking about everything from Iraq to the *E! Network*. It was almost as if the two were trying to avoid the topic. The snow was now beginning to blow around. After a few minutes, Scottie went back to his house. Jackie finished shoveling her sidewalk and went inside. As she sat in her kitchen thumbing through catalogs, she once again thought about her sister. One year, she thought—it couldn't be possible. She felt lucky to have such a good and caring neighbor as Scottie. He might have been angry when Jackie put up her fence in the back yard, but today, he surely was a friend.

*E*ach day, we perform one of the most ancient of all behaviors: interpersonal communication. We head off to work and greet people on the bus, in the office, in the carpool, or on the street. We talk to our roommates and discuss last night's party over breakfast. Or, we wake up and soon find ourselves in the middle of a heated exchange with a family member about dirty dishes. Although each of these situations differs, they all underscore the pervasiveness of interpersonal communication in our lives.

This chapter's Case in Point scenario between Jackie and Scottie represents one of these interpersonal encounters. In this scenario, Scottie established verbal contact with Jackie. In turn, Jackie moved the conversation from the weather to her sister's death. The entire dialogue lasted only a few minutes, but it carried enormous importance. Scottie and Jackie not only initiated a conversation—their conversation also showed just how close they are to each other. As you can tell from their conversation, they are more than just neighbors; they are also good friends. The content of their brief conversation gives us an idea that they have more than a superficial relationship with each other.

These dialogues take place all the time without our giving them a second thought. And we often feel content about the way we communicate with others. A national poll commissioned by the National Communication Association (*www.natcom.org*), called "Why Americans Communicate," reports that nearly two-thirds of U.S. citizens feel very comfortable communicating with others. Women are more likely than men to feel comfortable, and older respondents (55 years and older) are more comfortable than any other age group. This comfort level pertains to communication in informal settings such as talking to a friend, family member, or partner.

Yet, not everyone is comfortable talking to others. In fact, some people are quite nervous about communicating. The extent to which people exhibit anxiety about speaking to others is called **communication apprehension**. Communication apprehension is a legitimate and real experience that researchers believe usually negatively affects our communication with others (Daly, McCroskey, Ayres, Hopf, & Ayres, 2007; Richmond & McCroskey, 1998). People with communication apprehension can go to great lengths to avoid communication situations because communicating can make them feel shy, embarrassed, and tense. At times, some individuals find themselves fearful or anxious around people from different cultural groups. This **intercultural communication apprehension** (Wrench, Corrigan, McCroskey, & Punyanunt-Carter, 2006) not only impairs quality face-to-face conversations, but also can affect whether or not we wish to communicate with someone *at all*. We will return to culture and communication in Chapter 3.

Even if we don't suffer from communication apprehension, there are many times when we have difficulty getting our message across to others. We may feel unprepared to argue with a supervisor for a raise, to let our

communication apprehension

A fear or an anxiety pertaining to the communication process.

intercultural communication apprehension

A fear or anxiety pertaining to communication with people from different cultural backgrounds.

Communication Assessment Test
Personal Report of Communication Apprehension (PRCA)

Directions:

This instrument is composed of twenty-four statements concerning feelings about communicating with other people. Please indicate the degree to which each statement applies to you using the following five-point scale:

strongly agree = 1   agree = 2   undecided = 3   disagree = 4   strongly disagree = 5

There are no right or wrong answers. Please mark your first impression and answer quickly. You can take this test online. Go to your online Resource Center for *Understanding Interpersonal Communication* and look under the resources for Chapter 1. (To learn how to get started with your online Resource Center, see the inside front cover of this book.)

_4_ 1. I dislike participating in group discussions.

_2_ 2. Generally, I am comfortable while participating in group discussions.

_2_ 3. I am tense and nervous while participating in group discussions.

_2_ 4. I like to get involved in group discussions.

_5_ 5. Engaging in a group discussion with new people makes me tense and nervous.

_1_ 6. I am calm and relaxed while participating in group discussions.

_2_ 7. Generally, I am nervous when I have to participate in a meeting.

_2_ 8. Usually, I am calm and relaxed while participating in a meeting.

_1_ 9. I am calm and relaxed when I am called upon to express an opinion at a meeting.

_5_ 10. I am afraid to express myself at meetings.

_5_ 11. Communicating at meetings usually makes me feel uncomfortable.

_2_ 12. I am relaxed when answering questions at a meeting.

_2_ 13. While participating in a conversation with a new acquaintance, I feel very nervous.

_1_ 14. I have no fear of speaking up in conversations.

_5_ 15. Ordinarily, I am very tense and nervous in conversations.

_1_ 16. Ordinarily, I am very calm and relaxed in conversations.

_1_ 17. While conversing with a new acquaintance, I feel very relaxed.

_5_ 18. I'm afraid to speak up in conversations.

_4_ 19. I have no fear of giving a speech.

_2_ 20. Certain parts of my body feel tense and rigid while giving a speech.

_2_ 21. I feel relaxed while giving a speech.

_4_ 22. My thoughts become confused and jumbled when I am giving a speech.

_2_ 23. I face the prospect of giving a speech with confidence.

_4_ 24. While giving a speech, I get so nervous I forget facts I really know.

Scoring

There are four categories for scoring: **group discussions, meetings, interpersonal conversations, and public speaking.** To compute your scores, add or subtract the numbers you marked for each item as indicated below:

1. Group discussions

   18 + (plus) scores for items 2, 4, and 6 − (minus) scores for items 1, 3, and 5

   = Subtotal ___−5___

   6 − 11 =

(Continues)

2. Meetings   5 – 12 = -7

   18 + (plus) scores for items 8, 9, and 12 – (minus) scores for items 7, 10, and 11

   = Subtotal ___ -7 ___

3. Interpersonal conversations   7 – 15

   18 + (plus) scores for items 14, 16, and 17 – (minus) scores for items 13, 15, and 18

   = Subtotal ___ 8 ___

4. Public speaking   8 – 10

   18 + (plus) scores for items 19, 21, and 23 – (minus) scores for items 20, 22, and 24

   = Subtotal ___ 2 ___

To obtain your score, add your four subscores together. Your score should range between 24 and 120. If your score is below 24 or above 120, you have made a mistake in computation. Scores can range, in each context, from a low of 6 to a high of 30. Any score above 18 indicates some degree of communication apprehension.

From www.jamescmccroskey.com. Used by permission.

apartment manager know that the hot water is not hot enough, or to tell our partner, "I love you." At times throughout the day, we may struggle with what to say, how to say something, or when to say something. We also may struggle with listening to certain messages because of their content or the manner in which they are presented. In addition, communication may seem difficult when others don't respond as we'd wish or when others don't even seem to pay attention to us.

This book is about improving your ability to interact with other people. Improving your interpersonal communication skills will assist you in becoming more effective in your relationships with a variety of people, including those with whom you are close (e.g., family members, friends, coworkers) and those with whom you interact less frequently (e.g., health care providers, contractors, babysitters).

Throughout this course, you will see how research and theory associated with interpersonal communication informs everyday encounters. You will also be introduced to a number of useful communication skills. We believe that the theoretical and practical applications of interpersonal communication are intertwined to the extent that we cannot ignore the mutual influence of one upon the other—after all, theories inform practice, and practice grows out of theory. At the same time, we agree with Robert Craig (2003), a communication professor and researcher, who maintains that the communication discipline can influence and enhance people's lives only by being practical (p. 18). So, we take a practical approach with this book in the hope that you will be able to use what you learn about the theoretical foundations and practical applications to make effective communication choices in your own interpersonal relationships.

Our first task is to map out a general understanding of interpersonal communication. We begin this journey by providing a brief history of how interpersonal communication came about in the field of communication.

The Study of Interpersonal Communication

Let's explore a brief overview of the communication discipline to give you a sense of its evolution. For a more expansive view of the communication field, we encourage you to look at additional sources that provide a more comprehensive presentation (Craig, 2003; Friedrich & Boileau, 1999, Rogers & Chaffee, 1983; Shepherd, 1993). You can find the full citations for these sources in the References section at the end of this book.

Acknowledging our Past

What we call *communication studies* today has its origins in ancient Greece and Rome, during the formation of what we now know as Western civilization. Being skilled at communication was expected of all Greek and Roman citizens (that is, free land-owning and native-born men). For example, citizens were asked to judge murder and adultery trials, travel as state emissaries, and defend their property against would-be land collectors. This sort of public communication was viewed primarily as a way to persuade other people, and scholars such as Aristotle developed ways to improve a speaker's persuasive powers. His book, the *Rhetoric*, described a way of making speeches that encouraged speakers to incorporate logic, evidence, and emotions and to consider how the audience perceived the speaker's credibility and intelligence.

Aristotelian thinking dominated early approaches to communication for centuries. But as time went on, interest grew in providing speakers with practical ways to improve their communication skills in situations other than public persuasion. And in the modern era, communication scholars began moving beyond the focus on skills to form a more theoretical and philosophical approach to communication. They began trying to answer the question "How do I come to know, to believe, and to act?" in relation to communication. (See Harper, 1979, for more information in this area.)

Contemporary communication courses—like the one you're enrolled in now—were first taught in English departments in the early 1900s. These courses, staying true to early Greek and Roman thinking, emphasized public speaking and were taught by English teachers who had some training in public communication. The English department was considered the appropriate place for communication courses because it was believed that written and spoken communication were synonymous. However, scholars who specialized in the study of public speaking (we call them communication scholars today) were unhappy with this arrangement. They maintained that there were clear differences between the two forms of communication.

In 1913, this debate grew so intense that when the National Council of Teachers of English held its annual convention in Chicago, a group of public speaking teachers proposed that they form their own association, the National Association of Academic Teachers of Public Speaking. This was the beginning of the modern-day National Communication Association (NCA), an organization comprised of more than 8,000 communication teachers, researchers, and practitioners who study over 50 different areas of communication. One of the largest fields of the communication discipline is interpersonal communication, which explores communication within many different relationships, including those between parents and children, teachers and students, supervisors and employees, friends, and spouses, to name just a few.

Understanding the Present

Even though we engage in interpersonal communication daily, it is often difficult to disentangle from everything else we do. To arrive at the definition of interpersonal communication, it helps first to distinguish it from other types of communication. Scholars have identified the following kinds of situations in which human communication exists: intrapersonal, interpersonal, small group, organizational, mass, and public. You may notice that the communication department at your school is organized around some or all of these communication types. Many schools use these categories as an effective way to organize their curriculum and course offerings.

Note that these communication types build on each other because they represent increasing numbers of people included in the process. In addition, keep in mind that although these communication types differ from one another in some significant ways, they aren't mutually exclusive. For example, you may engage in both intrapersonal and interpersonal communication in a single encounter, or interpersonal communication may take place in an organizational context. With these caveats in mind, let's take a closer look at the six types of communication.

- *Intrapersonal communication:* Communication with ourselves. We may find ourselves daydreaming or engaging in internal dialogues even in the presence of another person. These are intrapersonal processes. Intrapersonal communication includes imagining, perceiving, or solving problems in your head. For instance, intrapersonal communication takes place when you debate with yourself, mentally listing the pros and cons of a decision before taking action.

- *Interpersonal communication:* The process of message transaction between people (usually two) who work toward creating and sustaining shared meaning. We will discuss this definition in more detail later in this chapter.

- *Small group communication:* Communication between and among members of a task group who meet for a common purpose or goal. Small group communication occurs in classrooms, the workplace, and in more social environments (for example, sports teams or book clubs).

- *Organizational communication:* Communication with and among large, extended environments with a defined hierarchy. This context also includes communication among members within those environments. Organizational communication may involve other communication types, such as interpersonal communication (for example, supervisor/subordinate relationships), small group communication (for example, a task group preparing a report), and intrapersonal communication (for example, daydreaming at work).

- *Mass communication:* Communication to a large audience via some mediated channel, such as television, radio, the Internet, or newspapers. At times, people seek out others using personal ads either on the Internet or in newspapers or magazines. This is an example of the intersection of mass communication and interpersonal communication.

- *Public communication:* Communication in which one person gives a speech to a large audience in person. Public communication is also often called public speaking. Public speakers have predetermined goals in mind, such as informing, persuading, or entertaining.

Each of these communication types is affected by two pervasive influences: culture and technology. In the twenty-first century especially, acknowledging these two influences is crucial to our understanding of interpersonal communication and human relationships. First, It's nearly impossible to ignore the role that culture plays as we communicate with others. We now live in a country where intercultural contact is commonplace, making effective communication with others even more critical than it would be ordinarily. The ever-increasing presence of intercultural relationships—such as those between exchange students and their host families, and American parents and their children adopted from other countries—has prompted researchers to study the effects of these blended populations on communication effectiveness (e.g., Galvin, 2006). We will delve deeper into the topic of culture, community, and communication in Chapter 3.

Second, as you probably know from your own online experiences, it is now possible to communicate with another person without ever having face-to-face contact. Years ago, interpersonal communication was limited to sending letters or talking with someone personally. But today, relationships are routinely initiated, cultivated, and even terminated via electronic technology. This phenomenon has stimulated much recent research on technology, relationships, and interpersonal communication (e.g., Walther & Bazarova, 2007; Walther, Gay, & Hancock, 2005). Technology has not only made interpersonal communication easier and faster, it has shaped the very nature of our communication and our relationships. Our conversations have become abbreviated, such as when we look at our caller ID and answer the phone with "And when did you get home from vacation?" instead of "Hello?" We develop close relationships with others via online dating services (e.g., Match.com), and our personal web pages (e.g., MySpace.com and Facebook.com) allow us to have tens of millions of "friends." You will get a better sense of the extent of technology's influence on interpersonal relationships in Chapter 11.

Defining Interpersonal Communication

We define **interpersonal communication** as the process of message transaction between people to create and sustain shared meaning. There are three critical components embedded in this definition: process, message exchange, and shared meaning. Let's look at each in turn.

When we state that interpersonal communication is a **process**, we mean that it is an ongoing, unending vibrant activity that is always changing. When we enter into an interpersonal communication exchange, we are entering into an event with no definable beginning or ending, and one that is irreversible. For example, consider the moments when you first meet and begin communicating with classmates during a small group activity in class. Chances are that for the first few minutes everyone in the group feels a little awkward and uncertain. Yet, after you all introduce yourselves to one another, it's highly likely that you all feel more comfortable. This shift from feeling uncertain to feeling comfortable is the ongoing, irreversible interpersonal communication process in action.

The notion of process also suggests that it is not only individuals who change, but also the cultures in which they live. For instance, modern U.S. society is very different today than it was in the 1950s. The climate of the United States in the 1950s can be characterized as a time of postwar euphoria, colored by a concern about communism. The feminist movement of the 1970s had yet to occur, and for many white middle-class families, sex roles were traditional. Women's roles were more rigidly defined as nurturers and primary caretakers for children, whereas men's roles were relegated to emotionless financial providers. These roles influenced decision making in many families (Turner & West, 2006). Nowadays roles are less rigid. Many dads stay at home to care for children, and many moms work outside the home. And more than ever, couples make all kinds of decisions about the family together. Consider a couple communicating in the 1950s about a family issue and another couple discussing the same issue today. In what ways do you think the conversations would be similar or different?

The second element of our definition highlights **message exchange**, by which we mean the transaction of verbal and nonverbal *messages*, or information, being sent simultaneously between people. Messages, both verbal and nonverbal, are the vehicles we use to interact with others. But messages are not enough to establish interpersonal communication. For example, consider an English speaker stating the message, "I need to find the post office. Can you direct me there?" to a Spanish speaker. Although the message was stated clearly in English, no shared meaning results if the Spanish speaker is not bilingual.

Meaning is central to our definition of interpersonal communication because **meaning** is what people extract from a message. As you will learn in Chapter 4, words alone have no meaning; people attribute meaning to words. We create the meaning of a message even as the message unfolds. Perhaps our

interpersonal communication

The process of message transaction between two people to create and sustain shared meaning.

process

When used to describe interpersonal communication, an ongoing, unending, vibrant activity that always changes.

message exchange

The transaction of verbal and nonverbal messages being sent simultaneously between two people.

meaning

What communicators create together through the use of verbal and nonverbal messages.

have difficulties assimilating into U.S. culture, often illustrated by the use of language within the family. Language serves as a primary factor affecting the quality of relationships within the family (Soliz, Lin, Anderson, & Harwood, 2006). So, for example, if grandparents and grandchildren have difficulty communicating with each other because the grandparents speak primarily Spanish and the grandchildren speak primarily English, it's likely that meaning will be jeopardized.

The **social-emotional context** indicates the nature of the relationship that affects a communication encounter. For example, are the communicators in a particular interaction friendly or unfriendly, supportive or unsupportive? Or do they fall somewhere in between? These factors help explain why, for instance, you might feel completely anxious in one employment interview but very comfortable in another. At times, you and an interviewer may hit it off, and at other times you may feel intimidated or awkward. The social-emotional context helps explain the nature of the interaction taking place.

In the **historical context,** messages are understood in relationship to previously sent messages. Thus, when Billy tells Tina that he missed her while they were separated over Spring Break, Tina hears that as a turning point in their relationship. Billy has never said that before and, in fact, he has often mentioned that he rarely misses anyone when he is apart from him or her. Therefore, his comment is colored by their history together. If Billy regularly told Tina he missed her, she would interpret the message differently.

We will return to the notion of context often in this book. For now, keep in mind that context has a significant influence on our relationships with others. Further, context involves people and their conversations and relationships. If we don't consider context in our interactions with others, we have no way to judge our interpersonal effectiveness.

Although the linear model was highly regarded when it was first conceptualized, it has been criticized because it presumes that communication has a definable beginning and ending (Anderson & Ross, 2002). In fact, Shannon and Weaver (1999) later emphasized this aspect of their model by claiming people receive information in organized and discrete ways. Yet, we know that communication can be messy. We have all interrupted someone or had someone interrupt us. The linear model also presumes that listeners are passive and that communication occurs only when speaking. But we know that listeners often affect speakers and are not simply passive receivers of a speaker's message. With these criticisms in mind, researchers developed another way to represent the human communication process: the interactional model.

Feedback and the Interactional Model

To emphasize the two-way nature of communication between people, Wilbur Schramm (1954) conceptualized the **interactional model of communication.** Schramm's model shows that communication goes in two directions: from sender to receiver and from receiver to sender. This circular, or interactional,

social-emotional context

The relational and emotional environment in which communication occurs.

historical context

A type of context in which messages are understood in relationship to previously sent messages.

interactional model of communication

A characterization of communication as a two-way process in which a message is sent from sender to receiver and from receiver to sender.

Figure 1.2   Interactional model of communication

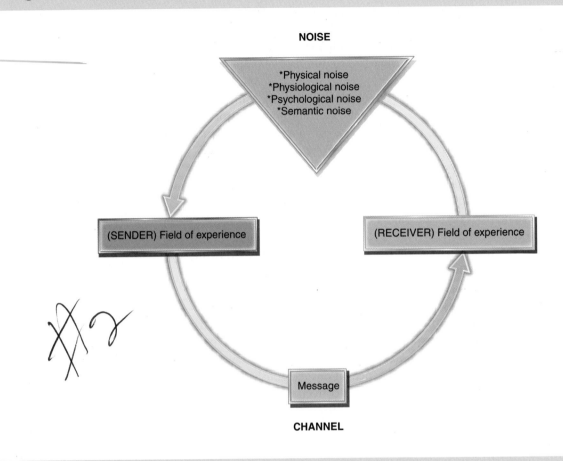

NOISE

*Physical noise
*Physiological noise
*Psychological noise
*Semantic noise

(SENDER) Field of experience

(RECEIVER) Field of experience

Message

CHANNEL

feedback

A verbal or nonverbal response to a message. See also internal feedback and external feedback.

internal feedback

The feedback we give ourselves when we assess our own communication.

external feedback

The feedback we receive from other people.

process suggests that communication is ongoing rather than linear. In the interactional model, individuals in a conversation can be both sender and receiver, but not both simultaneously (see Figure 1.2).

The interactional approach is characterized primarily by **feedback**, which can be defined as responses to people, their messages, or both. Feedback may be verbal (meaning we respond in words) or nonverbal (meaning we respond in facial expressions, body posture, and so forth). Feedback may also be internal or external. **Internal feedback** occurs when you assess your own communication (for example, by thinking "I never should have said that"). **External feedback** is the feedback you receive from other people (for example, "Why did you say that? That was dumb!").

A person can provide external feedback that results in important internal feedback for himself or herself. For example, let's say that Alexandra gives Dan the following advice about dealing with the death of his partner: "You feel sad as long as you need to. Don't worry about what other people think. I'm sick of people telling others how they should feel about something. These are your feelings." While giving Dan this external feedback, Alexandra may realize that her advice can also be applied to her own recent breakup. Although she may intend to send Dan a comforting message, she may also provide herself internal feedback as she deals with her relational circumstances.

Like the linear model, the interactional model has been criticized primarily for its view of senders and receivers—that is, one person sends a message to another person. Neither model takes into consideration what happens when nonverbal messages are sent at the same time as verbal messages. For example, when a father disciplines his child and finds the child either looking the other way or staring directly into his eyes, the father will "read" the meaning of the child's nonverbal communication as inattentive or disobedient. What happens if the child doesn't say anything during the reprimand? The father will still make some meaning out of the child's silence. The interactional view acknowledges that human communication involves both speaking and listening, but it asserts that speaking and listening are separate events and thus does not address the effect of nonverbal communication as the message is sent. This criticism led to the development of a third model of communication, the transactional model.

Shared Meaning and the Transactional Model

Whereas the linear model of communication assumes that communication is an action that moves from sender to receiver, and the interactional model suggests that the presence of feedback makes communication an interaction between people, the **transactional model of communication** (Barnlund, 1970; Watzlawick, Beavin, & Jackson, 1967) underscores the fact that giving and receiving messages is simultaneous and mutual. In fact, the word *transactional* indicates that the communication process is cooperative. In other words, communicators (senders and receivers) are both responsible for the effect and effectiveness of communication. In a transactional encounter, people do not simply send meaning from one to the other and then back again; rather, they build shared meaning.

A unique feature of the transactional model is its recognition that messages build upon each other. Further, both verbal and nonverbal behaviors are necessarily part of the transactional process. For example, consider Alan's conversation with his coworker Pauline. During a break, Pauline asks Alan about his family in Los Angeles. He begins to tell Pauline that his three siblings all live in Los Angeles and that he has no idea when they will be able to "escape the prison" there. When he mentions "prison," Pauline looks confused. Seeing Pauline's puzzled facial expression, Alan clarifies that he hated Los Angeles because it was so hot, people lived too close to each other, and he felt that he was being watched all the time. In sum, he felt like he was in a prison. This example shows how much both Alan and Pauline are actively involved in this communication interaction. Pauline's nonverbal response to Alan prompted him to clarify his original message. As this interaction shows,

transactional model of communication

A characterization of communication as the reciprocal sending and receiving of messages. In a transactional encounter, the sender and receiver do not simply send meaning from one to the other and then back again; rather, they build shared meaning through simultaneous sending and receiving.

Figure 1.3 Transactional model of communication

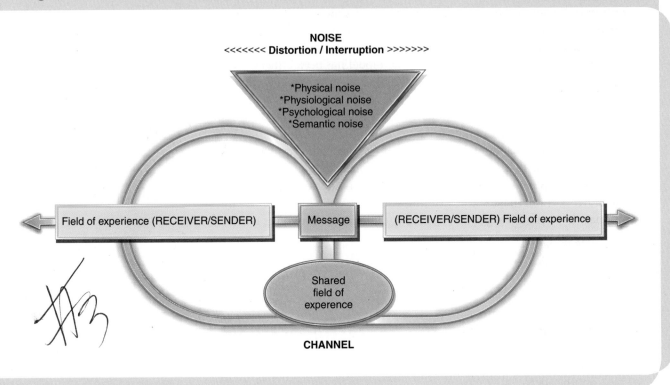

Note that the transactional model in Figure 1.3 is characterized by a common field of experience between communicator A and communicator B. The **field of experience** refers to a person's culture, past experiences, personal history, and heredity, and how these elements influence the communication process.

People's fields of experience overlap at times, meaning that people share things in common. Where two people's fields of experience overlap, they can communicate effectively. And as they communicate, they create more overlap in their experiences. This process explains why initial encounters often consist of questions and answers between communicators, such as "Where are you from?", "What's your major?", "Do you ski?" The answers to these questions help establish the overlap in the communicators' experiences: "Oh, I was in Chicago over the holidays last year," "Really, that's my major, too," "Yeah, I don't ski either." Further, fields of experience may change over time.

For instance, in class, Rhonda and Marcy have little in common and have little overlap in their fields of experience. They just met this term, have never taken a course together before, and Rhonda is eighteen years older than

---

field of experience

The influence of a person's culture, past experiences, personal history, and heredity on the communication process.

labels or representations for feelings, concepts, objects, or events. Words are symbols. For instance, the word *table* represents something we sit at. Similarly, the word *hate* represents the idea of hate, which means strong feelings for someone or something.

Words like *fear* suggest that symbols may be somewhat abstract, and with this abstraction comes the potential for miscommunication. For instance, consider how hard it would be for someone who has never attended college to understand the following:

> I have no idea what the *prereqs* are. I know that the *midterm* is pretty much *objective*. And the prof doesn't like to follow the *syllabus* too much. I wish that stuff was in the *undergrad* catalog. I'm sure I'd rather do an *independent study* than take that class.

Because the verbal symbols used in this message are not understood by everyone, the message would be lost to someone who had never encountered words such as those italicized. This example underscores the importance of developing a transactional viewpoint because communication requires mutual understanding. In Chapter 4, we look in more detail at the importance of language in interpersonal relationships.

Interpersonal Communication Is Rule-Governed

Consider the following examples of communication rules:

- As long as you live under my roof, you'll do what I say.
- Always tell the truth.
- Don't talk back.
- Always say "thank you" when someone gives you a present.
- Don't interrupt while anyone is talking.

You probably heard at least one of these while growing up. We noted earlier that rules are important ingredients in our relationships. They help guide and structure our interpersonal communication. Rules essentially say that individuals in a relationship agree that there are appropriate ways to interact in their relationship. Like the rules in our childhood, most of the rules in our relationships today tell us what we can or can't do. Susan Shimanoff (1980) has defined a **rule** as "a followable prescription that indicates what behavior is obligated, preferred, or prohibited in certain contexts" (p. 57). In other words, Shimanoff, like many other communication researchers, thinks that we can choose whether or not we wish to follow a rule. Ultimately, we must decide whether the rule must be adhered to or can be ignored in our interpersonal exchanges.

To understand this principle, consider the Chandler family, a family of three that finds itself homeless. The Chandlers live day to day in homeless shelters in a large city in the South. The family members agree on a communication rule explicitly stating that they will not discuss their economic situation in public. This rule requires all family members to refrain from talking

rule

A prescribed guide that indicates what behavior is obligated, preferred, or prohibited in certain contexts.

From birth, we are taught how to communicate interpersonally, most significantly by our family. As we grow older, we refine our skills as we interact with a wider and wider group of people, such as our teachers, friends, coworkers, and partners.

about what led to their homelessness. Each member of the family is obligated to keep this information private, an intrafamily secret of sorts. Whether or not people outside the Chandler family agree on the usefulness of such a rule is not important. Yet, one test of the rule's effectiveness is whether or not family members can refrain from discussing their circumstances with others. Further, if the rule is not followed, what will the consequences be? Rules, therefore, imply choice, and participants in a relationship may choose to ignore a particular rule.

Interpersonal Communication Is Learned

People obviously believe that interpersonal communication is a learned process. Otherwise, why would we be writing this book, and why would you be taking this course? Yet, as we mentioned at the beginning of this chapter, we often take for granted our ability to communicate. Still, we all need to refine and cultivate our skills to communicate with a wide assortment of people. As our book's theme underscores, you must be able to make informed communication choices in changing times.

You're in this course to learn more about interpersonal communication. But you've also been acquiring this information throughout your life. We learn how to communicate with one another from television, our peer group, and our partners. Early in our lives, most of us learn from our family. Consider this dialogue between Laura Reid and her 7-year-old son, Tucker:

Tucker: Mom, I saw Holly's dad driving a motorcycle today.

Laura: Really? That must've been cool to see. Holly's dad's name is Mr. Willows.

Tucker: What's his name?

Laura: Mr. Willows.

Tucker: No, Mom—what's his real name?

Laura: Honey, I told you. Mr. Willows.

Tucker: Doesn't he have a name like I do?

Laura: Little kids call him Mr. Willows. Grownups call him Kenny.

Tucker: Why can't I call him Kenny?

Laura: Because you're not a grownup and because he is older than you, you should call him Mr. Willows.

Clearly, Laura Reid is teaching her child a communication rule she believes leads to interpersonal effectiveness. She tells her son that he should use titles for adults. Implied in this teaching is that kids do not have the same conversational privileges as adults. Interestingly, this learned interpersonal skill evolves with age. For example, at age 24, what do you think Tucker will call Kenny Willows? This awkwardness about names is frequently felt by newlyweds as they become members of their spouse's family. Does a husband call his wife's mother "Mom," or does he call her by her first name? Of course, his mother-in-law may ask to be called "Mom," and yet her son-in-law may be uncomfortable with accommodating her request, especially if his own biological mother is still alive.

Interpersonal Communication Has Both Content and Relationship Levels

Each message that you communicate to another contains information on two levels. The **content level** refers to the information contained in the message. The words you speak to another person and how you say those words constitute the content of the message. Content, then, includes both verbal and nonverbal components. A message also contains a **relationship level**, which can be defined as how you want the receiver of a message to interpret your message. The relational dimension of a message gives us some idea how the speaker and the listener feel about each other. Content and relationship levels work simultaneously in a message, and it is difficult to think about sending a message that doesn't, in some way, comment on the relationship between the sender and receiver (Knapp & Vangelisti, 2005). In other words, we can't really separate the two. We always express an idea or thought (content), but that thought is always presented within a relational framework. Consider the following example.

Father Paul is a Catholic priest who is the pastor of a large parish in the Rocky Mountains. Corrine Murphy is the parish administrative assistant. Both have been at the parish for more than ten years and have been good friends throughout that time. One of the most stressful times in the church is during the Christmas season. The pastor is busy visiting homebound parishioners, while Corrine is busy overseeing the annual holiday pageant. With this stress comes a

content level
The verbal and nonverbal information contained in a message that indicates the topic of the message.

relationship level
The information contained in a message that indicates how the sender wants the receiver to interpret the message.

REVISITING
CASEinPOINT

1. *Apply any of the principles of interpersonal communication to Jackie and Scottie's conversation.*

2. *Indicate the content and relational dimensions associated with Jackie and Scottie's interaction.*

Y*ou can answer these questions online under the resources for Chapter 1 at your online Resource Center for Understanding Interpersonal Communication.*
(To learn how to get started with your online Resource Center, see the inside front cover of this book.)

lot of shouting between the two. On one occasion, several parishioners hear Father Paul yell, "Corrine, you forgot to tell me about the Lopez family! When do they need me to visit? Where is your mind these days?" Corrine shoots back: "I've got it under control. Just quit your nagging!" The parishioners listening to the two were a bit taken aback by the way they yelled at each other.

In this example, the parishioners who heard the conversation were simply attuned to the content dimension and failed to understand that the ten-year relationship between Father Paul and Corrine was unique to the two of them. Such direct interpersonal exchanges during stressful times were not out of the ordinary. Father Paul and Corrine frequently raised their voices to each other, and neither gave it a second thought. In a case like this, the content should be understood with the relationship in mind.

In this chapter so far, we have explored the definition of interpersonal communication in some detail and have described several principles associated with interpersonal communication. Now that you know what interpersonal communication is, let's focus on some of the misconceptions about interpersonal communication.

Myths about Interpersonal Communication

Maybe it's the media. Maybe it's Hollywood. Maybe it's Dr. Phil or Oprah. Whatever the source, for one reason or another, people operate under several misconceptions about interpersonal communication. These myths impede our understanding and enactment of effective interpersonal communication.

Interpersonal Communication Solves All Problems

We cannot stress enough that simply being skilled in interpersonal communication does not mean that you are prepared to work out all of your relational problems. When you learn to communicate well, you may communicate clearly about a problem but not necessarily be able to solve it. Also, keep in mind that communication involves both talking and listening. Many students have told us during their advising appointments that sometimes when they try to "talk out a problem," they achieve no satisfaction. It seems, then, that with the emphasis the media place on talking, many students forget about the role of listening. We hope you leave this course with an understanding of how to communicate effectively with others in a variety of relationships. We also hope you realize that simply because you are talking does not mean that you will solve all of your relationship problems.

Interpersonal Communication Is Always a Good Thing

National best-selling self-help books and famous self-improvement gurus have made huge amounts of money promoting the idea that communication is the magic potion for all of life's ailments. Most often, communication is a good thing in our relationships with others. We wouldn't be writing this book if we didn't think that! Yet, there are times when communication results in less-than-satisfying relationship experiences. A relatively new area of research in interpersonal communication is called "the dark side" (Cupach & Spitzberg, 1994, 2004; Spitzberg & Cupach, 1998).

The **dark side of interpersonal communication** generally refers to negative communication exchanges between people. People can communicate in ways that are manipulative, deceitful, exploitive, homophobic, racist, and emotionally abusive (Cupach & Spitzberg, 1994). In other words, we need to be aware that communication can be downright nasty at times and that interpersonal communication is not always satisfying and rewarding. Although most people approach interpersonal communication thoughtfully and with an open mind, others are less sincere. To contrast the dark side, we also discuss the **bright side of interpersonal communication**, which focuses on the altruistic, supportive, and affirming reasons that people communicate with others. Look for discussions of the dark and bright sides of interpersonal communication throughout the chapters of this book.

Interpersonal Communication Is Common Sense

Consider the following question: If interpersonal communication is just a matter of common sense, why do we have so many problems communicating with others? We need to abandon the idea that communication is simply common sense.

It is true that we should be sure to use whatever common sense we have in our personal interactions, but this strategy will get us only so far. In some cases, a skilled interpersonal communicator may effectively rely on his or her common sense, but we usually also need to make use of an extensive repertoire of skills to make informed choices in our relationships. One problem with believing that interpersonal communication is merely common sense relates to the diversity of our population. As we discuss in Chapter 3, cultural variation continues to characterize U.S. society. Making the assumption that all people intuitively know how to communicate with everyone ignores the significant cultural differences in communication norms. Even males and females tend to look at the same event differently (e.g., Dow & Wood, 2006).

dark side of interpersonal communication

Negative communication exchanges between people, such as manipulation, deceit, and verbal aggression.

bright side of interpersonal communication

Altruistic, supportive, and affirming communication exchanges between people.

To rid ourselves of the myth of common sense, we simply need to take culture and gender into consideration.

Interpersonal Communication Is Synonymous with Interpersonal Relationships

We don't automatically have an interpersonal relationship with someone merely because we are exchanging interpersonal communication with him or her. Interpersonal communication *can* lead *to* interpersonal relationships, but an accumulation of interpersonal messages does not *automatically* result in an interpersonal relationship. Sharing a pleasant conversation about your family with a stranger riding on the bus with you doesn't mean you have a relationship with that person.

Relationships do not just appear. William Wilmot (1995) remarked that relationships "emerge from recurring episodic enactments" (p. 25). That is, for you and another person to develop an interpersonal relationship, a pattern of intimate exchanges must take place over time. Relationships usually will not happen unless two people demonstrate a sense of caring and respect, and have significant periods of time to work on their relational issues.

Your turn

E xplore the similarities and differences in the way you communicate with your neighbors, family, friends, and coworkers. If you like, you can use your student workbook or your **Understanding Interpersonal Communication** Online Resources to complete this activity.

Interpersonal Communication Is Always Face to Face

Throughout this chapter, most of our discussion has centered on face-to-face encounters between people. Indeed, this is the primary way that people meet and cultivate their interpersonal skills with each other. It is also the focus of most of the research in interpersonal communication. Yet, large numbers of people are beginning to utilize the Internet in their communication with others. This mediated interpersonal communication requires us to expand our discussion of interpersonal communication beyond personal encounters. In the spirit of inclusiveness, we incorporate technological relations into our interpretation of interpersonal communication and devote Chapter 11 to this important topic.

Thus far, this chapter has given you a fundamental framework for examining interpersonal communication. We close the chapter by examining a feature of the interpersonal communication process that is not easily taught and is often difficult to comprehend: ethics.

Interpersonal Communication Ethics

Communication ethicist Richard Johanneson (2002) concluded that "ethical issues may arise in human behavior whenever that behavior could have significant impact on other persons, when the behavior involves conscious choice of means and ends, and when the behavior can be judged by standards of right and wrong" (p. 1). In other words, ethics is the cornerstone of interpersonal communication.

Ethics is the perceived rightness or wrongness of an action or behavior. Researchers have identified ethics as a type of moral decision making, determined in large part by society (Pfeiffer & Forsberg, 2005). A primary goal of ethics is to "establish appropriate constraints on ourselves" (Englehardt, 2001, p. 1). Ethical decisions involve value judgments, and not everyone will agree with those values. For instance, do you tell racist jokes in front of others and think that they are harmless ways to make people laugh? What sort of value judgment is part of the decision to tell or not to tell a joke? In interpersonal communication, acting ethically is critical. As Raymond Pfeiffer and Ralph Forsberg (2005) concluded, "To act ethically is, at the very least, to strive to act in ways that do not hurt other people, that respect their dignity, individuality, and unique moral value, and that treat others as equally important to oneself " (p. 7). If we're not prepared to act in this way, one can conclude that we do not consider ethics important. Overall, being ethical means having respect for others, shouldering responsibility, acting thoughtfully with others, and being honest. The following section fleshes out these ethical behaviors more thoroughly.

Ethics is necessarily part of not only our personal relationships, but our work relationships as well. To get a sense of the interplay between ethics and various jobs, consider Table 1.1 on page 34, which shows what the U.S. public views as being the most and least ethical occupations. See if you agree with how the country views ethical occupations and if your career choice is found among the top 23 listed. What do you think the rankings look like today?

ethics

The perceived rightness or wrongness of an action or behavior, determined in large part by society.

Five Ethical Systems of Communication

There are many ways to make value judgments in interpersonal communication. Researchers have discussed a number of different ethical systems of communication relevant to our interpersonal encounters (e.g., Andersen, 1996; Englehardt, 2001; Jensen, 1997). We will discuss five of them here. As we briefly overview each system, keep in mind that these systems attempt to let us know what it means to act morally.

"Miss Dugan, will you send someone in here who can distinguish right from wrong?"

Table 1.1 Ethics on the job: Views of the most ethical occupations

Occupation	1999 Rating*	2006 Rating*
Nurses	73%	84%
Druggists/pharmacists	69%	73%
Veterinarians	63%	71%
Medical doctors	58%	69%
Dentists	52%	62%
Engineers	50%	61%
Clergy	56%	58%
College teachers	52%	58%
Police officers	52%	54%
Psychiatrists	N/A	38%
Bankers	30%	37%
Chiropractors	26%	36%
Journalists	24%	26%
State governors	24%	22%
Business executives	23%	18%
Lawyers	13%	18%
Stockbrokers	16%	17%
Senators	17%	15%
Members of Congress	11%	14%
Insurance salespeople	10%	13%
HMO managers	10%	12%
Advertising personnel	9%	11%
Car salespeople	8%	7%

*Based on those who responded "very high" or "high" in ethics.

From *USA Today*, December 12, 2006, p. 8A.

categorical imperative

An ethical system, based on the work of philosopher Immanuel Kant, that advances the notion that individuals follow moral absolutes. The underlying tenet in this ethical system suggests that we should act as an example to others.

Categorical Imperative

The first ethical system, the **categorical imperative**, is based on the work of philosopher Immanuel Kant (Kuehn, 2001). Kant's categorical imperative refers to individuals following moral absolutes. This ethical system suggests that we should act as though we are an example to others. According to this system, the key question when making a moral decision is: What would happen if everyone did this? Thus, you should not do something that you wouldn't feel is fine for everyone to do all the time. Further, Kant believed that the consequences of actions are not important; what matters is the ethical principle behind those actions.

For example, let's say that Mark confides to Karla, a coworker, that he has leukemia. Karla tells no one else because Mark fears his health insurance will be threatened if management finds out. Elizabeth, the supervisor, asks Karla if she knows what's happening with Mark because he misses work and is always tired. The categorical imperative dictates that Karla tell her boss the truth, despite the fact that telling the truth may affect Mark's job, his future with the company, and his relationship with Karla. The categorical imperative requires us to tell the truth because Kant believed that enforcing the principle of truth telling is more important than worrying about the short-term consequences of telling the truth.

Utilitarianism

The second ethical system, **utilitarianism**, was developed in 1861 by John Stuart Mill (Capaldi, 2004). According to this system, what is ethical is what will bring the greatest good for the greatest number of people. Unlike Kant, Mill believed the consequences of moral actions are important. Maximizing satisfaction and happiness is essential. For example, suppose you're over at a friend's house and her younger sister is crying incessantly. You notice your friend grabbing her sister, shaking her, and yelling for her to be quiet. Afterward, you observe red marks on the child's arms. Do you report your friend to the authorities? Do you remain quiet? Do you talk to your friend?

Making a decision based on utilitarianism or what is best for the greater good means that you will speak out or take some action. Although it would be easier on you and your friend if you remained silent, doing so would not serve the greater good. According to utilitarianism, you should either talk to your friend or report your friend's actions to an appropriate individual.

The Golden Mean

The **golden mean**, a third ethical system, proposes that we should aim for harmony and balance in our lives. This principle, articulated more than 2,500 years ago by Aristotle (Metzger, 1995), suggests that a person's moral virtue stands between two vices, with the middle, or the mean, being the foundation for a rational society.

Let's say that Cora, Jackie, and Lester are three employees who work for a large insurance company. During a break one afternoon, someone asks what kind of childhood each had. Cora goes into specific detail, talking about her abusive father: "He really let me have it, and it all started when I was 5," she begins before launching into a long description. On the other hand, Jackie tells the group only, "My childhood was okay." Lester tells the group that his was a pretty rough childhood: "It was tough financially. We didn't have a lot of money. But we really all got along well." In this example, Cora was on one extreme, revealing too much information. Jackie was at the other extreme, revealing very little, if anything. Lester's decision to reveal a reasonable amount of information about his childhood was an ethical one; he practiced

utilitarianism

An ethical system, developed by John Stuart Mill, that suggests that what is ethical will bring the greatest good for the greatest number of people. In this system, consequences of moral actions, especially maximizing satisfaction and happiness, are important.

golden mean

An ethical system, articulated by Aristotle, that proposes a person's moral virtue stands between two vices, with the middle, or the mean, being the foundation for a rational society.

the golden mean by providing a sufficient amount of information but not too much. In other words, he presented a rational and balanced perspective. In this case, note that revealing too much and revealing too little may make another awkward or uncomfortable. Finding the "balance" in self-disclosure is especially difficult, a topic we discuss in greater detail in Chapter 8.

Ethic of Care

An **ethic of care**, the fourth ethical system, means being concerned with connection. Carol Gilligan first conceptualized an ethic of care by looking at women's ways of moral decision making. She felt that because men have been the dominant voices in society, women's commitment toward connection has gone unnoticed. Gilligan (1982) initially felt that an ethic of care was a result of how women were raised. Although her ethical principles pertain primarily to women, Gilligan's research applies to men as well. Some men adopt the ethic, and some women do not adopt the ethic. In contrast to the categorical imperative, for instance, the ethic of care is concerned with consequences of decisions.

For instance, suppose that Ben and Paul are having a conversation about whether it's right to go behind a person's back and disclose that he or she is gay (called *outing* a person). Ben makes an argument that it's a shame that people won't own up to being gay; they are who they are. If someone hides his or her sexuality, Ben believes that it's fine to "out" that person. Paul, expressing an ethic of care, tells his friend that no one should reveal another person's sexual identity. That information should remain private unless an individual wishes to reveal it. Paul explains that outing someone would have serious negative repercussions for the relationships of the person being outed and thus shouldn't be done. In this example, Paul exemplifies a symbolic connection to those who don't want to discuss their sexual identity with others.

Significant Choice

The fifth ethical system, **significant choice**, is an ethical orientation conceptualized by Thomas Nilsen (Nilsen, 1966). Nilsen argued that communication is ethical to the extent that it maximizes people's ability to exercise free choice. Information should be given to others in a noncoercive way so that they can make free and informed decisions. For example, if you place a personal ad on the Internet and fail to disclose that you are married, you are not ethical in your communication with others. However, if you give information regarding your relationship status and other details, you are practicing the ethical system of significant choice.

Understanding Ethics and Our Own Values

Ethics permeates interpersonal communication. We make ongoing ethical decisions in all our interpersonal encounters. Should someone's sexual past

ethic of care

An ethical system, based on the concepts of Carol Gilligan, that is concerned with the connections among people and the moral consequences of decisions.

significant choice

An ethical system, conceptualized by Thomas Nilsen, underscoring the belief that communication is ethical to the extent that it maximizes our ability to exercise free choice. In this system, information should be given to others in a noncoercive way so that people can make free and informed decisions.

Table 1.2 Ethical systems of interpersonal communication

Ethical System	Responsibility	Action
Categorical imperative	To adhere to a moral absolute	Tell the truth
Utilitarianism	To ensure the greatest good for the greatest number of people	Produce favorable consequences
Golden mean	To achieve rationality and balance	Create harmony and balance for the community and the individual
Ethic of care	To establish connection	Establish caring relationships
Significant choice	To enable free choice	Maximize individual choice

Adapted from Englehardt, 2001.

be completely revealed to a partner? How do you treat an ex-friend or ex-partner in future encounters? Is it ever okay to lie to protect your friend? These kinds of questions challenge millions of interpersonal relationships.

Raymond Pfeiffer and Ralph Forsberg (2005) conclude that when we are confronted with ethical decisions, "we should not ignore our society's cultural, religious, literary, and moral traditions.

Our values have emerged from and are deeply enmeshed in these traditions. They often teach important lessons concerning the difficult decisions we face in life" (p. 8).

The five ethical systems, summarized in Table 1.2, can give you strategies for making ethical decisions. However, making sense of the world and of our interpersonal relationships requires us to understand our own values. And, these values are apparent not only in our face-to-face conversations, but our online conversations as well. Ethical behavior is essential when we communicate with people whom we don't see or with whom we have no shared physical space. We return to this topic later in the book.

We need to understand that because ethical choices can have lasting physical, emotional, financial, and psychological consequences, a sense of ethics should guide us on a daily basis. Being aware of and sensitive to your decisions and their consequences will help you make the right choices in these changing times.

"On the Internet, nobody knows you're a dog."

Choices for Changing Times: Competency and Civility

Ethics & Choice

We close Chapter 1 by reiterating two themes that guide this book: choice and changing times. Throughout this text, you will explore many topics associated with interpersonal communication. We encourage you to consider the importance of choice and change as you read the material.

Lenora Watkins was clearly in a bind. She had dated Luke for about a month. She didn't have any serious complaints about him but felt that Luke was sending her mixed messages. One day, he'd come over to her dorm room, and they'd sit together studying on the bed. The next time they were together, Luke would act distant, not wanting to even hold her hand. This back-and-forth intimacy was driving Lenora nuts, and she was quite frustrated with the situation.

Lenora thought nothing could be much worse than her current experiences with Luke, so she let her friend Carmen set her up with a coworker. On a coffee date, Lenora met Rodney, a professional who had divorced about three months ago. Lenora and Rodney got along great, and she felt less frustration with him than with Luke. They started dating regularly, and Lenora enjoyed his company a lot.

Lenora wasn't sure what she should do in this situation. Although neither Luke nor Rodney had said they expected an exclusive relationship with her, she knew they probably assumed she wasn't dating anyone else. Plus, she just felt funny trying to juggle the two relationships. She felt her silence to each of the men about the other was a lie of omission, but she wasn't sure what would happen if she told them the truth.

Lenora faces an ethical dilemma. Discuss the ethical problems pertaining to her relationships with Luke and Rodney. How should she handle the question of whether to tell them about each other? Justify your answers by using one or more of the ethical systems of communication (categorical imperative, utilitarianism, golden mean, ethic of care, or significant choice).

Go to your online Resource Center for *Understanding Interpersonal Communication* to access an interactive version of this scenario under the resources for Chapter 1. The interactive version of this scenario allows you to choose an appropriate response to this dilemma and then see what consequences your choice brings about. You can also compare your answers to the questions at the end of the scenario to those provided by the authors and, if requested, email your response to your instructor. (To learn how to get started with your online Resource Center, see the inside front cover of this book.)

communication competency

The ability to communicate with knowledge, skills, and thoughtfulness.

First, we believe that you have an abundance of choices available to you in your communication with others, and we hope that you will always choose to become a more effective communicator. Yet, we know that our communication with others is sometimes filled with anxiety, confusion, unpleasantness, excitement, and angst. Having a toolbox of ways to adapt and respond appropriately to all sorts of communication situations will help you achieve the meanings you intend to convey.

At the core of communication effectiveness are two behaviors: competency and civility. **Communication competency**, or the ability to communicate with knowledge, skills, and thoughtfulness, should be foremost when trying to meet a communication challenge. When we are competent, our communication is both appropriate and effective. We use communication appropriately when we accommodate the cultural expectations for communicating, including using the rules, understanding the roles, and being "other-centered." When we are effective, we have acquired meaning and each communicator has achieved his or her goals in a conversation or a relationship.

As you read the following chapters, you will acquire a lot of knowledge about interpersonal communication. You will also be asked to apply that knowledge as you consider several interpersonal skills that we discuss at the end of each chapter. Developing a large repertoire

As Joseph Forgas (2002) states, perception and individual identity go hand in hand. This intersection is the focus of our chapter. We begin by explaining the perception process.

Understanding Perception: A Seesaw Experience

In most of our interpersonal encounters, we form an impression of the other person. These impressions, or perceptions, are critical to achieving meaning. The process of looking at people, things, activities, and events can involve many factors. For instance, in a face-to-face meeting with a teacher to challenge a low grade on a paper, you would probably notice not only your instructor's facial reactions and body position but also your own. You might also be attentive to the general feeling you get when going into the instructor's office. And you would probably prepare for the encounter by asking other students what their experiences with the instructor had been with respect to grade challenges.

Perceiving an interpersonal encounter, then, involves much more than hearing the words of another person. Perception is an active and challenging process that involves all five senses: touch, sight, taste, smell, and hearing. Through perception, we gain important information about the interpersonal communication skills of others and of ourselves. For our purposes, then, we define **perception** as a process of using our senses to respond to stimuli. The perception process occurs in four stages: attending and selecting, organizing, interpreting, and retrieving. Because perception is the foundation of all of our interpersonal communication, we will describe each stage (see Table 2.1 on page 48).

Attending and Selecting

The first stage, **attending and selecting**, requires us to use our visual, auditory, tactile, and olfactory senses to respond to stimuli in our interpersonal environment. When we are attentive and selective, we are **mindful**. Ellen Langer (1989) believes that mindful communicators pay close attention to detail. Being mindful means being observant and aware of your surroundings. In the case of interpersonal communication, this includes engaging your senses. For example, take Dr. Gomez's mindfulness as he attended to the parents' grief, his own personal reaction to the news, and his perceptions of how the couple might perceive him as a medical professional. Further, he is attentive and focused. He saw the couple's sorrowful expressions (sight), held the mother's hand (touch), and listened as they talked about their situation (hearing).

Dr. Gomez was in a situation that called for mindfulness, but not every situation requires complete mindfulness. We are constantly bombarded with stimuli that make it almost impossible to focus on every detail of an encounter.

perception

The process of using our senses to understand and respond to stimuli. The perception process occurs in four stages: attending and selecting, organizing, interpreting, and retrieving.

attending and selecting

The first stage of the perception process, requiring us to use our visual, auditory, tactile, and olfactory senses to respond to stimuli in our interpersonal environment.

mindful

Having the ability to engage our senses so that we are observant and aware of our surroundings.

Table 2.1 Stages of the interpersonal perception process

Stage	Description	Example
Attending and selecting	First stage in the perception process. It involves sorting out stimuli. We choose to attend to some stimuli and to ignore others.	At the campus library, Kendrick notices his friend talking to a woman in one of his classes he had wanted to meet and date.
Organizing	Second stage in the perception process. It involves categorizing stimuli to make sense of them.	Kendrick creates the belief that his friend and the woman are close.
Interpreting	Third stage in the perception process. It involves assigning meaning to stimuli.	Kendrick decides not to ask his classmate out for a date because she is already dating his friend.
Retrieving	Fourth stage in the perception process. It involves recalling information we have stored in our memories.	Kendrick remembers that the two were together at a concert on campus a few weeks earlier.

As a result, we use **selective perception**. When we selectively perceive, we decide to attend to things that fulfill our own needs, capture our own interests, or meet our own expectations. We pay attention to some things while ignoring others. You can explore this idea further in an article that discusses how we attend to and select what is important to us from the sometimes overwhelming number of messages we receive each day. Go to your online Resource Center for *Understanding Interpersonal Communication* to access *InfoTrac College Edition Exercise 2.1: Attending to What Is Important* under the resources for Chapter 2. Read "Bet You Can't Remember How to Tie the Bows on Your Life Jackets," available through InfoTrac College Edition.

In our relationships with others, we use selective perception all the time. For example, let's say that Luke has decided to end his relationship with Melissa. He explains that he thinks it is in her best interest as well as his for them to break up. However, he says that he has learned a lot while in the relationship. Luke continues talking, telling Melissa several of the things he feels he learned from being with her, and explains that he is grateful to have spent time with her.

As Melissa selectively perceives this unexpected conversation, she probably attends to the reason why Luke is breaking up with her. Regardless of everything else Luke says, Melissa listens for a particular piece of information. As a result, she filters and ignores other information, such as what Luke learned while being in the relationship. As would most people in such a situation, Melissa wants to know what motivated Luke's decision to break up. In addition to selectively perceiving his words, Melissa also selectively attends to

selective perception

Directing our attention to certain stimuli while ignoring other stimuli.

tion, **retrieving**, asks us to recall information stored in our memories. At first glance, retrieving appears to be pretty straightforward. Yet, as you think about it further, you'll see that the retrieval process involves selection as well. At times, we use **selective retention**, a behavior that recalls information that agrees with our perceptions and selectively forgets information that does not. Here is an example that highlights the retrieval process and some potential conflict associated with it.

Crystal sits with her friends as they talk about Professor Wendall. She doesn't really like what she hears. They talk about how boring the professor is and that his tests are too hard. They also make fun of his Southern drawl as they imitate his teaching. Crystal remembers that she had Professor Wendall for a class more than two years ago, but doesn't recall him being such a bad professor. In fact, she remembers the biology course she took from him as challenging and interesting. It doesn't make sense that her friends don't like Professor Wendall.

So, why do Crystal's friends and Crystal perceive Professor Wendall differently? Crystal has retrieved information about her professor differently. He may have ridiculed students, but Crystal doesn't recall that. She remembers his accent, but she does not remember it causing any problems. She also recollects Wendall's exams to be fair; she never received anything below a grade of B. Crystal's retrieval process, then, has influenced her perception of Professor Wendall in the classroom. When we exercise selective retention in the perception process, then, it affects our communication with others.

So far, we have examined the perception process and its components. As we know, interpersonal communication can be difficult at times. Understanding how perception functions in those encounters helps clarify potential problems. We now turn our attention to several influences on our perception process. As you will learn, a number of factors affect the accuracy of our perceptions.

Influences on Perception

When we perceive activities, events, or other people, our perceptions are a result of many variables. In other words, we don't all perceive our environment in the same way because individual perceptions are shaped by individual differences. We now discuss five factors that shape our perceptions: culture, sex and gender, physical factors, technology, and our sense of self.

Culture

Culture is an important teacher of perception (Martin & Nakayama, 2007) and provides the meaning we give to our perceptions (Chen & Starosta, 2006). In Chapter 3, you will learn how culture pervades our lives and affects communication. With regard to perception, culture dictates how something should be organized and interpreted. For instance, Bantu refugees from Somalia perceive time differently after they arrive in the United States. In Somalia,

retrieving

The fourth and final stage of the perception process, in which we recall information stored in our memories.

selective retention

Recalling information that agrees with our perceptions and selectively forgetting information that does not.

they do not have wall clocks or watches, but in the United States, they learn to be punctual and watch the clock. In addition, William Hamilton (2004) notes:

> Bantu parents learn that hitting their children is discouraged, though that was how they were disciplined in Africa. . . . they learn that Fourth of July fireworks are exploded to entertain not kill, and that being hit by a water balloon, as Bantu children were in one incident at school, is a game and not a hateful fight. (p. A14)

As another example, in the United States, most people expect others to maintain direct eye contact during conversation. This conversational expectation is influenced by a European American cultural value. However, traditional Japanese culture does not dictate direct eye contact during conversation (McDaniel, 2005), so we may feel a classmate from Japan is not listening to us during conversation when he or she doesn't maintain eye contact. As a final illustration, the teachings of Islam and Christianity guide many Lebanese American families in virtually every decision of life, including birth, death, education, courtship, marriage, divorce, and contraception (Hashem, 1997). This adherence to religious principles may be difficult for someone without any religious connection to understand. Recall that each time you communicate with another person, you're drawing upon relational schema, a topic we discussed earlier. It may be difficult for two people with differing cultural backgrounds to sustain meaning if they are using two different schemata. We highlight ways to improve competency in this area at the end of the chapter.

To better understand how perceptions stemming from cultural beliefs affect people in important aspects of their lives, read the article "Asian-

Our culture influences how we perceive ourselves and others. By the same token, when we immerse ourselves in another culture, our perception of ourselves and others can evolve and change.

© Thompson/Anthro-Photo

Americans Face Great Wall; Perceptions, Cultural Traditions Hinder Advancement to Top Corporate Ranks," available through InfoTrac College Edition. Go to your online Resource Center for *Understanding Interpersonal Communication* to access **InfoTrac College Edition Exercise 2.2: Cultural Perceptions and the Glass Ceiling** under the resources for Chapter 2.

You can see, then, that cultural heritage affects how people perceive the world. In turn, that same cultural heritage affects how people communicate with and receive communication from others. Cultural variation is sometimes the reason we can't understand why someone does something or the reason why others question our behavior. Although it's natural to believe that others look at things the same way you do, remember that cultures can vary tremendously in their practices, and these differences affect perception.

Sex and Gender

Sex refers to the biological make-up of an individual (male or female). **Gender** refers to the learned behaviors a culture associates with being a male or female. For example, we have a masculine or feminine gender. If we possess both masculine and feminine traits in equally large amounts, we are called *androgynous*. Possessing relatively low amounts of masculinity and femininity is termed *undifferentiated* (see Figure 2.1). It is possible to be a masculine female or a feminine male.

Researchers have investigated the relationship between perception and sex. Looking at perceptions of body type, researchers found that boys and

sex

The biological make-up of an individual (male or female).

gender

The learned behaviors a culture associates with being a male or female, known as masculinity or femininity.

Figure 2.1   Gender roles in communication

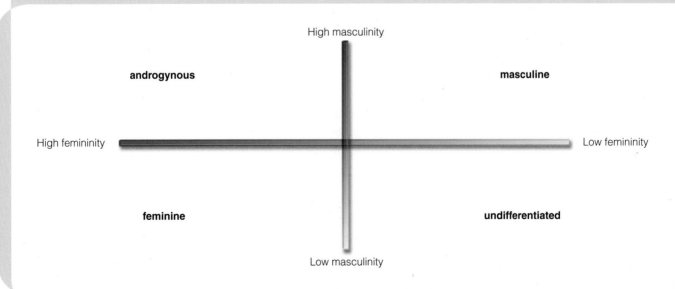

High masculinity

androgynous   masculine

High femininity   Low femininity

feminine   undifferentiated

Low masculinity

girls in kindergarten and second grade differed in preferences for body types. Girls preferred a thinner figure than boys, and girls perceived thinness as both attractive and feminine. Boys preferred more athletic builds by kindergarten and were indirectly communicating "preferences for being smart, moderately strong, and somewhat prone to fighting" (Miller, Plant, & Hanke, 1993, p. 56). Other researchers have noted that when asked to compare themselves with others, college-aged women—more than men—were inclined to compare themselves with professional models when evaluating their sexual attractiveness and weight (Franzoi & Klaber, 2007).

Many of these differences are a result of the way men and women have been raised. **Gender role socialization** is the process by which women and men learn the gender roles appropriate to their sex (for example, being masculine if you are biologically a male). This socialization affects the way the sexes perceive the world. Messages about masculinity and femininity are communicated to children early in life, and these messages stick with us into adulthood. Sandra Bem (1993) notes that when we understand and organize our world around masculinity and femininity, we are using a **gender schema**. Specifically, she believes that through a schema, we process and categorize beliefs, ideas, and events as either masculine or feminine. If new information doesn't fit our gender schema, Bem maintains that we simply discard it.

Think about your perceptions of the following situations:

- A 5-year-old boy playing house with a 6-year-old neighbor girl
- A retired elderly male dancing with another male at a New Year's Eve party
- A newborn girl wearing a pink dress with flowers
- An adolescent female helping her father change the oil in his car

gender role socialization

The process by which women and men learn the gender roles appropriate to their sex. This process affects the way the sexes perceive the world.

gender schema

A mental framework we use to process and categorize beliefs, ideas, and events as either masculine or feminine in order to understand and organize our world.

Do any of these situations contradict how you normally view male and female behavior? Does the age of the person make a difference? If so, why? What contributes to these perceptions? Parents? Teachers? Peers? Games? In all likelihood, each of these—in some way—has helped shape your current perceptions.

Men and women frequently look at things differently (Ivy & Backlund, 2003), depending on what gender schema they bring to a circumstance. As people sort out the various stimuli in their environment, gender cannot be ignored or devalued. Certainly, men and women can reject gender prescriptions and help society expand its perceptual expectations. However, most people continue to look at their worlds with rigid interpretations of the sexes, resulting in perceptions that may be distorted or inaccurate. To further explore the power of perception in relation to gender and communication, read the article "Exploring the Impact of Gender Role Self-Perception on Communication Style," available through InfoTrac College Edition. Go to your online Resource Center for *Understanding Interpersonal Communication* to access *InfoTrac College Edition Exercise 2.3: Sex, Gender, and Perception about Communication* under the resources for Chapter 2.

As you read and review the material, keep in mind two of the words in this book's title: "changing times." We live in a society that is more culturally diverse than ever. We describe this cultural complexity in this chapter and look at the significant issues associated with culture and communication. The words of Larry Samovar and Richard Porter (2004) underscore our rationale for this chapter: "What members of a particular culture value and how they perceive the universe are usually far more important than whether they eat with chopsticks, their hands, or metal utensils" (p. 24). Knowledge of others' cultural values and practices enhances intercultural communication.

For intercultural communication to occur, individuals don't have to be from different countries. In a diverse society such as the United States, we can experience intercultural communication within one state, one town, or even one neighborhood. You may live in an urban center where it's likely people from various cultural backgrounds live together. In the South End of Boston, for instance, it is common to see people with Caribbean, Cambodian, and Latino backgrounds all living on the same street. In Milwaukee, one would be able to find both Polish and Mexican communities on the south side of the city.

Trying to understand people who may think, talk, look, and act differently from us can be challenging at times. Just think about the words people use to describe those who may be culturally different from them: odd, weird, strange, unusual, and unpredictable. These associations have existed over centuries. Consider the words of fifth century Greek playwright Aeschylus: "Everyone is quick to blame the alien." As we discuss in this chapter, today, the "alien" takes many troubling shapes and forms, especially with anti-immigration perceptions permeating society.

Intercultural communication theorists (for example, Jackson, 2002) argue that humans cannot exist without culture. Our individuality is constructed around culture. As we learned in Chapter 2, our identities are shaped by our conversations and relationships with others and vice versa. Our cultural background enters into this mix by shaping our identity, our communication practices, and our responses to others. We tend to use other people as "guideposts for normative behavior" (Jackson, p. 360). In doing so, we can focus on how others from diverse cultures differ from us. For instance, when Jean from the United States meets Lee from China in her philosophy class, she might notice how Lee smiles more frequently than her U.S. counterparts. Jean might also observe that Lee is much more deferential to the professor than she and her U.S. friends are. Yet, this comparison is incomplete. Intercultural scholars believe that despite their cultural differences, people continue to have a great deal in common. This chapter explores both what factors culturally bind us as well as what elements divide us.

Defining Culture

Culture is a difficult concept to define, in part because it is complex, multidimensional, and abstract. Some researchers (e.g., Kroeber & Kluckhohn, 1993) have discovered over 300 different definitions for the word! For our purposes, we define **culture** as the shared, personal, and learned life experiences of a group of individuals who have a common set of values, norms, and traditions. The values of a culture are its standards and what it emphasizes most. Norms are patterns of communication. Traditions are the customs of a culture. These values, norms, and traditions affect our interpersonal relationships within a culture. It's almost impossible to separate values, norms, and traditions from any conversation pertaining to intercultural communication.

As we define the term culture, keep in mind that we are embracing a "global" interpretation. That is, we acknowledge culture to include commonly-held components such as race, ethnicity, physical ability, age, gender, and sex. Yet, we also believe that a person's religious identity, career path, sexual identity, and family background are all necessarily part of our discussions of culture. Our examples in this book reflect this expansive view of culture. We now look at three underlying principles associated with our definition of culture: culture is learned, culture creates community, and culture is multileveled.

Culture Is Learned

We aren't born with knowledge of the practices and behaviors of our culture. People learn the values, norms, and traditions of their culture through the communication of symbols for meaning. We learn about culture both consciously and unconsciously. We can learn about culture directly, such as when someone actually teaches us, and indirectly, such as when we observe cultural practices. In the United States, our family, friends, and the media are the primary teachers of our culture.

Let's look at an example of a learned ritual that varies depending on culture. Bradford Hall (2005) observes some differences in dating in New Zealand and the United States. In New Zealand, it is uncommon for someone to exclusively date another unless he or she has gone out with that person in a group of friends first. Even television shows in New Zealand suggest that romantic relationships begin in groups. Further, exclusive dating in New Zealand occurs only after the couple makes long-term relationship plans. As Hall observes (and as most of you already know), in the United States, exclusive dating does not have to be preceded by group interactions, and many people in exclusive dating relationships in the United States haven't made long-term plans.

When you have acquired the knowledge, skills, attitudes, and values that allow you to become fully functioning in your culture, you are said to be enculturated. **Enculturation** occurs when a person—either consciously or unconsciously—learns to identify with a particular culture and a culture's thinking, way of relating, and worldview. Enculturation allows for successful participation in a particular society and makes a person more accepted by that society. Learning about a society usually takes place within a family or

culture

The shared, personal, and learned life experiences of a group of individuals who have a common set of values, norms, and traditions.

enculturation

Occurs when a person—either consciously or unconsciously—learns to identify with a particular culture and a culture's thinking, way of relating, and worldview.

close relationships. Isa becomes enculturated, for instance, when as a little girl she learns the rules about not using profanity, dressing "like a girl," and going to church each Sunday. Although she is young, she is slowly being enculturated into the United States, and this process will continue throughout her lifetime.

Whereas enculturation occurs when you are immersed in your own culture, **acculturation** exists when you learn, adapt to, and adopt the appropriate behaviors and rules of a host culture. Acculturated individuals have effectively absorbed themselves into another society. However, you don't have to sacrifice your personal set of principles simply because you've found yourself in another culture. For example, some immigrants to the United States may attend school in a large city such as Phoenix or Miami. These individuals may adapt to the city by using its services, understanding the laws of the city, or participating in social gatherings on campus. Yet, they may return to many of their cultural practices while in their homes, such as participating in spiritual healings.

To sum up, enculturation is first-culture learning and acculturation is second-culture learning.

Explore how the media contribute to stereotypes of various cultures and influences what we learn about our own culture. If you like, you can use your student workbook or your **Understanding Interpersonal Communication** Online Resources to complete this activity.

Your turn

Culture Creates Community

Central to our definition of culture is the assumption that it helps to create a sense of community. We view **community** as the common understandings among people who are committed to coexisting together. Cultures create their own sets of values, norms, rules, and customs, which help them to communicate.

In the United States, communities are filled with a number of cultures within cultures, sometimes referred to as **co-cultures** (Orbe, 1998). For example, a Cuban American community, a Chinese American community, and a community of people with disabilities are all co-cultures within one larger culture (the United States). Each community has unique communication behaviors and practices, but each also subscribes to behaviors and practices embraced by the larger United States culture. Many times, the two cultures mesh effortlessly; however, sometimes a **culture clash**, or a conflict over cultural expectations, occurs. For instance, imagine how three European American students using slang while working on a group project might alienate a Mexican American group member who is still learning English. Or, consider the reaction a recently immigrated Islamic woman, who is accustomed to

acculturation

Occurs when a person learns, adapts to, and adopts the appropriate behaviors and rules of a host culture.

community

The common understandings among people who are committed to coexisting.

co-culture

A culture within a culture.

culture clash

A conflict over cultural expectations and experiences.

© J. Emilio Flores/Getty Images

wearing hijab (traditional Muslim head and body covering), might have to more revealing Western dress. Culture clashes are not necessarily bad; in fact, having the opportunity to view a situation from a different cultural point-of-view can be productive. Michael Jonas of the *Boston Globe* (August 5, 2007) observes that "culture clashes can produce a dynamic give-and-take, generating a solution that may have eluded a group of people with more similar backgrounds and approaches" (p. D2).

Culture Is Multileveled

On the national level of culture, we assume that people of the same national background share many things that bind them in a common culture: language, values, norms, and traditions. Thus, we expect Germans to differ from Hmong based on differing national cultures. However, as discussed in the previous section, cultures can be formed on other levels, such as generation, sexual identity, gender, race, and region, among others. For example, in many parts of the

For the most part, the United States embraces the notion of co-cultures. Although U.S. co-cultures often clash, most co-culture members balance their own cultural practices with those of the larger culture and sometimes even invite people outside their co-culture to participate in their traditions.

country, regionalisms exist. People who live in the middle of the United States (in states such as Kansas, Illinois, Iowa, Nebraska, Indiana, and Wisconsin) are often referred to as "Midwesterners." People who live in Vermont, New Hampshire, Maine, Massachusetts, Rhode Island, and Connecticut are called "New Englanders." Both Midwesterners and New Englanders have their own unique way of looking at things, but the two regions also share a great deal in common—namely, pragmatic thinking and an independent spirit.

Another example of a co-culture that is not based on nationality is a culture that develops around a certain age cohort. People who grew up in different time frames grew up in different cultural eras, as the labels we attach to various generations suggest—for example, Depression Babies of the 1930s or Flower Children of the 1960s. The culture of the Great Depression in the 1930s reflected the efforts of people trying to survive during troubling financial times. Thus, values of frugality and family unity dominated. In contrast, the 1960s was a prosperous era in which individualism and protest against the government flourished. As people age, they find it difficult to abandon many of the values they learned during childhood.

Furthermore, our interpersonal relationships can constitute "minicultures" (Wilmot, 2006). A "relational culture" (Galvin & Wilkinson, 2006) develops when an interpersonal relationship is characterized by a unique system of communication, including "nicknames, joint storytelling, inside jokes, and code words" (p. 10). Like the members of a particular generation described above, two people with their own relational culture share a common worldview, but it is one they have constructed themselves. We have given you a general framework for understanding culture. We continue by addressing the diversity that exists within the United States.

REVISITING CASE in POINT

1. Embedded in Brad and Miguel's conversation are some assumptions of culture. Identify how at least one assumption relates to their dialogue in the airport.

2. One of the assumptions to consider when defining culture relates to culture creating community. Within that assumption is the notion of a culture clash. Discuss the presence of elements associated with a culture clash in Brad's discussion with Miguel.

You can answer these questions online under the resources for Chapter 3 at your online Resource Center for Understanding Interpersonal Communication.

Diversity in the United States: A Nation of Newcomers

Intercultural contact is pervasive in the United States. This diversity affects family structure, corporations, religious institutions, schools, and the media. With more than 300 million citizens, our nation is a heterogeneous mix of various cultures. See Figure 3.1 for a look at how ancestral groups, and their root cultures, are distributed across the United States. The increase in diversity over the past several years is not without consequence. Rubin Martinez (2000) observes that our diversity can be challenging: "All across the country, people of different races, ethnicities, and nationalities, are being thrown together and torn apart . . . it is a terrifying experience, this coming together, one for which we have of yet only the most awkward vocabulary" (pp. 11–12).

Figure 3.1   Diversity in the United States

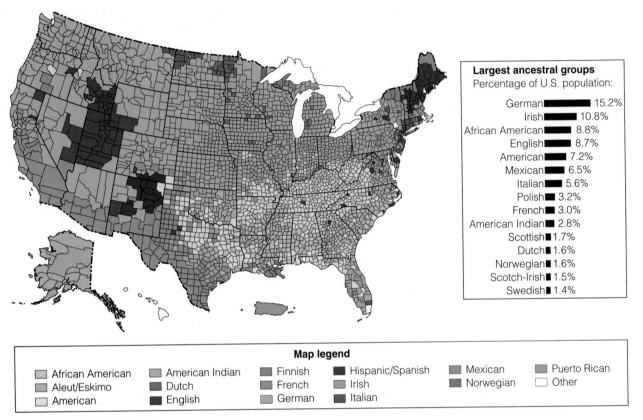

Largest ancestral groups
Percentage of U.S. population:

German	15.2%
Irish	10.8%
African American	8.8%
English	8.7%
American	7.2%
Mexican	6.5%
Italian	5.6%
Polish	3.2%
French	3.0%
American Indian	2.8%
Scottish	1.7%
Dutch	1.6%
Norwegian	1.6%
Scotch-Irish	1.5%
Swedish	1.4%

Map legend

African American	American Indian	Finnish	Hispanic/Spanish	Mexican	Puerto Rican
Aleut/Eskimo	Dutch	French	Irish	Norwegian	Other
American	English	German	Italian		

From *USA Today* July 1, 2004, p. 7A.

With the exception of Native peoples, who were the first cultural group in the United States, we live in a nation that experiences almost constant immigration. For example, Fred Jandt (2006) notes that Latinos, many from Mexico, are the fastest growing cultural group in the United States, growing considerably over the past decade in particular. The United States traditionally supports cultural newcomers. However, a backlash of sorts is increasing. For example, an "English only" movement has gained momentum across the country. Politicians and activists, feeling that the arrival of new cultural groups in the United States risks dividing the country along language and cultural lines, continue to try to make English the official language of the country. In 1996, the United States House of Representatives passed the English Language Empowerment Act, which would have made English the official language of the United States. It never became law, but it highlighted feelings by some that multiple cultures with multiple languages can cost the United States economically (Hayakawa, 1990).

Over the past several years, immigration has caused increased anxiety. The Migration Policy Institute (2007) notes that the September 11, 2001 terrorist attacks in the United States prompted security concerns about "illegal" immigration. Some of the more drastic reforms that have been advocated include building a large fence on the Mexican-American border, denying immigrant families access to health care, and deporting all undocumented immigrants to their native countries (http://blog.lib.umn.edu/ihrc/immigration/immigration _and_the_law). With over 700,000 legal immigrants and nearly 500,000 undocumented immigrants entering the country (Migration Policy Institute, 2007), this topic will continue to resonate within families and across society in general.

Almost 50 years ago, anthropologist Edward T. Hall (1959) noted that "culture is communication and communication is culture" (p.169). In other words, we learn how, where, why, when, and to whom we communicate through cultural teachings. Conversely, when we communicate, we reproduce and reinforce our cultural practices. Hall's words still apply today. The United States is more diverse than ever, and almost everyone has been exposed to this growing diversity in some way. The nation's growing diversity has been hotly debated, with some cultural critics believing that the increase in diversity results in honoring only those voices that support it (for example, McGowan, 2001). However, other writers (for example, Knott, 2006) contend that diversity allows for informed perspectives from many cultural backgrounds. Regardless of the divergent opinions on this matter, we cannot ignore that we now live in a country with expanding cultural variability.

Learning how to communicate effectively with members of different cultures is a hallmark of a thoughtful and effective communicator. Let's explore this issue further by examining the importance of intercultural communication.

Why Study Intercultural Communication?

Intercultural communication scholars Judith Martin and Thomas Nakayama (2008) note several reasons to study intercultural communication. We identify six "imperatives," or critical reasons, based on Martin and Nakayama's work and provide their application to interpersonal relationships. At the heart of this discussion is our belief that intercultural communication will continue to be important well beyond the class you are taking.

Technological Imperative

As developing countries continue to supply the United States with imported goods, as more U.S. companies send workers to jobs overseas, and as more people from other countries emigrate and find work in the United States, the ability to communicate across cultures will become increasingly necessary and valuable. For example, teleworkers in India who are employed by U.S. companies learn about many aspects of U.S. culture, including finance, sports, and entertainment, so they can better communicate with customers in the United States.

The extent to which technology has changed the United States cannot be overstated. The advent of the personal computer more than twenty years ago was just the beginning of a technological revolution. Following computers, a number of other technologies (including faxes, palm organizers, videophones, and, of course, the Internet) helped propel the United States into the twenty-first century.

These technological changes increase opportunities for intercultural communication. For example, consider Yolanda's experience with *eBay*, an online auction site. When Yolanda finds out that she holds the high bid on an antique handkerchief she wants to buy, she discovers that the seller is from a small town in Italy. Yolanda emails the seller and tells him that her grandmother has relatives in a town in northern Italy. He emails back to tell her that he, too, has relatives in that same town. As the two continue to email each other, they realize that both sets of relatives in Italy know each other! Later that year, they all get together electronically, an event they decide to repeat each year.

The implications of technology on our intercultural relationships continue to change even as we write this chapter. We revisit the subject of technology and interpersonal communication in Chapter 11.

© 2003 David Wells/The Image Works

Demographic Imperative

Earlier in this chapter, we noted that cultural diversity continues to shape and reshape the United States, and we provided information about the demographic changes in the United States. Yet, many co-cultures within the country reject the notion that blending into the national culture is ideal. Since dialogues about diversity began, writers and scholars have referred to the United States as a "melting pot," a metaphor that evokes a unified national character formed as a result of immigration. In the past, immigrants frequently changed their names, clothes, language, and customs to "fit in."

In contrast, metaphors for diversity in the United States include a symphony, stew, or

classes and accept challenges to power in interpersonal relationships. Although included on the list of cultures low in power distance, the United States is becoming higher in power distance because of the growing disparity between rich and poor (Jandt, 2006).

Intercultural encounters between people from high and low power distance cultures can be challenging. For instance, a supervisor from a high power distance culture may have difficulty communicating with employees who come from lower power distance cultures. Although the supervisor may be expecting complete respect and follow-through on directives, the employees may be questioning the legitimacy of such directives.

Masculinity-Femininity

Hofstede (2001) identifies the dimension of masculinity-femininity as the extent to which cultures represent masculine and feminine traits in their society. Remember from our discussion of masculinity and femininity in Chapter 2 that masculinity is not the same as "male," and femininity is not the same as "female," although use of these terms still reinforces stereotypical notions of how men and women should behave. **Masculine cultures** focus on achievement, competitiveness, strength, and material success—that is, characteristics stereotypically associated with masculine people. Money is important in masculine cultures. Further, masculine cultures are those where the division of labor is based on sex. **Feminine cultures** emphasize sexual equality, nurturance, quality of life, supportiveness, and affection—that is, characteristics stereotypically associated with feminine people. Compassion for the less fortunate also characterizes feminine cultures.

Hofstede's (2001) research showed that countries such as Mexico, Italy, Venezuela, Japan, and Austria are masculine-centered cultures, where the division of labor is based on sex. Countries such as Thailand, Norway, the Netherlands, Denmark, and Finland are feminine-centered cultures, where a promotion of sexual equality exists. The United States falls closer to masculinity.

What happens when a person from a culture that honors such masculine traits as power and competition intersects with a person from a culture that honors such feminine traits as interdependence and quality of life? For example, suppose that a woman is asked to lead a group of men. In Scandinavian countries, such as Denmark and Finland, such a task would not be problematic. Many political leaders in these countries are feminine (and female), and gender roles are more flexible. Yet, in a masculine culture, a female leader might be viewed with skepticism and her leadership might be challenged.

Individualism-Collectivism

When a culture values **individualism**, it prefers competition over cooperation, the individual over the group, and the private over the public. Individualistic cultures have an "I" communication orientation, emphasizing self-concept

masculine culture

A culture that emphasizes characteristics stereotypically associated with masculine people, such as achievement, competitiveness, strength, and material success.

feminine culture

A culture that emphasizes characteristics stereotypically associated with feminine people, such as sexual equality, nurturance, quality of life, supportiveness, affection, and a compassion for the less fortunate.

individualism

A cultural mindset that emphasizes self-concept and personal achievement and that prefers competition over cooperation, the individual over the group, and the private over the public.

and personal achievement. Individualistic cultures, including the United States, Canada, Britain, Australia, and Italy, tend to reject authoritarianism (think, for instance, how many rallies have occurred in the United States denouncing U.S. Presidents and their policies), and typically support the belief that people should "pull themselves up by their own bootstraps."

Collectivism suggests that the self is secondary to the group and its norms, values, and beliefs. Group orientation takes priority over self-orientation. Collectivistic cultures tend to value duty, tradition, and hierarchy. A "we" communication orientation prevails. Collectivistic cultures such as Columbia, Peru, Pakistan, Chile, and Singapore lean toward working together in groups to achieve goals. Families are particularly important, and people have higher expectations of loyalty to family, including taking care of extended family members.

Interestingly, the collectivistic and individualistic orientations intersect at times. For instance, in the Puerto Rican community, a collectivistic sense of family coexists with the individualistic need for community members to become personally successful. Hector Carrasquillo (1997) observed that "a Puerto Rican is only fully a person insofar as he or she is a member of a family" (p. 159). Still, Carrasquillo points out that younger Puerto Ricans have adopted more independence and have accepted and adapted to the individualistic ways of the United States culture. We see, therefore, that even within one culture, the individualism-collectivism dimension is not static.

Hofstede's work regarding dimensions of culture is often applied to business settings. To read an article that discusses how Hofstede's dimensions of culture can be applied specifically to business negotiation, go to your online Resource Center for *Understanding Interpersonal Communication* and access *InfoTrac College Edition Exercise 3.1: Culture and Negotiation* under the resources for Chapter 3 and read "Next for Communicators: Global Negotiation."

collectivism

A cultural mindset that emphasizes the group and its norms, values, and beliefs over the self.

© Setboun/Corbis

© Digital Vision/Getty Images

In many Asian countries, doing things together underscores the collectivistic nature of society. In the United States, people sometimes have trouble identifying with the collectivistic value of placing the group before the individual. At the same time, they often embrace collectivistic values, such as the importance of family and tradition.

Consider the summary of Hofstede's four dimensions of culture provided in Table 3.2. As we did in the previous sections, we provide representative cultures as identified by Hofstede. Keep in mind that because his results are based on averages, you will most likely be able to think of individuals you know who are exceptions to the categorization of nations. For another summary of these concepts and an even more extensive list of representative countries, use your online Resource Center for Understanding Interpersonal Communication to access *Interactive Activity 3.2: Hofstede's Dimensions of Culture* under the resources for Chapter 3.

One additional cultural dimension merits consideration: context. Recall from Chapter 1 that context is the surrounding in which communication takes place. Intercultural communication theorists find that people of different cultures use context to varying degrees to determine the meaning of a message. Scholars have referred to this as context orientation theory (Hall & Hall, 1990). **Context orientation theory** answers the following question: Is meaning derived from cues outside of the message or from the words in the message?

The cultures of the world differ in the extent to which they rely on context. Researchers have divided context into two areas: high-context and low-context (Victor, 1992). In **high-context cultures**, the meaning of a message is primarily drawn from the surroundings. People in high-context cultures do

context orientation theory:
The theory that meaning is derived from either the setting of the message or the words of a message and that cultures can vary in the extent to which message meaning is made explicit or implicit.

high-context culture
A culture in which there is a high degree of similarity among members and in which the meaning of a message is drawn primarily from its context, such as one's surroundings, rather than from words.

Table 3.2 Hofstede's cultural dimensions

Dimension	Description
Uncertainty avoidance	• Cultures high in uncertainty avoidance desire predictability (for example, Greece, Japan).
	• Cultures low in uncertainty avoidance are unthreatened by change (for example, United States, Great Britain).
Distribution of power	• Cultures high in power distance show respect for status (for example, Mexico, India).
	• Cultures low in power distance believe power should be equally distributed (for example, United States, Israel).
Masculinity-femininity	• Masculine cultures value competitiveness, material success, and assertiveness (for example, Italy, Austria).
	• Feminine cultures value quality of life, affection, and caring for the less fortunate (for example, Sweden, Denmark).
Individualism-collectivism	• Individualistic cultures value individual accomplishments (for example, Australia, United States).
	• Collectivistic cultures value group collaboration (for example, Chile, Columbia).

not need to say much when communicating because there is a high degree of similarity among members of such cultures. Further, people read nonverbal cues with a high degree of accuracy because people share the same structure of meaning. Native American, Latin American, Japanese, Chinese, and Korean cultures are all high-context cultures. On a more fundamental level, high-context communities are less formal and decisions take into consideration the relationships between and among people.

In **low-context cultures**, communicators find meaning primarily in the words in messages, not the surroundings. In low-context cultures, meanings are communicated explicitly; very little of the conversation is left open to interpretation. As a result, nonverbal communication is not easily comprehended. Examples of low-context cultures include Germany, Switzerland, the United States, Canada, and France.

Think about how cultural differences in context might affect interaction during conflict episodes, job interviews, or dating. If one person relies mainly on the spoken word and the other communicates largely through nonverbal messages, what might be the result?

So far in this chapter, we have discussed why you need to understand intercultural communication. We're confident that you are beginning to appreciate the cultural diversity in your lives and that you are prepared to work on improving your intercultural communication skills. A critical step toward understanding your culture and the cultures of others is to understand the problems inherent in intercultural communication. We examine five such challenges now.

Challenges of Intercultural Communication

Although intercultural communication is important and pervasive, becoming an effective intercultural communicator is easier said than done. In this section, we explain five obstacles to intercultural understanding: ethnocentrism, stereotyping, anxiety and uncertainty, misinterpretation of nonverbal and verbal behaviors, and the assumption of similarity.

Ethnocentrism

Ethnocentrism is the process of judging another culture using the standards of your own culture. Ethnocentrism is derived from two Greek words, *ethno*, or nation, and *kentron*, or center. When combined, the meaning becomes clear: nation at the center. Ethnocentrism is a belief in the superiority of your own culture. Myron Lustig and Jolene Koester (1999b) claim that cultures "train their members to use the categories of their own cultural experiences when judging the experiences of people from other cultures" (p. 146). Normally,

low-context culture

A culture in which there is a high degree of difference among members and in which the meaning of a message must be explicitly related, usually in words.

ethnocentrism

The process of judging another culture using the standards of our own culture.

Language Evolves

As time passes, some words become out of date and aren't used any longer. For example, the words *petticoat, girdle, dowry,* and even *typewriter* are becoming obsolete and disappearing from our vocabulary. Some expressions that were popular in earlier times simply aren't used now, illustrating that language is susceptible to fads and fashion. If you are younger than 80 years old, you probably have never used the phrase *the bees' knees,* 1920s slang that meant something was wonderful or "hot." In the 1950s and 1960s, it was common for people to say "toottle-loo" instead of "goodbye," and when couples wanted to go find a romantic spot, they'd tell others that they were "going to the submarine races," although there was no evidence of any water nearby! Some researchers talk of words and phrases as having "careers," in the course of which their meaning may undergo dramatic changes (Bowdle & Gentner, 2005).

Sometimes words experience a revival after they had been popular during an earlier era. For example, the word *groovy* was popular in the 1960s, fell out of favor for a while, and then became trendy again in the late 1990s with the release of the popular Austin Powers movies. *Groovy*'s revival didn't last long among the larger population, but smaller segments of society still use the word frequently. Sometimes our vocabulary changes as a result of social changes. For example, we don't use the word *Negro* anymore, but instead favor *African American.* These sorts of language changes might be ridiculed as political correctness and thought of as over-concern for how things are said. But confusing political correctness with important language reform is a mistake. Changing language to give people respect and to be accurate is a goal that shouldn't be trivialized. Further, using language that is appropriate to a culture's evolution strengthens a person's credibility.

Because verbal symbols are so powerful, they can symbolize prejudicial attitudes that we should eliminate (Mills, 1981). For instance, the words *colored, Negro, Afro-American, African American,* and *person of color* reflect changes in the position of black people in the United States. The words are not synonyms but actually have different meanings (McGlone, Beck, & Pfiester, 2006). *African American* communicates an emphasis on ethnicity rather than race, and *person of color* attempts to be more positive than *nonwhite.*

Similarly, the language used to describe people with disabilities has evolved. For example, when Dale tells his parents about his friend Abby, who uses a wheelchair because she has muscular dystrophy, he calls her a *person with a disability.* He doesn't use the word *handicapped* or *crippled* because language reform has helped him see people in wheelchairs as people first, not as their disabilities. He knows Abby as a great friend with a biting sense of humor who uses a wheelchair to get around. To further explore language reform, use your online Resource Center for *Understanding Interpersonal Communication* to access **Interactive Activity 4.1: Politically Correct Language** under the resources for Chapter 4.

Some college campuses are making efforts to accommodate transgender students, including using pronouns that those in the transgender community favor: *ze* in place of *he* or *she* and *hir* instead of *him* or *her* (Bernstein, 2004). This accommodation is important for ease and accuracy of communication. For example, when Natalie wants to refer to a friend, Noel, who identifies as transgender, she can simply say, "ze is a friend of mine" instead of "he or she is a friend of mine."

Verbal symbols continue to evolve and their meanings change. For instance, the words *calling card* used to mean an engraved card that you left at the home of someone whom you had just visited. Today, we still use the term *calling card*, but now it refers to prepaid cards for making phone calls. Similarly, the word *gay* used to refer to being happy and lighthearted, as in "we'll have a gay old time." Today, *gay* is a sexual identity. Incidentally, the term *gay* was chosen intentionally by people in gay communities because of the positive associations it carried from its former meaning.

People have coined new words such as *Googling, metrosexual, hyperlink, Crackberry* (referring to the addictive qualities of Blackberries and other electronic devices), and *blog* to name a few. These new words give labels to recent innovations. As Paul McFedries (2004) observes, "when there's a new invention, service, trend or idea, we need a new way to describe these things. The emerging vocabulary becomes a mirror to the culture" (p. 12).

"I'm hearing a lot of buzzwords from you, but I'm not getting a buzz."

Finally, vocabularies tend to reflect the current times. The second edition of the *Oxford Dictionary of English* (2003) contained 3,000 new words and the themes they expressed centered on terrorism, technology, and television ("Are you suffering from data smog?" 2003). The new words included *24/7* (all the time), *counterterrorism* (military or political activities designed to thwart or prevent terrorism), *dirty bomb* (a conventional bomb containing material that is radioactive), *egosurfing* (searching the Internet for references to oneself), and *bada bing* (a term from *The Sopranos* used to emphasize that something will happen effortlessly and predictably).

Words Are Powerful

Certain words have the power to affect people dramatically. As we've said previously, words are arbitrary symbols, so their power is not intrinsic; it derives from our having agreed to give them power. As we mentioned above, these agreements change over time. For example, in the 17th century, the word "blackguard" was a potent insult but that's no longer the case. But other words (like "ass") have taken on power they didn't have in the 17th century (Duck, 2007).

People have made many words powerful. For instance, in 2004, CNN reported that the state of Georgia was considering banning the word *evolution* in the science curriculum in the public schools ("Georgia considers banning 'evolution'," 2004). The school superintendent said that the *concept* of evolution would still be taught but that the *word* would no longer be used. This case points to the power that Georgians gave the term *evolution,* although in the end, the word was not banned.

In 2002, in one of his more famous speeches, President Bush labeled North Korea, Iraq, and Iran an "axis of evil." Some critics thought Bush began a war of words with that phrase. On its editorial page, *USA Today* said that Bush's rhetoric was inflammatory as well as inaccurate because the three countries' political positions differed from one another. The editorial concluded by stating that "treating Iran, Iraq and North Korea as a unified, monolithic axis—vulnerable to the same rhetoric and tactics—is a formula for failure, not to mention an invitation to a multifront war" ("'Axis of evil' remark sparks damaging backlash," 2002, p. 16A). Others might argue that Bush's phrase was an example of strong, motivational rhetoric. Either way, it's a dramatic example of the power of words. To read an interesting student editorial about the media's use of the terms *terrorist* and *suicide bomber,* use your online Resource Center for *Understanding Interpersonal Communication* to access **Interactive Activity 4.2: The Power of Words** under the resources for Chapter 4.

The power of words in the English language is illustrated by a study looking at how the phrase *think positive* affected breast cancer patients (Kitzinger, 2000). The study found that in general, the phrase *think positive* sent a message that if you don't get better it's because you're not being positive enough. This phrase, then, had a great deal of power, often making patients feel inadequate or responsible for their own illness.

Communication Assessment Test
Vocabulary Test

Sharpen your vocabulary by testing yourself with the following sentence-completion questions. After making your choice, explain why you think it is correct. You can take this test online. Go to your online Resource Center for *Understanding Interpersonal Communication* and look under the resources for Chapter 4.

1. Scrooge, in the famous novel by Dickens, was a _____ ; he hated all humankind.

   A. misanthrope   D. hedonist

   B. hypochondriac   E. sybarite

   C. philanthropist

2. Businesspeople must widen their horizons; a _____ attitude will get them nowhere in this age of globalization.

   A. moderate   D. diversified

   B. petrified   E. comprehensive

   C. parochial

3. Our bookshelves at home display a range of books on wide-ranging subjects in many languages, reflecting the _____ tastes of our family members.

   A. anomalous   D. furtive

   B. limited   E. eclectic

   C. arcane

4. Plastic bags are _____ symbols of consumer society; they are found everywhere you travel.

   A. rare   D. fleeting

   B. ephemeral   E. covert

   C. ubiquitous

5. Although some people think that only poor and poorly educated people use slang, this idea is _____.

   A. accurate   D. widespread

   B. popular   E. ineffectual

   C. erroneous

6. Dr. Stuart needs to _____ his thesis with more data; as it stands, his argument is _____.

   A. support, profound

   B. bolster, acceptable

   C. refine, satisfactory

   D. buttress, inadequate

   E. define, succinct

7. Through the nineteenth century, the classics of Western civilization were considered to be the _____ of wisdom and culture, and _____ people, by definition, knew them well.

   A. foundation, average

   B. epitome, uneducated

   C. cornerstone, obtuse

   D. font, ecclesiastical

   E. repository, educated

8. In this biography, we're given a glimpse of the writer _____ pursuing the path of the poet despite _____ and rejection slips.

   A. doggedly, disappointment

   B. tirelessly, encouragement

   C. sporadically, awards

   D. successfully, acclaim

   E. unsuccessfully, failure

9. In keeping with his own _____ in international diplomacy, Churchill proposed a personal meeting of heads of government, but the effort was doomed to failure because the temper of the times was _____.

   A. ideas, pluralistic

   B. predilections, inimical

   C. aversions, hostile

(Continues)

D. impulses, amicable

E. maxims, salacious

10. The subtle shades of meaning, and still subtler echoes of association, make language an instrument which only very skilled users can employ with _____ and _____.

A. confidence, aloofness

B. self-assurance, certainty

C. sincerity, hope

D. conservatism, alacrity

E. eloquence, ruthlessness

Answers

1. A	3. E	5. C	7. E	9. B
2. C	4. C	6. D	8. A	10. B

Modified from "Sentence Completion Minitest 4" from www.majortests.com, 2005. Test created by Helen Mathur.

In another example of how much power people give words, both conservative and liberal groups have requested that certain (different) words be banned from student text books (Ravitch, 2003). Words such as *devil, dogma,* and *cult,* and words that make comparisons, such as *economically disadvantaged,* have all been considered dangerous, and groups have asked to ban them. The fact that people label a word as taboo indicates that they think it is highly charged and powerful.

After a word becomes taboo, it often becomes more powerful. For instance, Robin's daughter Kate was 10 years old before she knew that all families didn't ban the word *fat.* Robin had struggled with her weight all her life and was very sensitive about her body. As a result, the family never used the word *fat,* and it became a very powerful word in their house. While visiting a friend, Kate was surprised when she heard the family joking around about gaining weight and calling each other fat. Even though her friend's family found it acceptable to use the word *fat,* Kate still couldn't bring herself to use the forbidden word.

Meanings for Verbal Symbols May Be Denotative or Connotative

Denotative meaning refers to the literal, conventional meaning that most people in a culture have agreed is the meaning of a symbol. Denotation is the type of meaning found in a dictionary definition. For instance, Merriam-Webster Online (2004) defines the word gun as follows:

1. *a: a piece of ordnance usually with high muzzle velocity and comparatively flat trajectory*

   b: a portable firearm (as a rifle or handgun)

   c: a device that throws a projectile

2. *a: a discharge of a gun especially as a salute or signal*

   b: a signal marking a beginning or ending

denotative meaning

The literal, conventional meaning of a verbal symbol that most people in a culture have agreed is the meaning of that symbol.

connotative meaning

The meaning of a verbal symbol that is derived from our personal and subjective experience with that symbol.

concrete

Able to be seen, smelled, tasted, touched, or heard.

referent

The thing a verbal symbol represents.

abstract

Not able to be seen, smelled, tasted, touched, or heard.

framing theory

A theory that argues that when we compare two unlike things in a figure of speech, we are unconsciously influenced by this decision.

These definitions form the denotative meaning of the word *gun*. Denotative meanings can be confusing; because the dictionary provides more than one meaning for *gun*, your listener must decide if you are using definition 1a, 1b, 1c, 2a, or 2b.

The **connotative meaning** of a term varies from person to person. Connotative meanings derive from people's personal and subjective experience with a verbal symbol. For example, someone who had a close friend or relative shot to death would have a different emotional or connotative meaning for *gun* than would a hunter or a member of the National Rifle Association. Although both of these people would be aware of the denotative meanings of *gun*, their definition of the word would be colored by their personal connotative meanings.

Words Vary in Level of Abstraction

You can place a word on a continuum from concrete to abstract. If a word is **concrete**, you are able to detect its **referent** (the thing the word represents) with one of your senses. Stated another way, concrete words are those that you can see, smell, taste, touch, or hear. The more a word restricts the number of possible referents, the more concrete the word is. For instance, if Sara has 15 relatives but only 3 brothers, brother is a more specific, concrete term than *relative,* and *Scott* (the name of one of Sara's brothers) is more specific than either of the two other terms. The word *relative* is the term with the fewest restrictions, so it is the most **abstract**. We can envision a ladder of abstraction (see Figure 4.2) that begins with the most concrete symbol for a referent and moves to the most abstract.

Figure 4.2   The ladder of abstraction

Some referents are naturally somewhat abstract. Ideas like love and democracy do not have terms that correspond to the lower rungs of the ladder of abstraction. Language skills allow us to talk about the concepts involved in abstract terms. For example, when we speak about *justice,* we use other abstract terms, such as *fairness,* to get our message across. To make our ideas more concrete so others can better understand our meaning, we often use figures of speech such as metaphors and similes. Metaphors equate two terms—for example, "*Love* is a *roller-coaster ride.*" Similes make comparisons using the word *like* or *as*—for example, "*Justice* is like *redistributing portions of a pie.*"

Although they do not provide perfect descriptions, figures of speech can be beautiful, allowing language to soar to poetic heights and enabling us to see something in a new way. Yet, it is also true that some metaphors are used so often that they become "frozen" or "conventional" and we don't even recognize that they are metaphoric ("my mood is down") (Sopory, 2006). Sometimes the comparisons provided by metaphors and similes don't help us understand meaning better, but rather mislead us. One theory about how figures of speech affect us is **framing theory** (Lakoff, 2003). Framing theory argues that when we compare two unlike things in a figure of speech, we are unconsciously influenced by the comparison. For example, comparing differences between men and women to war (i.e. the battle of the sexes) focuses our thinking on oppositions and a basic animosity between the sexes. We don't consciously reflect on this—the metaphor just causes us to make this association. Imagine how our thinking might differ if we instead used the metaphor "gender union" (DeFrancisco & Palczewski, 2007) to talk about the sexes.

When referents are not right in front of us, we can visualize them through the **process of abstraction** (the ability to move up and down the ladder of abstraction from specific to general and vice versa). For instance, let's say

The NewsHour with Jim Lehrer/ © MacNeil-Lehrer Productions

FORMER CAPT. PHILLIP CARTER
U.S. ARMY

IPC *in the* News

The power of metaphor to bring two separate ideas together is illustrated in a *USA Today* article that discusses how military officials and government spokespeople talk about the war in Iraq. The article observes that sports metaphors are no longer used to talk about the war: "No one will ever characterize anything again as a 'slam dunk'." Instead, comments like those of retired Army captain Phillip Carter on PBS's *NewsHour* compare the war to liquids: "You squeeze the bad guys out of Baghdad, and they pop like a water balloon up into the Diyala province." The article speculates that liquid metaphors may be useful because of the "amorphous nature of the enemy" as well as the fact that everyone can relate to them—who hasn't played with a water balloon? The article also cautions against throwing around all such metaphors casually: "The military should tell it like it is, not dress up the war in cutesy language."

Beehner, L. (2007, June 4) A squirt or a surge? Both are miscast war metaphors. *USA Today,* p. 11A.

process of abstraction

The ability to move up and down the ladder of abstraction from specific to general and vice versa.

that Jay wants to tell his friends about his fabulous new red and white Mini Cooper. As he uses descriptors to talk about his car in its absence, his friends are able to imagine it pretty clearly. Later Jay sees a friend, Lois, who just totaled her car. Jay decides to tell Lois about his new car, but he uses words that are less concrete, leaving out the brand name and color so that Lois won't be too envious. To read an interesting article that examines how journalists tend to move up and down the ladder of abstraction, check out "The Ladder of Abstraction" by using your online Resource Center for *Understanding Interpersonal Communication* to access *InfoTrac College Edition Exercise 4.1: Moving Up and Down the Ladder of Abstraction.*

Because words vary in their level of abstraction, meaning is often ambiguous. This ambiguity may be unintentional or strategic. For instance, if Jane lacks the verbal skills of clarity and audience analysis, her communication may seem vague, even though she doesn't intend it to be. However, sometimes it may serve a purpose to be ambiguous. Researchers have described this phenomenon in two ways: strategic ambiguity and equivocation.

Your turn

*R*eflect on ambiguity in verbal symbols by tracking language you hear in conversation and in the media, particularly in political speeches and advertising.
If you like, you can use your student workbook or your **Understanding Interpersonal Communication** Online Resources to complete this activity.

Strategic ambiguity refers to how people talk when they do not want others to completely understand their intentions (Eisenberg, 1984). In organizations people (especially at the management level) may leave out cues on purpose to encourage multiple interpretations by others. It is possible that ambiguity moderates tensions in an organization. To promote harmony, leaders of organizations may have to be ambiguous enough to allow for many interpretations while simultaneously encouraging agreement (Eisenberg). This strategy can also be used by a person in a conflict. Saying something like "I am not sure about that" allows several interpretations and may achieve the end of the argument.

Equivocation is a type of ambiguity that involves choosing your words carefully to give a listener a false impression without actually lying. For instance, if your grandmother sends you a birthday gift that you don't like, but you value your relationship with your grandmother and don't want to hurt her feelings, you might equivocate in your thank-you. You might say: "Thanks so much for the sweater. It was so thoughtful of you to think about keeping me warm in the cold winters!" You have not said the sweater was attractive, nor have you said you liked it, so you haven't lied overtly. However, if you are a good equivocator, you have given your grandmother the impression that you are really pleased with a sweater that you, in fact, dislike. Keep in mind that such a tactic could have long-term consequences. In this case, you could receive similar unwanted sweaters for several birthdays to come.

strategic ambiguity

Leaving out cues in a message on purpose to encourage multiple interpretations by others.

equivocation

A type of ambiguity that involves choosing our words carefully to give a listener a false impression without actually lying.

Equivocating involves saying things that are true but misleading. It should be no surprise that the language of advertising makes use of equivocation. When an ad says that a car's seats "have the look and feel of fine leather" that means that they are *not* made of fine leather, but the use of the words *fine leather* leads an unsuspecting listener to think that they are. In addition, the word *virtually* is a good equivocal word. The phrase *virtually spotless* means that the described item may have some spots on it, but the phrase leads you to believe otherwise.

Sometimes *euphemisms* are a kind of equivocal speech. **Euphemisms** are milder or less direct words substituted for other words that are more blunt or negative. They are used to reduce the discomfort related to an unpleasant or sensitive subject. For example, we say we're going to the *restroom* even though we're not planning to rest, we refer to a person's *passing* rather than their death, or we talk about *adult entertainment* rather than pornography.

Factors Affecting Verbal Symbols

We understand and use words differently depending on a variety of factors. In this section, we discuss the relationships between verbal symbols and each of the following: culture and ethnicity, gender, generation, and context. Although we discuss these factors in isolation, they can form many combinations. For example, an elderly African American man living in the United States talking to his granddaughter at home uses verbal symbols quite differently than a young Asian woman living in Korea speaking to a group of business associates at an annual meeting.

Culture and Ethnicity

On the most basic level, culture affects language (and vice versa) because most cultures develop their own language. Thus, people of Kenya tend to speak Swahili, and those living in Poland usually speak Polish. This section addresses some of the many other ways culture and ethnicity relate to language.

Let's first look at idioms. An **idiom** is a word or a phrase that has an understood meaning within a culture, but that meaning doesn't come from exact

euphemism

A milder or less direct word substituted for another word that is more blunt or negative.

idiom

A word or a phrase that has an understood meaning within a culture but whose meaning is not derived by exact translation.

REVISITING CASEINPOINT

1. How does the conversation between Carlos and Liz illustrate the idea that the meaning for words is both connotative and denotative?

2. When Carlos says, "I was wondering if we could grab a cup of coffee later," how is he using the levels of abstraction of language strategically?

You can answer these questions online under the resources for Chapter 4 at your online Resource Center for Understanding Interpersonal Communication.

translation. Thus, people who are learning a language have to learn the meaning of each idiom as a complete unit; they cannot simply translate each of the words and put their meanings together. For example, in English we say "it was a breeze" when we mean that something was easy. If someone tried to translate "it was a breeze" without knowing it functions as an idiom, they would mistake the statement's meaning. However, a listener also has to pay attention to context. If "it was a breeze" is the response to the question "What messed up all the papers I had laid out under the window?" English speakers know not to access the statement's idiomatic meaning but rather to rely on the meaning of each word.

Let's look at another example. Madeline works for the International Student Center at Western State University, and some of the international students tell her that U.S. students are unfriendly. When they parted company with a group of U.S. students, they said, those students said "see you later," but the U.S. students made no attempt to do so. The international students believed that the U.S. students failed to keep their promise for future social interactions. Madeline explained to the international students that "see you later" is an example of a particular type of idiom called phatic communication. **Phatic communication** consists of words and phrases that are used for interpersonal contact only and are not meant to be translated directly word for word. This type of communication can be thought of as content-free because listeners are not supposed to think about the meaning of the statement; rather, they are expected to respond to the polite contact the speaker is making. When you see someone and say "Hi, how are you doing?" you probably don't really want to know how the details about how the other person is doing—you're just making contact. "How's it going?" or "How are you doing?" should elicit a response such as "Okay—how about you?" If you said "how's it going?" to your acquaintance Katy, and she started to tell you about her recent breakup or the big fight she had with her brother, you would likely be surprised and might think that Katy was odd.

Now we'll discuss some verbal behaviors thought to characterize two specific groups, African Americans and Mexican Americans. There are many

phatic communication

Communication consisting of words and phrases that are used for interpersonal contact only and are not meant to be translated verbatim.

tions. Nonverbal communication is an integral part of the communication process and always a part of our relationships with others.

This chapter explores nonverbal communication and its importance in our lives. We focus our discussion on how nonverbal behavior functions, both directly and indirectly, in our daily activities. Before we move on in our discussion about nonverbal communication, let's spend a few moments defining it. **Nonverbal communication** encompasses all behaviors—other than spoken words—that communicate messages and have shared meaning between people. This definition has three associated parameters. First, electronic communication (a subject we return to in Chapter 11) is not included in our definition. Second, when we note that there is "shared meaning," we are saying that a national culture agrees on how to construe a behavior. For example, in many co-cultures in the United States, when a parent sees a child do something unsafe, the parent might wag his or her index finger. The child must know the meaning behind this nonverbal shaming technique to respond to the parent's reprimand. Third, as we mentioned in Chapter 4, verbal and nonverbal communication usually work together to create meaning.

Nonverbal communication is central to our relational lives. Howard Giles and Beth Le Poire (2006) thoughtfully illustrate that the way people communicate nonverbally influences 1) how relationships are established, maintained, and dissolved, 2) the diagnosis of health-related problems such as autism, 3) the number of sexual partners a person has, 4) how babies show emotional distress, 5) marital satisfaction and stability, and 6) perceptions of beauty. These reasons are just a snapshot of why the area of nonverbal communication is valued and essential to discuss in a book on interpersonal communication.

nonverbal communication

All behaviors other than spoken words that communicate messages and create shared meaning between people.

"Say what's on your mind, Harris—the language of dance has always eluded me."

Nonverbal communication competence requires us to be able to encode and decode nonverbal messages (Burgoon & Hoobler, 2002). We also have to use nonverbal communication ourselves to get across our meaning. Being able to adapt to people around you is a hallmark of a competent nonverbal communicator. **Interaction adaptation theory** suggests that individuals simultaneously adapt their communication behavior to the communication behavior of others (Burgoon, Stern, & Dillman, 1995). Thus, the better we are able to adapt, the better we are able to understand the meaning of a message. Suppose, for example, that Rosa and her roommate, Nadine, are in a noisy place talking about a conflict they've had pertaining to their apartment's cleanliness. Nadine is practicing interaction adaptation if, when Rosa leans forward to talk about the topic, Nadine simultaneously leans forward to listen to the story. This "postural echo" suggests that Nadine is not only mirroring Rosa's behavior but that she is also trying to understand Rosa's meaning.

With our definition of nonverbal communication established, we're now ready to explore some of the principles of nonverbal communication before moving on to discuss nonverbal communication codes and cultural variations in nonverbal communication.

Principles of Nonverbal Communication

Although it is often overlooked, nonverbal communication is a vital aspect of interpersonal communication. Consider times when we don't say a word but manage to "say" so much. Imagine, for example, hugging a close friend at her father's funeral. In this situation, nonverbal communication is probably more comforting than any words you could say. This apparent inconsistency of efficient communication without words is what makes nonverbal communication so important in our conversations with others. We now explore four principles of this type of communication.

Nonverbal Communication Is Often Ambiguous

One reason nonverbal communication is so challenging in our relationships is that our nonverbal messages often mean different things to different people, which can lead to misunderstandings. Compared to verbal messages, nonverbal messages are usually more ambiguous. For example, suppose that Lena prolongs her eye contact with Todd and, in turn, Todd refocuses on Lena. While Lena may be showing some attraction to Todd, he may be returning the eye contact because he believes that something is wrong. Clearly, the same nonverbal behavior (eye contact) can elicit two different meanings.

Mark Hickson, Don Stacks, and Nina-Jo Moore (2004) capture the challenge of nonverbal communication by noting that it is more difficult to understand because it is intangible and more abstract. A major reason for this ambiguity is that many factors influence the meaning of nonverbal behav-

interaction adaptation theory

A theory that suggests individuals simultaneously adapt their communication behavior to the communication behavior of others.

iors, including shared fields of experience, current surroundings, and culture. Consider the following conversation between a father and son as they talk about the son's staying out past his curfew:

Father: Look, I told you to be home by 11! It's past midnight now. And get that smirk off your face!

Son: First, dad, you might have told me 11, but you also didn't say anything when I asked if I could stay out till 12. You didn't say anything for sure. I mean, like, you were changing the oil on the truck when I asked you. You didn't even look at me. I couldn't hear you that much while you were under the car. And, how am I . . .

Father: You heard what you wanted to hear. I told you . . .

Son: I swear, Dad. I thought my curfew was midnight. And I've stayed out till midnight before.

This scenario suggests a few things about the ambiguous nature of nonverbal communication. First, the father seems to be annoyed by his son's smirk. Is he truly smirking, or is the father misinterpreting his son's facial expression because he is angry? Second, the son took his dad's verbal message about the 11 p.m. deadline less seriously because his father neglected to make eye contact when delivering it. In addition, the son thought that his dad hesitated when he asked about a later curfew, and also claimed that he couldn't clearly hear his father's response from under the car, further eroding the power of the father's verbal communication. In this example, ambiguity results from the interaction of the verbal and nonverbal behaviors of both the father and son.

© Ryan McVay/The Image Bank/Getty Images

The ambiguity of nonverbal gestures can lead to misunderstandings. For example, if someone winks at you, is he flirting with you, letting you in on a joke, showing affection, or does he simply have something in his eye?

Nonverbal Communication Regulates Conversation

People use nonverbal communication to manage the ebb and flow of conversations. Nonverbal regulators allow speakers to enter, exit, or maintain the conversation. Who talks when and to whom, referred to as **turn-taking**, is based primarily on nonverbal communication. For instance, if we want a chance to speak, we usually lean forward, toward the speaker. When we don't want to be interrupted in a conversation, we may avoid eye contact and keep our vocal pattern consistent so that others don't have an opportunity to begin talking until we are finished. When we are ready to yield the conversation to another, we typically stop talking, look at the other person, and perhaps make a motion with our hands to indicate that it is now okay for the other person to respond.

We can also yield the conversation floor by raising or lowering our pitch level to stress our last word or syllable. As we mentioned earlier, we are often unconscious of such behaviors. For example, let's say that Bruce, a student in Professor Brownstone's biology class, decides to challenge a grade. When Bruce arrives at Professor Brownstone's office, the straight-A student launches into a rehearsed, detailed story about not having enough time to study because he was sick with the flu. He avoids making eye contact with Professor Brownstone and doesn't pause to allow the professor to react until he has finished his entire memorized speech. As he finishes his last sentence, "I know that you have a policy on make-ups, but I think I have an extenuating situation," he looks up to meet the professor's eyes and raises the pitch level of his voice so that his statement almost becomes a question. Whether or not he realizes it, Bruce uses nonverbal communication to regulate the conversation with his professor. At first he prevents his professor from entering the exchange, and then he uses the pitch of his voice to yield the floor.

Nonverbal Communication Is More Believable than Verbal Communication

Although, as we noted earlier, nonverbal communication is often ambiguous, people believe nonverbal messages over verbal messages. You've no doubt heard the expression "actions speak louder than words." This statement suggests that someone's nonverbal behavior can influence a conversational partner more than what is said. For instance, a job candidate being interviewed may verbally state her commitment to being professional, yet if she wears jeans and arrives late to the interview, these nonverbal cues will cause the interviewer to regard her statement with skepticism.

Consider how Esther reacts to the nonverbal communication of the customers at a local gas station where she is an attendant. She makes judgments about people based on their appearance. For example, Esther is more inclined to give the store's restroom key to someone who appears calm than to some-

turn-taking

In a conversation, nonverbal regulators that indicate who talks when and to whom.

one who looks rushed, nervous, and sweaty. However, as we learned in Chapter 2, her perception may be inaccurate or incomplete.

Nonverbal Communication May Conflict with Verbal Communication

Although nonverbal and verbal communication frequently operate interdependently, sometimes our nonverbal messages are not congruent with our verbal messages. We term this incompatibility a **mixed message**. When a friend asks you, "What's wrong?" after observing you with tears in your eyes, and you reply "Nothing," the contradiction between your nonverbal and verbal behavior is evident. When a physician frowns as she reveals to her patient that the prognosis "looks good," she gives a mixed message. Or, consider a wife, who after being asked by her husband if she loves him, shouts, "Of course I love you!" Most of us would agree that angrily shouting to express our affection sends a mixed message.

mixed message

The incompatibility that occurs when our nonverbal messages are not congruent with our verbal messages.

When confronted with a mixed message, people have to choose whether to believe the nonverbal or the verbal behaviors. Because children are generally not sophisticated enough to understand the many meanings that accompany nonverbal communication, they rely on the words of a message more than the nonverbal behaviors (Morton & Trehub, 2001). However, most children understand nonverbal messages such as shaking the head for "no" and a finger to the lips for "keep quiet." In contrast, adults who encounter mixed messages pay the most attention to nonverbal messages and neglect much of what is being stated. The multiple messages that originate from the eyes, voice, body movement, facial expressions, and touch usually overpower the verbal message.

REVISITING CASEinPOINT

1. *Identify one principle of nonverbal communication and apply it to Mark Mattson's perception of his mother.*

2. *How has Julia Mattson's appearance regulated any conversation between Mark and her?*

You can answer these questions online under the resources for Chapter 5 at your online Resource Center for Understanding Interpersonal Communication.

To further explore how our nonverbal behaviors often conflict with our verbal messages, check out "Your Body Speaks Volumes, but Do You Know What It Is Saying?" available through InfoTrac College Edition. Use your online Resource Center for *Understanding Interpersonal Communication* to access *InfoTrac College Edition Exercise 5.1: What Is Your Body Language Saying?* To read about mixed messages in a specific context, business negotiations, access *Interactive Activity 5.1: Mixed Messages in Negotiations.*

Nonverbal Communication Codes

Extensive study of nonverbal communication indicates that we employ several different forms of nonverbal codes in our conversations with others. Later in the chapter, we will look at a number of these codes and discuss their cultural implications. In this section, we examine a classifying system articulated by Burgoon et al. (1996), which is set out in Table 5.1. This system includes visual-auditory codes, contact codes, and place and time codes.

Visual-Auditory Codes

As their name reflects, visual-auditory codes include categories of nonverbal communication that you can see and hear. These categories are kinesics (body movement), physical appearance (such as attractiveness), facial communication (such as eye contact), and paralanguage (such as pitch and whining).

Kinesics (Body Movement)

Body communication is also called **kinesics**, a Greek word meaning "movement." Kinesics refers to the study of body motions and how people use them to communicate. Kinesic behavior is wide-ranging; it can include anything from staying put at a party after being asked to leave, to gesturing during a speech.

The primary components of kinesics are gestures and body posture/ orientation. Gestures have been analyzed for almost 2,500 years. For example, writings by the Greek philosopher Aristotle explained that gestures are impor-

kinesics

The study of a person's body movement and its effect on the communication process.

Table 5.1　Categories of nonverbal communication

Code	Nonverbal Category
Visual-auditory	Kinesics (*body movement*)
	Physical appearance (*body size, body artifacts, attractiveness*)
	Facial communication (*eye contact, smiling*)
	Paralanguage (*pitch, rate, volume, speed, silence*)
Contact	Haptics (*touch*)
	Space (*personal space, territoriality*)
Place and time	The environment (*color, lighting, room design*)
	Chronemics (*time*)

tant when delivering a public speech. Further, Michael Corballis (2002) notes that gestures preceded verbal communication by tens of thousands of years.

What can we learn from gestures? First, we need to consider the context of gestures to understand them. Think about the gestures that the following individuals would use: parking lot attendant, nurse, radio disc jockey, landscaper, and auctioneer. What gestures would they have in common? What gestures are unique to these occupations? In the classroom setting, gestures such as raising a hand, writing on a chalkboard, pointing, and waving at a student to come sit in a particular seat are common. Janet Bavelas (1994) describes the following gesture types:

Many people use gestures to communicate nonverbally on the job, particularly when they work in a noisy environment or need to communicate with one another silently. Do you commonly use gestures in your workplace? What do they communicate?

- **Delivery gestures** signal shared understanding between communicators. Clifton, for example, nods his head to let his friend, Kaitlin, know that he understands what she is talking about.

- **Citing gestures** acknowledge another's feedback. For instance, in a conversation with her employee, Ms. Rasmussen uses a citing gesture when she disagrees with what her employee is saying; she raises her hand, palm flat to the receiver, her index finger extended upward.

- **Seeking gestures** request agreement or clarification from the speaker. For instance, we may extend both our arms out, keep our palms flat, and shrug. This gesture is used when someone is communicating "I don't know what you mean."

- **Turn gestures** indicate that another person can speak or are used to request the conversation floor. We referenced this nonverbal communication earlier in the chapter when we discussed the regulating function of nonverbal messages. Turn gestures include pointing at another to indicate it is his or her turn, or extending your hand outward and rotating your wrist in a clockwise motion to show that the other person should continue speaking.

In addition to gestures, our body posture and orientation reveal important information. Posture is generally a result of how tense or relaxed we are. For example, your body posture would differ depending on whether you were reading this chapter while you were alone in your room or in the campus library. **Body orientation** is the extent to which we turn our legs, shoulders, and head toward (or away) from a communicator. Albert Mehrabian (1981) found that body orientation affects conversations. For example, when people communicate with those of higher status, they tend to stand directly facing him or her. Conversely, those with higher status tend to use a leaning posture when speaking to subordinates.

To further explore how we use our bodies to convey interpersonal feelings and attitudes, use your online Resource Center for *Understanding Interpersonal Communication* to access *Interactive Activity 5.2: Feelings, Attitudes, and Kinesics*.

delivery gestures

Gestures that signal shared understanding between communicators in a conversation.

citing gestures

Gestures that acknowledge another's feedback in a conversation.

seeking gestures

Gestures that request agreement or clarification from a sender during a conversation.

turn gestures

Gestures that indicate that another person can speak or that are used to request to speak in a conversation.

body orientation

The extent to which we turn our legs, shoulders, and head toward (or away) from a communicator.

REVISITING
CASEINPOINT

1. Identify several areas of nonverbal communication pertaining to Mark and Julia Mattson.

2. Looking at physical appearance specifically, how does Mark make a decision associated with his mother's mental and physical competency? Do you believe his impending decision is appropriate?

You can answer these questions online under the resources for Chapter 5 at your online Resource Center for Understanding Interpersonal Communication.

Physical Appearance

In interpersonal exchanges, physical appearance plays a role in our evaluations of others ("How could he have done that?! He is such a good-looking guy"). Physical appearance encompasses all of the **physical characteristics** of an individual, including body size, skin color, hair color and style, facial hair, and facial features (for example, nose size, skin texture, and so on).

How does physical appearance influence our interpersonal communication? Although we are unable to discuss every aspect of physical appearance, a few thoughts merit attention. Certainly, skin color has affected the communication process. Even today—decades after civil rights legislation took effect—some people won't communicate with people who are of a particular race or ethnicity. Body size, too, can influence our interpersonal relationships. Do you find yourself making judgments about people who appear overweight or too thin? What is your first assessment of a person who is more than six feet tall? What is your initial impression of a bodybuilder? Do you evaluate women who shave their body hair differently from women who choose not to shave?

Body artifacts refer to our possessions and how we decorate ourselves and our surroundings. Clothing, for example, can convey social status or group identification. In the corporate world, tailored clothing bolsters one's status among many peers. During Kwanzaa, a holiday celebration in African American communities, participants frequently wear traditional African clothing, which serves as a nonverbal connection among African Americans. People who wear religious symbols, such as a crucifix or the Star of David, may be exhibiting religious commitments. Military clothing is usually accompanied by medals or stripes to depict rank, which suggests military accomplishment. Body piercings and tattoos can communicate many different messages; those who have them are often viewed as nonconformists, and may be rated poorly by employers. Walking down the street with your iPod, talking on your cell phone while standing in a line at Burger King, or wearing Ray-Ban sunglasses and a Red Sox (or Yankees!) hat backwards are all examples of bodily artifacts.

Physical appearance also includes the level of attractiveness of the interpersonal communicators. Research (e.g., Floyd, 2006) exists on interpersonal attractiveness. Mark Knapp and Judith Hall (2005) have compiled a number

physical characteristics

Aspects of physical appearance, such as body size, skin color, hair color and style, facial hair, and facial features.

body artifacts

Items we wear that are part of our physical appearance and that have the potential to communicate, such as clothing, religious symbols, military medals, body piercings, and tattoos.

of conclusions based on their review of the research findings. Two seem particularly pertinent to our discussion. First, generally speaking, people seek out others who are similar to themselves in attractiveness, just as they seek out others who are similar to themselves in other characteristics. If you are a non-smoker, are you likely to be compatible with a smoker? If you are vegetarian, will you be attracted to a carnivore? Although people are not so narrow and simplistic that they use only one behavior to determine attractiveness, it is true that we are interested in being around those people who are similar to us.

Second, Knapp and Hall (2005) note that physically attractive people are often judged to be more intelligent and friendly than those not deemed attractive. This conclusion resonates in a number of different environments, including the classroom. For example, researchers note that physically attractive students are viewed as more intelligent and friendly than less attractive students (Ritts, Patterson, & Tubbs, 1992). However, in the business setting, "more attractive women in executive roles are often the victims of prejudice, taken less seriously and often resented, thus feeling the pressure to come up with glasses and hairstyles that project a more severe aura" (Jones, 2004, p. 3B). We should make an effort not to allow our judgments of other people to be based on their level of physical attractiveness.

Imagine yourself...

...at work

You are J.T.'s supervisor at a data-processing company. J.T. has been a conscientious employee for over seven years, but in the past month, you have noticed that his appearance has changed. His shirts are always wrinkled, his hair is continually messy, and other employees have privately complained to you about his body odor. Although J. T. is a productive worker and has been cited as "Employee as the Month" several times over the years, you feel you need to approach him, both because you fear something might be wrong and you worry about the effect his disheveled appearance could have on his relationships with his colleagues. Knowing what you do about the importance of physical appearance to interpersonal communication, how do you go about talking to J. T. about his appearance?

Facial Communication

More than any other part of the body, the face gives others insight into how someone is feeling. Our facial expressions cover the gamut of emotional meaning, from eagerness to exhaustion. We often have difficulty shielding authentic feelings from others because we usually don't have much control over our facial communication. This fact further explains the point we made earlier in this chapter, that people tend to believe our nonverbal codes over our verbal codes—it's tough to hide our feelings. While looking at an infant or toddler, try suppressing a smile. When talking to a parent who has lost a child in a war, repressing a sad look on your face is probably impossible. It's simply too challenging to control a region of our body that is so intimately connected to our emotions.

The part of the face with the most potential for communication is the eye. Eye contact is a complex part of human behavior. For most of us, a single eye movement communicates on multiple levels. If we hold a glance for a split second, in a certain context that glance may be interpreted in an intimate way

(Bates & Cleese, 2001), even if we don't intend to send such a message. We can look directly into someone's eyes to communicate interest, power, or anger. We roll our eyes to signal disbelief or disapproval. We avoid eye contact when we are uninterested, nervous, or shy. Our eyes also facilitate our interactions. We look at others while they speak to get a sense of their facial and body communication. Simultaneously, others often look at us while we speak. We also make judgments about others simply by looking at their eyes, deciding if they are truthful, uninterested, tired, involved, or credible. Although our conclusions may be erroneous, most people rely on eye contact in their conversations.

Finally, smiling is one of the most recognizable nonverbal behaviors worldwide. Although in some contexts a smile can have a negative effect, it usually has a positive effect on an encounter. In an experiment testing the effects of smiling on helping behavior, Nicolas Gueguen and Marie-Agnes De Gail (2003) report that smiling at others encourages them to assist in tasks. Studying 800 passersby, the research team had eight research assistants ask others for help. One group of assistants smiled at some of the people exiting a grocery store. A few seconds later, passersby had an opportunity to help an assistant who dropped a computer diskette on the ground. Results showed that the previous smile of a stranger enhanced later helping behavior. That is, those who were smiled at earlier were more likely to help the stranger with the computer disk.

Smiling at another nearly always results in a more pleasant encounter. However, smiling at ill-conceived times may prompt others to react unfavorably. In conflict, for instance, smiling is often perceived as an inappropriate behavior. Smiling during a heated exchange can aggravate an already difficult situation, unless the smile is well timed to ease tensions. Smiling has multiple meanings (for example, a smirk and a sneer communicate two different things), so context is definitely important when we interpret another's smile.

For an interactive look at how our eyes, mouth, and tilt of the head provide clues about our emotions, use your online Resource Center for *Understanding Interpersonal Communication* to access **Interactive Activity 5.3: Eyes, Mouth, and Tilt of Head**. And to read an interesting article about emotions that are recognized across cultures, access **InfoTrac College Edition Exercise 5.2: Universal Facial Expressions** to check out "Emotions Revealed: Recognizing Facial Expressions."

Paralanguage (Voice)

To introduce the concept of paralanguage, let's examine the story of Charles. A few years ago, Charles contracted HIV, the virus that can lead to AIDS. Charles is frequently an upbeat man, and everyone around him enjoys his company. However, sometimes his best friend, Melissa, can hear a "voice" that is different from the one Charles normally uses. For example, sometimes when Charles says that he feels fine and that no one should be concerned about his health, Melissa hears a different message. During such conversations, Charles frequently lapses into silence. He pauses awkwardly as he talks

and all of it is conducted at the point in the communication process that we call hearing.

We introduced you to the issue of stimuli in Chapter 2. With respect to its relationship to working memory theory, consider the following. When Polly sits at The Coffee Bean drinking coffee and reading the morning paper, she hears all types of noises, including people ordering coffee, couples laughing, the door squeaking as it opens and closes, and even the hum of the fluorescent lights. However, she is not paying attention to these background noises. Instead, she is hearing the stimuli without thinking about them. Polly must be able to tune out these stimuli because otherwise she wouldn't be able to concentrate on reading the paper. For instance, Polly's tuning out the stimuli around her might cause her not to register a fight occurring outside the coffee shop, and so she may not immediately do anything about it (e.g., tell one of the shop employees). However, she may unconsciously store "the fight scene," and retrieve it in the future (say, if she engages in a conversation about street crime).

Like Polly, we find ourselves hearing a lot of stimuli throughout our day, whether it's the buzz of lights, music in a restaurant, or the sounds of cars passing on the street. Most of us are able to continue our conversations without attending to these noises.

Being a good listener is much more than letting in audible stimuli. Listening is a communication activity that requires us to be thoughtful. The choices we make when we listen affect our interpersonal encounters. People often take listening for granted as a communication skill in interpersonal relationships. As Harvey Mackay (2001) of the International Communication Association concluded, "listening is the hardest of the 'easy' tasks." Unlike hearing, listening is a learned communication skill. People often have a difficult time describing what being an effective listener is, but seem to know when another person is not listening. Within this framework, we define **listening** as the dynamic, transactional process of receiving, responding to, recalling, and rating, stimuli and/or messages from another. When we listen, we are making sense of the message of another communicator.

Listening is dynamic because it is an active and ongoing way of demonstrating that you are involved in an interpersonal encounter. Further, listening is transactional because both the sender and the receiver are active agents in the process, as we discussed in Chapter 1. In other words, listening is a two-way street. Merely showing that we are listening is a necessary but insufficient way to maintain relationships. We need others to show us they know we are listening.

The remaining four concepts of the definition require a more detailed discussion. We already know that hearing is the starting point in the listening process. Stimuli have to be present, but much more, is required. The **four "Rs" of listening** —receiving, responding, recalling, and rating—make up the listening process (see Figure 6.1 on page 188). Each of the following sections discusses a component of the listening process and the specific skill it requires, including a few recommendations for improving that skill.

Take a moment to notice all the auditory stimuli around you. On an average day, how much stimuli do you think you ignore so that you can concentrate on a task or on another person's message?

listening

The dynamic, transactional process of receiving, recalling, rating, and responding to stimuli, messages, or both.

four "Rs" of listening

The four components of the listening process: receiving, responding, recalling, and rating.

Figure 6.1   The listening process

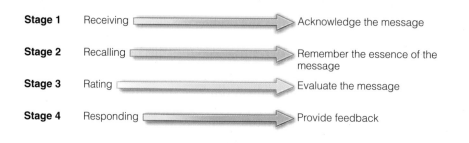

Stage 1   Receiving ⟶ Acknowledge the message

Stage 2   Recalling ⟶ Remember the essence of the message

Stage 3   Rating ⟶ Evaluate the message

Stage 4   Responding ⟶ Provide feedback

Receiving

When we receive a message, we hear and attend to it. **Receiving** involves the verbal and nonverbal acknowledgment of communication. We are selective in our reception and usually screen out those messages that are least relevant to us. Perhaps one reason we don't receive every message is that our attention spans are rather short, lasting from around two to twenty seconds (Wolvin & Coakley, 1996). Our short-term memory, then, affects the receiving process.

When we are receiving, we are being mindful, a concept we discussed in Chapter 2. Mindfulness, you may recall, means we are paying close attention to the stimuli around us. Mindful listening requires us to be engaged with another person as he or she communicates. We can also become **mindless**, which means we aren't paying attention to the stimuli around us. Imagine what your life would be like if you were always mindful—you would be over-whelmed in your communication activities. Being mindless at times is neces-sary, but keep in mind that some stimuli that are perceived as unimportant can be beneficial (think about listening to the rain falling as a way to reduce stress).

The following two suggestions should improve your ability to receive messages effectively. First, eliminate unnecessary noises and physical barriers to listening. If possible, try to create surroundings that allow you to receive a message fully and accurately. Talking on a cell phone, watching MTV, or cleaning house while receiving a personal message are poor listening habits. Second, try not to interrupt the reception of a message. Although you may be tempted to cut off a speaker when he or she communicates a message about which you have a strong opinion, yield the conversational floor so you can receive the entire message and not simply a part of it.

Responding

Responding means giving feedback to another communicator in an interper-sonal exchange. Responding suggests the transactional nature of the interper-sonal communication process. That is, although we are not speaking to

receiving

The verbal and nonverbal acknowledgment of a message.

mindless

Being unaware of the stimuli around us.

responding

Providing observable feedback to a sender's message.

Jason Harris

Jason Harris

Our nonverbal behaviors can provide important feedback to others about whether or not we're really listening to what they're saying. Compare the nonverbal behavior of the man in the photo on the left and the man in the photo on the right. Which person do you think is listening effectively?

another person, we are engaged in communicating by listening. This suggests that responding is critical to achieve interpersonal meaning.

Responding, which lets a speaker know that the message was received, happens during and after a conversation. We provide both nonverbal and verbal feedback to someone as he or she talks and, at times, our feedback continues even though the conversation has ended.

Feedback, as you learned in Chapter 1, can be nonverbal, verbal, or both. Margaret Imhof (2003) differentiated between good and bad listeners in a pool of U.S. and German communicators. Good listeners provided feedback while maintaining frequent eye contact, displaying an open body position (e.g., body position angled toward speaker), and paraphrasing or restating relevant statements. Poor listeners jumped to conclusions, talked only about themselves, displayed a closed body position (e.g., arms closed, body positioned away from speaker), and interrupted.

You can enhance the way you respond in several ways. Adopting the other's point of view is important. This skill (which we talk about later in this chapter) is particularly significant when communicating with people with cultural backgrounds different from your own. Also, take ownership of your words and ideas. Don't confuse what you say with what the other person says. Finally, don't assume that your thoughts are universal; not everyone will agree with your position on a topic.

Recalling

Recalling involves understanding a message, storing it for future encounters, and remembering it later. We have sloppy recall if we understand a message when it is first communicated but forget it later. When we do recall a conversation, we don't recall it word-for-word; rather, we remember a personal version

recalling

Understanding a message, storing it for future encounters, and remembering it later.

(or essence) of what occurred (Bostrom, 1990). Recall is immediate, short-term, or long-term (Bostrom & Waldhart, 1988), and people's recall abilities vary.

Suppose another person criticizes you for recalling a conversation incorrectly. You might simply tell the other person that he or she is wrong. This is what happens in the following conversation between Matt and Dale. The two have been good friends for years. Matt is a homeowner who needed some painting done, and Dale verbally agreed to do it. Now that Dale has given Matt the bill, the two remember differently their conversation about how the bill was to be paid:

Dale: Matt, I remember you said you'd pay the bill in two installments. We didn't write it down, but I remember your words: "I can pay half the bill when you give it to me and then the other half two weeks later." Now you're telling me you didn't say that. What's up with that?

Matt: That's not it at all. I recall telling you that I would pay the bill in two installments *only* after I was satisfied that the work was finished. Look, I know this is not what you want to hear, but the hallway wall is scratched and needs to be repainted. I see gouges on the hardwood floors by the living room, and look at the paint drips on the molding in the dining room.

Dale: I told you that I would come in later to do those small repairs, and you said you'd pay me.

Matt: I don't remember the story that way.

Matt and Dale clearly have different recollections of their conversation. Their situation is even more challenging because both money and friendship are involved.

A number of strategies can help you improve your ability to later recall a message. First, repeating information helps to clarify terms and provide you an immediate confirmation of whether the intended message was received accurately. Second, using *mnemonic* (pronounced "ni-MON-ik") devices as memory-aiding guides will likely help you recall things more easily. Abbreviations such as MADD (for Mothers Against Drunk Driving) and PETA (People for the Ethical Treatment of Animals) use acronyms as mnemonic devices. Finally, chunking can assist you in recalling. **Chunking** means placing pieces of information into manageable and retrievable sets. For example, if Matt and Dale discussed several issues and sub-issues—such as a payment schedule, materials, furniture protection, paint color, timetables, worker load, and so on—chunking those issues into fewer, more manageable topics (for example, finances, paint, and labor) may have helped reduce their conflict.

chunking

Placing pieces of information into manageable and retrievable sets.

rating

Evaluating or assessing a message.

Rating

Rating means evaluating or assessing a message. When we listen critically, we rate messages on three levels: We decide whether or not we agree with the message, we place the message in context, and we evaluate whether the message has value to us.

You don't always agree with messages you receive from others. However, when you disagree with another person, you should try to do so from the other's viewpoint. Rating a message from another's field of experience allows us to distinguish among facts, inferences, and opinions (Brownell, 2002) and these three are critical in evaluating a message. Although we briefly explored facts and inferences in Chapter 2, let's refresh you on the subject. Facts are verifiable and can be made only after direct observation. Inferences fill in a conversation's "missing pieces" and require listeners to go beyond what was observed. **Opinions** can undergo changes over time and are based on a communicator's beliefs or values.

When we evaluate a message, we need to understand the differences among facts, inferences, and opinions. Let's say, for example, that Maggie knows the following:

- Her best friend, Oliver, hasn't spoken to her in three weeks.
- Oliver is healthy and calling other people.
- Maggie has called Oliver several times and has left messages on his answering machine.

These are the facts. If Maggie claims that Oliver is angry at her, doesn't care about her well-being, or has redefined the relationship without her knowledge, she is not acting on facts. Rather, she is using inferences and expressing opinions. Maggie's conclusions may not be accurate at all.

opinion
A view, judgment, or appraisal based on our beliefs or values.

Here are two recommendations that will help you improve your ability to rate messages. First, detect speaker bias, if possible. At times, you may find it difficult to listen to a message and to evaluate its content. The cause of this problem may be the speaker's bias; information in a message may be distorted because a speaker may be prejudiced in some way. Second, listeners should be prepared to change their position. After you have rated a message, you may want to modify your opinions or beliefs on a subject. Avoid being the know-it-all and try to become more flexible in your thinking.

So far, we have distinguished hearing from listening and introduced you to the components of

REVISITING CASEinPOINT

1. Explain how hearing a message, rather than listening to a message, in a campaign office can have lasting effects.

2. How might Jacqueline have been a more effective listener by practicing the "four Rs" of listening?

You can answer these questions online under the resources for Chapter 6 at your online Resource Center for Understanding Interpersonal Communication.

the listening process. To read about another listening model (prepare, receive, process, store, and respond), read the article "Power Up Your Listening Skills," available through InfoTrac College Edition. Go to your online Resource Center for *Understanding Interpersonal Communication* to access *InfoTrac College Edition Exercise 6.1: Listening Model* under the resources for Chapter 6.

The Importance of Listening

Although we like to think that we are good listeners, the truth is that we all need help in this area. Listening is an ongoing interpersonal activity that requires lifelong training. Active listening, a behavior we discuss in more detail later in the chapter, is particularly crucial. Because we listen for a variety of important reasons (see Figure 6.2), listening needs to be a high priority in our lives. Let's offer a few more reasons why studying this topic has lasting value.

Listening is essential to our relationships with others, whether they are coworkers, family members, friends, or other important people in our lives. Listening is used at least three times as much as speaking and at least four times as much as reading and writing (Grognet & Van Duzer, 2002).

Employers rank listening as the most important skill on the job (Career Solutions Training Group, 2000). Listening expert Michael Purdy suggests that hourly employees spend 30 percent of their time listening, managers 60 percent, and executives 75 percent or more (Purdy, 2004). Liz Simpson (2003), a writer for the *Harvard Management Communication Letter,* offers the

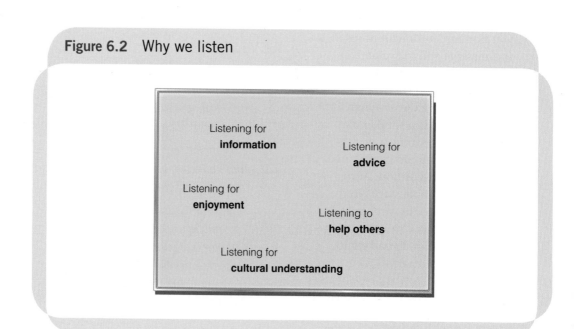

Figure 6.2   Why we listen

Listening for **information**

Listening for **advice**

Listening for **enjoyment**

Listening to **help others**

Listening for **cultural understanding**

following advice to those in the workplace: "To see things from another's point of view and to build trust with her [him], you have to listen closely to what she [he] says" (p. 4).

Listening has been called a twenty-first century skill (Bentley, 2000; Grau & Grau, 2003) because it is now more important than ever. Sheila Bentley (2000) remarked that "new technology and changes in current business practices have changed whom we listen to, what we are listening for, when we listen to them, and how we listen to them" (p. 130). Listening errors can influence worker productivity (Barker & Watson, 2001) and good listening is considered to be the "doorway to leadership, for every executive, manager, and supervisor" (Simonton, 2005, p. 22). Writing from a corporate vantage point, Jennifer Grau and Carole Grau (2003) note that "expanding listening capability and well-developed conflict management skills are not dispensable management tools" (p. 3). To read an article about the importance of listening in the workplace and to check out listening skill training offered to business managers, go to your online Resource Center for *Understanding Interpersonal Communication* to access **Interactive Activity 6.1: Listening in the Workplace** under the resources for Chapter 6.

Good listening skills are valuable in other types of interpersonal relationships as well. For example, successful medical students must develop effective listening skills because, on average, a medical practitioner conducts approximately 150,000 medical interviews with patients during a 40-year career (Watson, Lazarus, & Thomas, 1999). More recent research reported by Donaghue (2007) shows that doctor-patient communication, of which listening is identified as paramount, is especially pivotal in health care. Many hospitals, responding to national surveys on patient satisfaction, are now requiring assessments of a physician's listening skills for fear of malpractice suits. Answers to questions such as "During this hospital stay, how often did doctors listen carefully to you?" will now be collated and provided to patients to use to make health care choices.

Other contexts require skill in listening. In the educational context, researchers have found that effective listening is associated with more positive teacher-student relationships (Wolvin & Coakley, 2000). On the home front, many family conflicts can be resolved by listening more effectively (Greenhaus & Friedman, 2000; Turner & West, 2006). And, in our friendships, some research has shown that the intimacy level between two friends is directly related to the listening skills brought into the relationship (Karbo, 2006).

Although it dates to the 1940s (Nichols, 1948), the topic of listening is clearly relevant today. You would have trouble thinking of any interpersonal relationship in your life that doesn't require you to listen. Improving your listening skills will help improve your relational standing with others. To read an interesting article that reinforces the importance of listening and that offers steps to effective listening, go to your online Resource Center for *Understanding Interpersonal Communication* to access **Interactive Activity 6.2: The Importance of Listening.**

Before we discuss the listening process further, we should point out that not everyone has the physical ability to hear. Although our discussion in this chapter focuses on those who are able to hear physiologically, we are aware that many individuals rely on another communication system to create and share symbols: **American Sign Language (ASL)**. ASL is the third most popular language in the United States after English and Spanish. A visual rather than auditory form of communication, ASL is composed of precise hand shapes and movements. According to the "About ASL" page of a website dedicated to American Sign Language (www.aslinfo.com), approximately half a million people communicate in this manner in the United States and Canada alone. In fact, ASL is seen as a natural communication method for visual learners who aren't hearing-impaired, making it commonplace in many schools across the country (Toppo, 2002). The hard-of-hearing and deaf community has embraced ASL, and it is used to create and to sustain communication within the community.

At this point, you can see how important the skill of listening is in our interpersonal communication with others. Yet, for a number of reasons, people don't listen well. We now present several reasons why we don't always listen effectively in our relationships with others.

Your turn Think about how being a good listener affects your family relationships. If you like, you can use your student workbook or your **Understanding Interpersonal Communication** Online Resources to complete this activity.

The Barriers: Why We Don't Listen

People don't want to acknowledge that they are often poor listeners. As we present the following context and personal barriers to listening, try to recall times when you have faced these obstacles during interpersonal encounters. We hope that making you aware of these issues will enable you to avoid them or deal with them effectively. Table 6.1 presents examples of these obstacles in action.

Noise

American Sign Language (ASL)

A visual rather than auditory form of communication that is composed of precise hand shapes and movements.

As we mentioned earlier in Chapter 1, the physical environment and all of its distractions can prevent quality listening. Noise, you will remember, is anything that interferes with the message. Suppose, for instance, that a deaf student is trying to understand challenging subject matter in a classroom. Attempting to communicate the professor's words, the signer begins to sign words that are incorrect because she does not understand the content. Or, the signs are slurred or incoherent because the signing is too fast. These dis-

Maryland—offer courses on the topic. Most students' preparation in listening is limited to a chapter such as the one you are reading now. Very few companies offer their employees training in listening (Brownell, 2002).

Preoccupation

Even the most effective listeners become preoccupied at times. When we are preoccupied, we are thinking about our own life experiences and everyday troubles. Those who are preoccupied may be prone to what Anita Vangelisti, Mark Knapp, and John Daly (1990) call **conversational narcissism**, or engaging in an extreme amount of self-focusing to the exclusion of another person. Those who are narcissistic are caught up in their own thoughts and are inclined to interrupt others. Most of us have been narcissistic at one time or another; think of the many times you've had a conversation with someone while you were thinking about your rent, your upcoming test, or your vacation plans. Although such personal thoughts are important, they can obstruct our listening.

Preoccupation can also result from focusing on the technology in front of us. How many times have you been on the phone and typing at your computer at the same time? How often have you been told to "listen up" by a friend, only to simultaneously text message another friend. This preoccupation with technology while others are communicating with us can undercut effective and engaged listening.

conversational narcissism

Engaging in an extreme amount of self-focusing during a conversation, to the exclusion of another person.

"I'm sorry, I didn't hear what you said. I was listening to my body."

Listening Gap

We generally think faster than we speak. In fact, research shows that we speak an average rate of 150 to 200 words per minute, yet we can understand up to 800 words per minute (Wolvin & Coakley, 1996). That is, we can think about three or four times faster than we can talk. The **listening gap** is the time difference between your mental ability to interpret words and the speed at which they arrive to your brain. When we have a large listening gap, we may daydream, doodle on paper, or allow our minds to wander. This drifting off may cause us to miss the essence of a message from a sender. It takes a lot of effort to listen to someone. Closing the listening gap can be challenging for even the most attentive listeners.

Poor Listening Habits

The six behaviors set out in Table 6.2 and described in this section are poor listening habits that we may have picked up over the years. Although some of these occur more frequently than others in conversations, each is serious enough to affect the reception and meaning of a message.

Selective Listening

You engage in **selective listening**, or spot listening, if you attend to some parts of a message and ignore others. Typically, you selectively listen to those parts of the message that interest you. For an example of how spot listening can be problematic, consider what happens when jurors listen to a witness's testimony. One juror may listen to only the information pertaining to *where* a witness was during a crime to assess the witness's credibility. Another juror may selectively listen to *why* a witness was near the crime scene. Their spot listening prevents them from receiving all relevant information about the crime. Controlling for selective listening first requires us to glean the entire

listening gap

The time difference between our mental ability to interpret words and the speed at which they arrive at our brain.

selective listening

Responding to some parts of a message and rejecting others.

Table 6.2   How to overcome poor listening habits

Poor listening habit	Strategy for overcoming habit
Selective listening	Embrace entire message
Talkaholism	Become other-oriented
Pseudolistening	Center attention on speaker
Gap filling	Fill gap by mentally summarizing message
Defensive listening	Keep self-concept in check
Ambushing	Play fair in conversations

message. Attending to only those message parts that interest you or tuning out because you believe that you know the rest of a message may prompt others to question your listening skills.

Talkaholism

Some people become consumed with their own communication (McCroskey & Richmond, 1995). These individuals are **talkaholics**, defined as compulsive talkers who hog the conversational stage and monopolize encounters. When talkaholics take hold of a conversation, they interrupt, directing the conversational flow. And, of course if you're talking all the time, you don't take the time to listen. For instance, consider Uncle Randy, the talkaholic in the Norella family. The nearly thirty members of the Norella clan who gather each Thanksgiving dread engaging Uncle Randy in conversation because all he does is talk. And talk. Some family members privately wonder whether Randy understands that many of his more than two dozen relatives would like to speak. But without fail, Uncle Randy comes to dinner with story after story to tell, all the while interrupting those who'd like to share their stories, too.

Not all families have an Uncle Randy, but you may know someone who is a talkaholic—that is, someone who won't let you get a word in edgewise. If you are a talkaholic and have the urge to interrupt others, take a deep breath and remain silent while the other person finishes speaking. If you find yourself talking in a stream of consciousness without much concern for the other person, you are susceptible to becoming a talkaholic. Remember that other people like to talk, too.

Pseudolistening

We are all pretty good at faking attention. Many of us have been indirectly trained to **pseudolisten**, or to pretend to listen by nodding our heads, by looking at the speaker, by smiling at the appropriate times, or by practicing other kinds of attention feigning. The classroom is a classic location for faking attention. Professors have become adept at spotting students who pseudolisten; they usually laugh a bit later than others in the class and have a glazed

talkaholic

A compulsive talker who hogs the conversational stage and monopolizes encounters.

pseudolisten

To pretend to listen by nodding our heads, looking at the speaker, smiling at the appropriate times, or practicing other kinds of attention feigning.

look. You can correct this poor listening habit by making every effort to center your attention on the speaker.

Gap Filling

Listeners who think that they can correctly guess the rest of the story a speaker is telling and who don't need the speaker to continue are called **gap fillers**. Gap fillers often assume they know how a narrative or interpersonal encounter will unfold. Further, gap fillers also frequently interrupt; when this happens, the listener alters the message, and its meaning may be lost. Although an issue may be familiar to listeners, they should give speakers the chance to finish their thoughts.

Defensive Listening

Defensive listening occurs when people view innocent comments as personal attacks or hostile criticisms. Consider Jeannie's experiences. As the owner of a small jewelry shop in the mall, she is accustomed to giving directions to her small staff. Recently, one of her employees commented: "Look, Jeannie, I think you could get more young girls in here if you brought in some rainbow beads. The young ones love them." Jeannie's response was immediate: "Well. . ..here's what I recommend: Why don't you find a lot of money, get your own store, and then you can have all of the rainbow beads you want! I've been in this business for almost ten years, and I think I know what to buy! Why is it that everyone thinks they know how to run a business?"

Jeannie's response fits the definition of defensive listening. Those who are defensive listeners often perceive threats in messages and may be defensive because of personal issues. In the preceding example, Jeannie may not have any animosity toward her employee; she simply may have misinterpreted the comment. To ensure that you are not a defensive listener, keep your self-concept in check. Don't be afraid to ask yourself the following question: Am I too quick to defend my thoughts?

Ambushing

People who listen carefully to a message and then use the information later to attack the individual are **ambushing**. Ambushers want to retrieve information to discredit or manipulate another person. Gathering information and using it to undercut an opponent is now considered routine in politics. Divorce attorneys frequently uncover information to discredit their client's spouse. Ambushing in this manner should be avoided; words should never be viewed as ammunition for a verbal battle.

What are some of your poor listening habits? To help you identify areas in which you can improve your listening, go to your online Resource Center for *Understanding Interpersonal Communication* to access *Interactive Activity 6.3: Identify Your Listening Problems* under the resources for Chapter 6. To read about

gap fillers

Listeners who think they can correctly guess the rest of the story a speaker is telling and don't need the speaker to continue.

defensive listening

Viewing innocent comments as personal attacks or hostile criticisms.

ambushing

Listening carefully to a message and then using the information later to attack the sender.

listening style

A predominant and preferred approach to listening to the messages we hear.

people-centered listening style

A listening style associated with concern for other people's feelings or emotions.

strategies you can use to become a better listener, access *Interactive Activity 6.4: Overcome Bad Listening Habits*.

By now, it should be obvious that your listening skills affect your personal and professional relationships with others. Next, we focus on the styles of listening and then on the influence of culture on the listening process.

Styles of Listening

Typically, we adopt a style of listening in our interpersonal interactions. A **listening style** is a predominant and preferred approach to the messages we hear. We adopt a listening style to understand the sender's message. Researchers have identified four listening styles (Johnston, Weaver, Watson, & Barker, 2000): people-centered, action-centered, content-centered, and time-centered. We call this a P-A-C-T between communicators (see Figure 6.3).

People-Centered Listening Style

The style associated with being concerned with other people's feelings or emotions is called the **people-centered listening style**. People-oriented listeners try to compromise and find common areas of interest. Research shows that people-centered listeners are less apprehensive in groups, meetings, and interpersonal situations than other types of listeners (Sargent, Weaver, & Kiewitz, 1997; Watson & Barker, 1995). People-centered listeners quickly notice others' moods and provide clear verbal and nonverbal feedback.

Action-Centered Listening Style

The **action-centered listening style** pertains to listeners who want messages to be highly organized, concise, and error-free. These people help speakers focus on what is important in the message. Action-centered listeners want speakers to get to the point; they grow impatient when people tell stories in a disorganized or random fashion. They also **second-guess** speakers—that is, they question the assumptions underlying a message (Kirtley & Honeycutt, 1996). If a

Imagine yourself...

...with a mechanic at the garage

Driving to a friend's house, you hear an odd rattle coming from the front of your car and a squeak in the dash. You stop the vehicle and look under the hood, but can't seem to find anything wrong. That evening you make an appointment with a local garage to find out what the problem is. After placing the car on the lift and searching underneath it, the mechanic approaches you in the waiting area. He tells you that the noises are being caused by a problem with your steering shaft and that fixing it won't cost more than $50. You are so relieved to hear this good news that you tune out the rest of the mechanic's report. You fail to listen to him tell you that he has found a host of other problems unrelated to the noises you were hearing. Unfortunately, you agree to have the mechanic "get it all fixed," which he interprets to mean that he'll fix *all* the problems discovered, not just the steering shaft. As you wait beyond an hour, you check into the status of the repair, only to find out that "getting it all fixed" will cost about $250. You now have to confront the mechanic. How do you explain your faulty listening skills to him? In this situation, which barriers to listening might you have encountered? Which poor listening habits might you have exhibited?

action-centered listening style

A listening style associated with listeners who want messages to be highly organized, concise, and error-free.

second-guess

To question the assumptions underlying a message.

Figure 6.3   Styles of listening

People-centered

Action-centered

Content-centered

Time-centered

second-guesser believes a message is false, he or she develops an alternative explanation which they view as more realistic.

Action-centered listeners also clearly tell others that they want unambiguous feedback. For instance, as an action-centered listener, a professor may tell her students that if they wish to challenge a grade, they should simply delineate specific reasons why they deserve a grade change and what grade they feel is appropriate.

Content-Centered Listening Style

Individuals who engage in the **content-centered listening style** focus on the facts and details of a message. Content-centered listeners consider all sides of an issue and welcome complex and challenging information from a sender. However, they may intimidate others by asking pointed questions or by discounting information from those the listener deems to be non-experts. Content-centered listeners are likely to play devil's advocate in conversations. Therefore, attorneys and others in the legal profession are likely to favor this style of listening in their jobs.

Time-Centered Listening Style

When listeners adopt a **time-centered listening style**, they let others know that messages should be presented succinctly. Time-oriented listeners discourage wordy explanations from speakers and set time guidelines for conversations, such as prefacing a conversation with "I have only five minutes to talk."

content-centered listening style

A listening style associated with listeners who focus on the facts and details of a message.

time-centered listening style

A listening style associated with listeners who want messages to be presented succinctly.

Some time-centered listeners constantly check their watches or abruptly end encounters with others.

Which listening style is the best? It depends on the situation and the purpose of the interpersonal encounter. You may have to change your listening style to meet the other person's needs. For example, you might need to be a time-centered listener for the coworker who needs information quickly, but you might need to be person-centered while speaking to your best friend about his divorce. However, remember that just because you adjusted your style of listening does not mean that the other person adjusted his or her style. You will both have to be aware of each other's style. Know your preferred style of listening, but be flexible in your style depending on the communication situation.

Our listening style is often based on our cultural background. We now turn our attention to the role of culture in listening. When speakers and listeners come from various cultural backgrounds, message meaning can be affected.

Culture and the Listening Process

As we learned in Chapter 3, we are all members of a culture and various co-cultures. We understand that cultural differences influence our communication with others. Because all our interactions are culturally based, cultural differences affect the listening process (Brownell, 2002). Much of the research in this area pertains solely to race, ethnicity, and ancestry.

Recall from Chapter 3 our discussion of individualistic and collectivistic cultures. We noted that the United States is an individualistic country, meaning that it focuses on an "I" orientation rather than a "we" orientation. Individualistic cultures value direct communication, or speaking one's mind. Some collectivistic cultures, such as Japan, respect others' words, desire harmony, and believe in conversational politeness

Ethics & Choice

Four fraternity brothers were sitting in the lounge of their fraternity house on a cold winter day. Gabe Walther listened to his friends talk about their roommates, and wondered who was telling the truth. First, Patrick related a story about how his roommate had tried to commit suicide but couldn't work up the guts to swallow all of the sleeping pills. Gabe then listened to Victor's tale about his roommate stealing a copy of the biology final exam. And then Chris told the group about his roommate's financial problems.

Finally, Patrick spoke directly to the group: "Listen, guys, I've got to tell you something that I don't want repeated to anyone. This story is something I heard about a week ago, and it's about Professor Weinberg." Gabe knew that he was about to hear another story based on gossip. He was fed up with all of the stories and what he felt were violations of trust among the guys in the house.

Gabe Walther was obviously struggling with an ethical dilemma: Should he continue to sit through the gossip and listen to the stories, or should he excuse himself and leave? He didn't want his friends to think he was a prude, but he also didn't want to hear all these malicious rumors. He thought to himself: "Man, these guys have got to get a life. I just can't sit here and listen to this stuff."

What would you advise Gabe to do? Should he politely leave the lounge? Or, should he tell his housemates that he disliked their gossip? What ethical system of communication should be followed in this example (categorical imperative, utilitarianism, ethic of care, golden mean, significant choice)?

 Go to your online Resource Center for *Understanding Interpersonal Communication* to access an interactive version of this scenario under the resources for Chapter 6. The interactive version of this scenario allows you to choose an appropriate response to this dilemma and then see what consequences your choice brings about. You can also compare your answers to the questions at the end of the scenario to those provided by the authors and, if requested, email your response to your instructor.

(Lewis, 1999). While listening to others, communicators need to remember that differences in feedback (direct or indirect) may affect message meaning.

Richard Lewis (1999) suggests that listening variations across cultures affect the ability to be an effective salesperson. For example, Lewis points out that for the French, listening for information is the main concern. For citizens of several Arab countries, however, listening is done for know-how or for gain. And Lewis indicates that people in some cultures, such as Germany, do not ask for clarification; asking a presenter to repeat himself or herself is seen as a sign of impoliteness and disrespect. As a practical application of this information, consider how a salesperson's recognition of these cultural differences might positively affect his or her company's bottom line.

Donal Carbaugh (1999) offers additional information on ways that culture and listening work together. Looking at listening as a personal opportunity to interrelate with the environment, Carbaugh cites an example of the Blackfeet Indians:

> Blackfeet listening is a highly reflective and revelatory mode of communication that can open one to the mysteries of unity between the physical and spiritual, to the relationships between natural and human forms, and to the intimate links between places and persons. (p. 265)

In fact, Native American communities have come together to form an "Intertribal Monitoring Association on Indian Trust Funds" (www.imaitrustfunds .org) with the sole purpose of having "listening conferences." Representatives from various tribal nations gather to listen to how the Federal Government is adhering to Trust Fund Standards, to provide tribal forums, to keep up-to-date on policies and regulations on federal initiatives, among others. These listening conferences have been taking place for over 15 years.

The common thread in these examples is the notion that cultures vary in their value systems and yet, listening remains a critical part of the various cultural communities. Staying culturally aware of these variations as you consider the message of another person is important.

What strategies can you use to become a better listener with individuals from various cultures? First, don't expect every-

REVISITING
CASEinPOINT

1. *Choose one style of listening and apply it to Jacqueline and her volunteer work in a political campaign.*

2. *Consider the listening styles and discuss whether one style is more useful than another for Jacqueline, who serves as a director of volunteers.*

Y*ou can answer these questions online under the resources for* Chapter 6 at your online Resource Center for Under- standing Interpersonal Communication.

one else to adapt to your way of communicating. Second, accept new ways of receiving messages. Third, wait as long as possible before merging another's words into your words—don't define the world on your terms. Finally, seek clarification when possible. Asking questions in intercultural conversations reduces our processing load, and we are better equipped to translate difficult concepts as they emerge (Hall, 2005).

We spend the rest of the chapter reviewing effective listening skills you should practice. Improving your listening habits is a difficult, often lifelong, process, so you shouldn't expect changes to your listening behaviors to happen overnight.

Choices for Effective Listening

This section outlines six primary skills for improving listening. Whether we communicate with a partner, boss, friend, family member, coworker, or others, we all must choose whether we will develop good or bad listening habits. Let's explore the following guidelines for effective listening.

Evaluate Your Current Skills

The first step toward becoming a better listener is assessing and understanding your personal listening strengths and weaknesses. First, think about the poor listening habits you have seen others practice. Do you use any of them while communicating? Which listening behaviors do you exhibit consistently, and which do you use sporadically? Also, which of your biases, prejudices, beliefs, and opinions may interfere with receipt of a message?

In addition, we have stresses and personal problems that may affect our listening skills. For example, if you were told that your company was laying off workers, how would this affect your communication with people on a daily basis? Could you be an effective listener even though you would find yourself preoccupied with the financial and emotional toll you would experience if you were downsized? In such a situation, it would be nearly impossible to dismiss your feelings, so you should just try to accept them and be aware that they will probably affect your communication with others. To take a listening quiz that was developed for insurance agents but that is applicable to everyone, read the article "Are You a Good Listener? Take the Skills Quiz," available through InfoTrac College Edition. Go to your online Resource Center for *Understanding Interpersonal Communication* to access *InfoTrac College Edition Exercise 6.2: Are You a Good Listener?* under the resources for Chapter 6.

Prepare to Listen

After you assess your listening abilities, the next step is to prepare yourself to listen. Preparation requires both physical and mental activities. You may have to locate yourself closer to the source of the message (of course, depending on who the speaker is, your physical proximity will vary). If you have problems concentrating on a message, try to reduce or remove as many distractions as possible, such as the TV or stereo. Place yourself in a situation where you will not be distracted by looking out a window or watching other people interact.

To prepare yourself mentally, do your homework beforehand if you are going to need information to listen effectively. For example, if you want to ask your boss for a raise, you would want to have ready a mental list of the reasons why you deserve a raise and possible responses to reasons why you do not. If you are a student, reading the material before class will make the lecture or discussion much more meaningful because you will have the background knowledge to be able to offer your thoughts on issues as they arise. In your personal relationships, you should be mentally prepared to consider other points of view as well as your own.

Provide Empathic Responses

When we use empathy, we tell other people that we value their thoughts. **Empathy** is the process of identifying with or attempting to experience the thoughts, beliefs, and actions of another. Empathy tells people that although we can't feel their exact feelings or precisely identify with a current situation, we are trying to co-create experiences with them. As Judi Brownell (2002) observed: "you do not *reproduce* the other person's experiences. Rather, you and your partner work together to *produce,* or co-create, meanings" (p. 185). We show we're responsive and empathic by giving well-timed verbal feedback throughout a conversation, not simply when it is our turn to speak. Doing so suggests a genuine interest in the sender's message and has the side benefit of keeping us attentive to the message. To show empathy, we must also demonstrate that we're engaged nonverbally in the message. This can be accomplished through sustained facial involvement (avoiding a blank look that communicates boredom), frequent eye contact (maintaining some focus on the speaker's face), and body positioning that communicates interest.

Learning to listen with empathy is sometimes difficult. We have to show support for another while making sure that we are not unnecessarily exacerbating negative feelings. For instance, consider the following dialogue between two friends, Camilla and Tony. Camilla is angry that her boss did not positively review her work plan:

empathy

The process of identifying with or attempting to experience the thoughts, beliefs, and actions of another.

Empathy is an important component of listening. By providing empathic responses, we show that we value another person's thoughts and feelings. In the process, we may even help alleviate that person's anxiety, which is a useful emotional support skill.

© Richard Lord/The Image Works

Dilbert © Scott Adams/Dist. by United Features Syndicate, Inc.

Camilla: He's self-righteous, that's all there is to it. He didn't even tell me that my idea made sense. I think he's just jealous because he didn't come up with it first.

Tony: Yeah, I bet you're right. He really didn't show you any respect. And because he's the boss, I'm sure he wanted to take credit.

Although Tony meant to show empathy, he may have unintentionally perpetuated the idea that Camilla's boss was a "bad" man. Because Tony seems to be supporting her thoughts, Camilla will have a difficult time changing her perception of her boss. This negative view won't help Camilla in future conversations with her boss. Now, consider an alternative response from Tony that doesn't reinforce Camilla's negative perception:

Camilla: He's self-righteous, that's all there is to it. He didn't even tell me that my idea made sense. I think he's just jealous because he didn't come up with it first.

Tony: I know you're pretty frustrated and angry at him. You sound like you want to quit. I know that it has to be pretty rough for you, but hang in there.

In this example, Tony not only demonstrated some empathic listening skills but helped Camilla redirect her thinking about her boss. When Tony changed the direction of the conversation in this way, Camilla could consider less resentful impressions of the situation. Helping others alleviate their anxiety is a necessary emotional support skill for many interactions (Burleson, 2003). To read an article that reinforces the notion that empathy is key to effective listening, check out "Leaders Know How to Listen," available through InfoTrac College Edition. Go to your *Understanding Interpersonal Communication* to access **InfoTrac College Edition Exercise 6.3: Empathy and Listening** under the resources for Chapter 6.

Use Nonjudgmental Feedback

Most of us provide feedback without any concern for how the receiver will interpret it. When we give **nonjudgmental feedback**, we describe another's

nonjudgmental feedback

Feedback that describes another's behavior and then explains how that behavior made us feel.

behavior and then explain how that behavior made us feel. As we discussed in Chapter 4, centering a message on your own emotions without engaging in accusatory finger-wagging can help reduce interpersonal conflict.

Consider the difference between the following statements:

- "You are so rude to come in late. You made me a nervous wreck! You're pretty inconsiderate to make me feel this way!"

- "When you come home so late, I really worry. I thought something had gone wrong."

In heated moments especially, taking ownership of your feelings and perceptions, as in the second statement, is difficult. Owning your feelings rather than blaming others for your feelings results in more effective interpersonal communication.

Practice Active Listening

We define active listening as a transactional process in which a listener communicates reinforcing messages to a speaker. When we actively listen, we show support for another person and his or her message. Active listeners *want to* listen rather than feel *obligated to* listen. Particularly in close relationships with others, demonstrating that you are actively involved in the conversation will help both your credibility as a communicator and your relationship standing with others. Additional elements of active listening are paraphrasing, dialogue enhancers, questions, and silence. We briefly discuss each of these in the following subsections.

Paraphrasing

paraphrasing

Restating the essence of a sender's message in our own words.

Active listening requires **paraphrasing**, or restating the essence of another's message in our own words. Paraphrasing is a perception check in an interpersonal encounter; it allows us to clarify our interpretation of a message. When paraphrasing, try to be concise and simple in your response. For instance, you can use language such as "In other words, what you're saying is . . ." or "I think what I heard is that you . . ." or "Let me see if I get this right." Such phrases show others that you care about understanding the intended meaning of a message. To read an article that reinforces the benefits of paraphrasing, check out "Practice Listening Skills as a Leader," available through Info-Trac College Edition. Go to your *Understanding Interpersonal Communication* to access *InfoTrac College Edition Exercise 6.4: Paraphrasing and Listening* under the resources for Chapter 6.

dialogue enhancers

Supporting statements, such as "I see" or "I'm listening," that indicate we are involved in a message.

Dialogue Enhancers

Active listening requires us to show the speaker that even though we may disagree with his or her thoughts, we accept and are open to them. As we noted earlier, speakers need support in their conversations. **Dialogue enhancers** take the form of supporting expressions such as "I see" or "I'm listening." Dialogue enhancers should not interrupt a message. They should be used as indications that you are involved in the message. In other words, these statements enhance the discussion taking place.

Questions

Asking well-timed and appropriate questions in an interpersonal interaction can be a hallmark of an engaged active listener. Asking questions is not a sign of ignorance or stupidity. What questions demonstrate is a willingness to make sure you receive the intended meaning of the speaker's message. If you ask questions, you may receive information that is contrary to your instincts or assumptions, thereby avoiding gap filling, a problem we identified earlier. Don't be afraid to respectfully ask questions in your relationships with others. Your input will likely be met with gratitude as the other communicator realizes your desire to seek information.

Silence

Author Robert Fulghum (1989) comments in *All I Really Need to Know I Learned in Kindergarten* that silence is a big part of a satisfying life. It may seem strange to talk about the importance of being silent in interpersonal communication. In fact, in the self-help book sections in U.S. book stores, we

© Danny Lehman/Corbis

The value of silence is not lost on monks who take a vow of silence as part of their spiritual practice. In such a tradition, practicing silence is not meant as a way to reject others but as a means to clear away noise so the monks are better able to listen.

interpersonal explorer

Before you finish reading this chapter, take a moment to review the theories and skills discussed. How do you think the theories discussed in this chapter can help you better understand listening? In what ways can the skills discussed help you interact more effectively with other people in your life?

Theories that relate to listening

- **Working memory theory**
  We have the ability to simultaneously attend to multiple stimuli, to store other stimuli, and/or to retrieve information from long-term memory storage

Practical skills for improving listening

- Evaluate current personal listening skills
- Prepare to listen
- Provide empathy
- Use critical and nonjudgmental feedback
- Practice active listening techniques

Explore your interpersonal choices

Are you ready to explore your interpersonal choices regarding listening? Use your online Resource Center for *Understanding Interpersonal Communication* to access an interactive simulation that allows you to view the beginning of an interpersonal scenario regarding listening, make a choice about how the people in the scenario should proceed with their interaction, consider the consequences of your choice, and then see three possible outcomes to the interaction.

rarely find books on the importance of keeping quiet because the culture rewards talkativeness. Silence is a complicated concept in conversations. As communication ethicist J. Vernon Jensen (1997) stated, "silence can warmly bind friends together, but can chillingly separate individuals" (p. 151). We live in a society in which overt communication is embraced—just look at television talk shows for proof.

As the old saying goes, silence is golden. We should honor silence when another person is struggling with what to say. We need to allow the entire message to be revealed before jumping in. We also need to be silent because, at times, words are not needed. For example, after a conflict has been resolved and two people are looking at each other and holding each other's hands, they don't need to speak to communicate. Silence in this context may be more effective than words in making the people in the relationship feel closer.

However, silence is not always positive. It can also be used to manipulate or coerce another person in an interpersonal exchange. This is an example of the dark side of communication that we discussed in Chapter 1. For instance, giving someone "the silent treatment"—that is, refusing to talk to someone—may provoke unnecessary tension. Also, imposing your own code of silence in an encounter may damage a relationship. For example, if you chose to remain silent in an interpersonal conflict, you would most likely exacerbate the problem.

 Listening is one of the keys to success in all areas of your life. In addition to reading the advice given in this chapter, check out seven strategies to better listening by using your *Understanding Interpersonal Communication* online Resource Center to access *Interactive Activity 6.5: Keys to Better Listening* under the resources for Chapter 6. And for more techniques for better listening, including active listening, read the article "Improving Your Listening Skills," available through InfoTrac College Edition. Access *InfoTrac College Edition Exercise 6.5: Guidelines for Better Listening*.

CASE in POINT

REGINA CHEN AND ALLISON YANG

Each Saturday morning, graduate students Regina Chen and Allison Yang met for coffee, something they've done ever since they were undergraduate sophomores. This Saturday, however, was not a day just for chit chat. Although both women certainly had enough to talk about—including their courses, printer problems, and men—today would involve a different sort of conversation. Regina had something very important to tell her friend Allison.

As soon as Regina got her coffee, she darted over to Allison with an enormous grin. "Guess you can't imagine what *I'm* so happy about today," she said to her friend.

"Well," Allison said, "if you got another gorgeous guy to ask you out, I'm gonna leave this table now!"

"No, it's much, much better than that!," Regina responded, sitting down and leaning toward Allison. Although she was a bit nervous to tell Allison about the news, somehow she found a way: "I forgot to pick up my mail yesterday, and when I went downstairs this morning to the mailbox, I found a letter from the Stern Foundation. You know what's next, don't you?"

Allison shook her head quickly. "Tell me already!" she begged Regina.

"Well, I opened the letter and saw that I got the Federation Prize. Do you know what this means?! I am now the proud recipient of a $20,000 scholarship! *I can't believe this!* I never imagined that this last year of grad school I wouldn't have to worry about money issues. And now I can finish my thesis—without getting a job! This has to be the best day of grad school so far! Oh, listen, Ali—I know we both applied for this, and I'm sorry you didn't get it, but you *have* to be excited for me! Please tell me that you are!"

As soon as she finished talking, Regina pulled the letter out of her purse and put it on the table. Suddenly, however, she saw that Allison was not smiling. Regina's friend obviously didn't share in the excitement. "Wow," Allison said, calmly, looking out the window. "Look, I'm very happy for you. But I have to tell you, this is tougher than I thought. I really want my best friend to get good things, but this is a hard way to find out that I didn't get the money. Of course, like I said, I'm really happy. But you'll have to excuse me here. I'm not really all that into coffee talk today." Allison

Use your online Resource Center for *Understanding Interpersonal Communication* to watch a video clip of Regina and Allison's interaction.

> Access the resources for Chapter 7 and select "Regina" to watch the video (it takes a minute for the video to load). As you watch the video, consider the way in which Regina broke her news to Allison. Could she have done it in a way that better took into account Allison's potential emotional response? > You can respond to this and other analysis questions, and then click "Done" to compare your answers with those provided by the authors.

got up to leave. She felt ashamed of herself for not being able to really share in Regina's happiness. But she was so disappointed for herself that she had trouble not crying.

As Allison hugged her friend and left the café, Regina sat in a daze. She thought that maybe this hadn't been the most sensitive way of handling her good news with her friend. She thought that Allison would have been more excited about the award, but now she couldn't help but think that her best friend was now either envious, very sad, or both.

*E*veryone experiences the powerful impact of emotion: the joy of falling in love, the grief of losing a loved one, the pride in an accomplishment, the embarrassment of a public mistake, or the anger that boils up when we think someone is standing in the way of a cherished goal. In our opening Case in Point, Allison struggles with emotion when Regina gets an award that Allison wanted. Emotion affects our daily lives in powerful ways.

Experiencing emotion shapes our lives and our relationships. Emotion is often what we remember about interpersonal encounters. Jay barely remembers any of his high school teachers now that he's 32. But his ninth grade English teacher, Ms. Laurent, is someone he'll never forget. He often thinks of how she helped him feel proud of his work and optimistic about the future. Emotion often influences how we judge interpersonal interactions. For exam-

Emotion and interpersonal communication often go hand in hand. Not only does emotion influence how, when, and why we communicate with others, but our displays of emotion communicate messages themselves. For example, this family doesn't have to say a word to communicate their joy, gratitude, and relief when they receive a new house from Habitat for Humanity— their expressions say it all.

ple, when Andy thinks back to her friendship with Roz, she's glad it's over because of all the arguments between them, which left Andy feeling angry most of the time.

In this chapter, we investigate emotion and its powerful relationship to the interpersonal communication process. We all know intuitively how important emotion is, but often we don't have enough information about emotion—it isn't a subject discussed much in school. But when we don't pay attention to emotion, we can't be competent communicators. For instance, both Allison and Regina might have been helped in the opening Case In Point if they had information about emotion and became more emotionally competent. As with so many aspects of interpersonal communication, we need to gain adequate knowledge before we can develop our skills. Let's begin by defining emotion.

Defining Emotion: More than Just a Feeling

Defining the term *emotion* is complicated. Some researchers (for example, Fehr & Russell, 1984; Ortony, Clore, & Foss, 1987) argue that emotion involves only one person's feelings (like anger, fear, anxiety, happiness, and so forth). Other researchers include in their definition those emotions we feel in relationship with others like envy and love (Planalp & Fitness, 1999). Still other scholars (Buzzanell & Turner, 2003; Tracy, 2005) differentiate between *real* feelings and *manufactured* feelings that are produced because some outside norm dictates that they are appropriate. For instance, if you are a server in a restaurant, your job requires you to smile and act happy around your customers even if you've had a horrible day and don't feel like smiling at all. Manufacturing a feeling that you're not actually experiencing is called *emotion labor*.

In this book, we take an inclusive position and define **emotion** as the critical internal structure that orients us to, and engages us with, what matters in our lives: our feelings about ourselves and others. Thus, the term *emotion* encompasses both the internal feelings of one person (for instance, when Joe feels anxious before he meets Ana's parents) as well as feelings that can be experienced only in a relationship (for instance, when Joyce feels competitiveness when she hears how well Barb did on the chemistry exam). Emotion labor falls outside the definition we're using here.

The definition of emotion also rests on the notion of process; although we have names for discrete emotions such as fear, sadness, depression, ecstasy, and so forth, emotion is often experienced as a blend of several emotions (Oatley & Duncan, 1992). Think again of Allison from our opening Case In Point scenario. When she learns that Regina got the scholarship and she didn't, she feels disappointed, ashamed, envious, and happy for her friend all at once.

emotion

The critical internal structure that orients us to and engages us with what matters in our lives: our feelings about ourselves and others. Emotion encompasses both the internal feelings of one person (for instance, anxiety or happiness) as well as feelings that can be experienced only in a relationship (for instance, jealousy or competitiveness).

Strategic embarrassment is another example of an emotional blend. Although embarrassment is an unpleasant emotional state, people often plan embarrassing situations for others, and planning an embarrassing moment for someone else is often socially acceptable (Bradford & Petronio, 1998). For example, it is a common practice among adolescents to use strategic embarrassment in the following way (Bradford, 1993). Tom knows his friend, Jesús, is interested in Amy. He also knows that Jesús is shy and won't introduce himself to her. As Amy and Jesús pass in the school hallway, Tom purposely pushes Jesús into Amy. Jesús is embarrassed but recognizes that Tom actually helped him connect with Amy.

In a study illustrating how common emotional blends are, college students were asked to describe emotions they observed others communicating (Planalp, DeFrancisco, & Rutherford, 1996). The participants usually picked more than one emotion, even though the question was phrased to elicit a single emotion ("What emotion did you observe, e.g. anger, happiness, fear, etc.?"). Forty-five percent of the respondents chose two emotions for their answer, and 22 percent used three or more emotions. To explicate our definition of emotion more completely, we'll now discuss two category systems for emotion and explore the relationships among emotion, reason, and physicality (the body).

Two Category Systems for Emotion

To capture the complexity of emotion, some researchers have created category systems classifying common emotions in the U.S. These systems focus on attributes of emotion, such as **valence** (whether it reflects a positive or negative feeling), **activity** (whether it implies action or passivity), or **intensity** (how strongly felt it is).

One system (Russell, 1978, 1980, 1983) categorizes emotion along two dimensions at once: valence and activity. This system allows us to see how specific emotions cluster together depending on whether they are active-negative, active-positive, passive-negative, or passive-positive (see Figure 7.1). For example, when Luis feels an emotion such as excitement we can see on Figure 7.1 that it is positive and implies some action. When he feels an emotion like contentment, the figure shows that it's less positive and less active than excitement.

Another system for classifying individual emotion is based on its intensity. Robert Plutchik's (1984) emotion cone provides a graduated image of emotional range (see Figure 7.2). The lowest level of each vertical slice represents the mildest version of the emotion, and each successive level represents a more intense state. This system points to the impact of labeling an emotion with a particularly intense name. For example, if Jenna says she is bored in French class, that carries a much different meaning, and is far less intense, than if she says she loathes French. For another look at Plutchik's emotion cone and the various dimensions of emotion, go to your online Resource

valence

An attribute of emotion that refers to whether the emotion reflects a positive or negative feeling.

activity

An attribute of emotion that refers to whether the emotion implies action or passivity.

intensity

An attribute of emotion that refers to how strongly an emotion is felt.

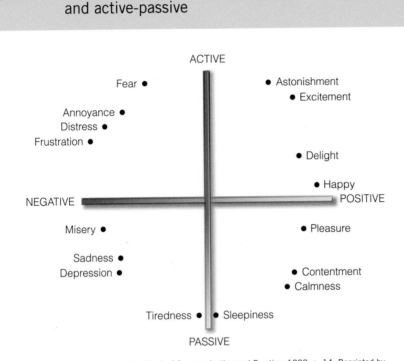

Figure 7.1 Category system for emotions: positive-negative and active-passive

From Guerrero, Anderson, Trost, eds. *Handbook of Communication and Emotion*, 1998, p. 14. Reprinted by permission of Elsevier.

Center for *Understanding Interpersonal Communication* to access **Interactive Activity 7.1: Emotion Cone** under the resources for Chapter 7.

Emotion, Reason, and the Body

From the preceding discussion, you can see that *emotion* is more than just feelings. It's more complicated than that. One of the complexities of emotion is that it's linked with the dualism that characterizes Western thought. **Dualism**, which originated in the 18th century with philosophers Immanuel Kant, and Rene Descartes, is a way of thinking that constructs polar opposite categories to encompass the totality of a thing, prompting us to think about it in an "either/or" fashion. For example, dualism encourages us to think about all of temperature as either hot or cold; all of gender as either feminine or masculine; all of a person as either good or bad. See Table 7.1 on page 221 for a listing of common dualisms that pervade our language and thinking.

When we phrase things as either/or choices we can't see a third (or fourth) possibility. Recall President George W. Bush's frequent comment after

dualism

A way of thinking that constructs polar opposite categories to encompass the totality of a thing. Dualism prompts us to think about things in an "either-or" fashion.

Figure 7.2   Emotion cone

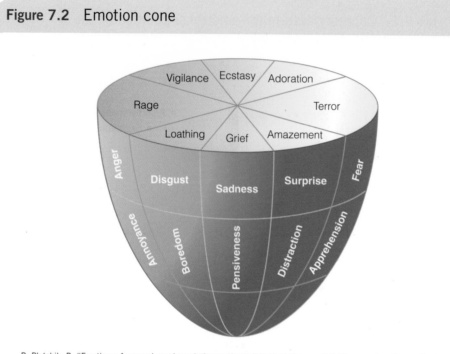

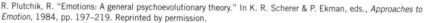

R. Plutchik, R. "Emotions: A general psychoevolutionary theory." In K. R. Scherer & P. Ekman, eds., *Approaches to Emotion*, 1984, pp. 197–219. Reprinted by permission.

September 11, 2001, that countries had to decide: They were *either* allied with the United States against terrorism, *or* they were against the United States and implicitly terrorists themselves. There is no room for a middle position in Bush's statement.

Dualism also encourages us to consider a person to be split into two parts—mind and body—that operate completely independently. The historic division between mind and body is further split when the mind is seen, in another dualism, as either reason or emotion.

Thinking about emotion as separate from reason and the body is reflected in medical school curricula. Many courses teach students to treat physical symptoms, but relatively few address the thoughts and feelings of patients and their families. And dualism is illustrated whenever someone says to another in a conflict: "Stop being hysterical about this! You have to be reasonable."

However, on some level we also understand that emotion, the body, and reason are inextricably linked. Our language can help us see the connections. Think about words we use to describe emotion: *heartache, heartsick, heartened, bighearted, heartless, heartfelt, light-hearted.* All these words indicate our instinctive knowledge of the connection among the mind, emotion, and the body.

Table 7.1 Common dualisms in western thought

hot ↔ cold	strong ↔ weak
male ↔ female	right ↔ wrong
good ↔ bad	public ↔ private
mind ↔ body	black ↔ white
reason ↔ emotion	thinking ↔ feeling
liberals ↔ conservatives	active ↔ passive

Further, experiencing emotion seems to affect people's physical functioning in ways that are not simply physical manifestations of the emotion. Journalist Bill Moyers (1993) interviewed Margaret Kemeny, a psychologist with training in immunology (the study of the immune system). She told him that evidence suggests that experiencing emotion has an effect on health. Based on her studies, she theorizes that prolonged depression makes people vulnerable to heart attacks and other debilitating diseases.

Psychiatrist Ana Fels agrees. A cardiologist referred a patient to her after a heart attack because the doctor hoped that treating the patient's depression would help stabilize the heart disease. Fels observed the relationship between body and emotion by stating, "Not only had his heart attack set off his depression, but his depression could worsen his heart disease" (Fels, 2002, p. D5). To read an interesting article about how the brain and body changes when recalling emotional experiences, go to your online Resource Center for *Understanding Interpersonal Communication* to access *Interactive Activity 7.2: Feeling Emotion.* For more about the links among emotion, the body, feeling, and the mind, access *Interactive Activity 7.3: Emotions, the Body, and the Mind.*

The reverse is also true: reason is dependent on emotion. Hunches and gut reactions show emotion in service of reason. Emotion helps us to decide between competing alternatives when all else is equal. How do you choose between a brown scarf and a black scarf when both look equally good with your coat? How do you choose whether to visit your friend Mark or your friend Sam, when you like them each the same? We would be paralyzed by indecision if we didn't have emotional responses to help us make decisions.

As we learned in Chapter 2, when we perceive something, we first attend to stimuli. So, let's say that stimuli is coming to you and you feel threatened in some way and that your safety is at risk. That is, you feel the emotion of fear. This insight involves reason. You must notice that something dangerous is happening (for example, someone approaches you looking threatening). In this step, you compare your knowledge of a non-dangerous event to what is actually happening, and you see the discrepancy (for example, you say to

© Ellen B. Senisi/The Image Works

IPC *in the* News

The relationship between reason and emotion is illustrated in a *USA Today* article discussing brain research that examined the role of emotion in decision making. The article reports on a study by neuroscientists showing that people use emotional biases in making so-called rational decisions. The lead researcher for this study says that to make healthy decisions, emotion and reason must be intertwined. He observes that what makes people rational isn't the suppression of emotion, but rather the tempering of emotion so that emotion and reason can work hand-in-hand. He also notes that one of the biggest insights from the study should be directed to educators, commenting that "our education system ignores the role of emotion in learning and decision making" (p. 6D). The results of the study show that we ought to be teaching about emotion in schools.

Vergano, D. (2006, August 7). Study: Ask with care. *USA Today*. p. 6D.

yourself, "I could have no one bothering me, but that's not happening"). You also have to determine the importance of this behavior and evaluate the context (for example, you and this person are friends playing football, or you are walking down a dark street and the person is a stranger). All these judgments are part of the cognitive element of emotion. Emotion also has a physiological component. For example, if someone approaches you with a scowl on his or her face, you are likely to experience physiological reactions such as accelerated heart rate, breathing changes, a lump in your throat, and tense muscles. Table 7.2 presents a listing of common emotions with their accompanying cognitive and physical elements.

Explaining Emotion: Biology and Social Interaction

Many theories help us understand emotion. We will now review two theories that explain how emotions originate: the biological and social (Hochschild, 1983). These theories help us understand emotion more comprehensively.

The Biological Theory of Emotion

Proponents of the biological theory agree with Charles Darwin and others (Hochschild, 1983) that emotion is mainly biological, related to instinct and energy. Because advocates of this view believe that emotions are similar across many types of people, they propose that people from a variety of cultures should experience feelings in the same manner.

Further, this theory assumes that emotion exists separately from thought and that we need thought only to bring a preexisting emotion to our conscious awareness. For example, let's say that Maura is arguing with her friend, Barbara, about how to plan a campus event. While they talk, Maura is thinking about advancing her ideas in the argument and is not paying any attention to the emotion she is experiencing. However, as she walks away from Barbara, she notices that she's slightly irritated because Barbara disagrees with her about the best way to advertise the event. Although Maura had been

Table 7.2 Emotions, physical reactions, and cognitions

Emotions	Physical Reactions	Cognitions
Joy	Warm temperature Fast heartbeat	"I am so happy, and this feels different"
Anger	Fast heartbeat Tense muscles	"I feel anger, and I want to do something"
Sadness	Lump in throat Tense muscles	"I am feeling sadness wash over me"
Shame	Hot flushes Fast heartbeat	"I am ashamed. What can I do?"

experiencing emotion during the argument, she needed introspection, or thought, to bring it to her attention.

Darwin placed importance on observable emotional expressions, not the meaning associated with them. Darwin argued that these "gestures" of emotion were remnants of prehistoric behaviors that served important functions. For instance, when we bare our teeth in rage, our behavior is a remnant of the action of biting. When we hug someone in an expression of love, our action is a remnant of the act of copulation. And when our mouths form an expression of disgust, our action is a remnant of the need to regurgitate a poisonous substance or spoiled food. Thus, in the biological theory, "emotion . . . is our experience of the body ready for an imaginary action" (Hochschild, 1983, p. 220). Furthermore, Darwin argued that people enact these gestures as a result of experiencing emotion. However, he also asserted that the opposite is true—that is, when people enact a certain gesture, they experience the related emotion. Darwin also believed that these emotive gestures (with a few exceptions, such as weeping and kissing) are universal, meaning that they cross all cultures.

The Social Interaction Theory of Emotion

The social interaction theory (Gerth & Mills, 1964) acknowledges that biology affects emotion and emotional communication. However, proponents of this theory are also interested in how people interact with their social situation before, during, and after the experience of emotion. In this way, the theory adds social factors, like interactions with others, to the biological basis for explaining emotion.

Our biology has a tremendous effect on our emotional expression. Smiling is a good example of an inherent human behavior—we don't have to be taught to smile to express happiness, pleasure, and many other emotions.

© Reuters/Corbis

For example, let's say that Catherine finds out on Tuesday that her best friend, Lola, is having a party on Friday. Lola hasn't invited Catherine. The social theory is interested in the following questions: What elements in Catherine's cultural milieu contribute to how she perceives being left off the guest list? That is, do any contextual elements affect her experience of emotion? For example, if Catherine's birthday is coming up, she might think Lola is giving her a surprise party. The biological theory of emotion considers these questions unimportant, but they are central to the social theory.

Like the biological theory, the social theory talks about gesture. However, the social theory focuses on how the reactions of others to our gestures help us define what we are feeling. For example, let's say that Catherine tells another friend, Allen, about not being invited to the party, and she starts to cry because she feels hurt. Allen interprets Catherine's tears as a manifestation of anger, saying to Catherine, "You must be really mad!" Catherine hears this and agrees, "Yes, I can't believe that jerk didn't invite me after all the times she's been to my parties!" Catherine's sense of her own emotional experience may have been confused before she talked to Allen, but his interpretation swayed her and influenced how she labeled her emotion.

See Table 7.3 for a comparison of the biological and social theories. To take a look at several other theories of emotion, including the "common sense" theory, use your online Resource Center for *Understanding Interpersonal Communication* to access *Interactive Activity 7.4: Theories of Emotion.*

Now that we have defined emotion and discussed some theories that help us understand it, we are ready to address our primary concern in this chapter: how emotion relates to interpersonal communication.

Table 7.3 The biological and social theories of emotion

	The biological theory	The social theory
Definition of emotion	Biological processes	Feeling states resulting from social interaction
Relationship of emotions to cognitions	Separate	Interrelated
Assumption of universality	Yes	No
Concern with subjective meaning	No	Yes

Emotion and Communication

Emotion clearly affects interpersonal communication. It influences how we talk to others, how others hear what we say and how our communication affects our relational outcomes (Theiss & Solomon, 2007). For example, people who feel betrayed by a relational partner have many communication choices to express their feelings. Research shows that if they use explicit strategies to forgive their partner, their relationships improve (Waldron & Kelley, 2005). Emotion permeates communication from birth to death. One study showed that the emotion embodied in the final conversation with a loved one before death makes a big difference in the survivor's ability to cope with the loss (Keeley, 2007).

Interpersonal communication can be influenced by the feelings of those around us through **emotional contagion**, or the process of transferring emotions from one person to another. Emotional contagion occurs when one person's feelings "infect" those around him or her. You have probably experienced emotional contagion yourself. Think of a time when you were with a friend who communicated in a nervous manner. Didn't you find yourself becoming nervous, too, just watching her fidget? Or you may have become depressed yourself after spending time with a friend who expressed that he was down in the dumps. Conversely, if you are around someone who expresses positive feelings, you usually find your own mood brightening and your communication becoming more upbeat. Daniel Goleman (2006) calls this *emotional afterglow*.

In examining the relationship between interpersonal communication and emotion, we need to clarify several terms: emotional experience, emotional communication, communicating emotionally, and emotional effects. **Emotional experience** refers to feeling emotion and thus is intrapersonal in nature (Belle felt nervous before her interview). **Emotional communication** means actually talking about the experience of emotion to someone else (Essie told Patrick how she was feeling about the possibility of adopting a child as a single mom). **Communicating emotionally** suggests that the emotion itself is not the

emotional contagion

The process of transferring emotions from one person to another.

emotional experience

The feeling of emotion.

emotional communication

Talking about an emotional experience.

communicating emotionally

Communicating such that the emotion is not the content of the message but rather a property of it.

content of the message but rather a property of it (Roberto yells at his wife Tessa, telling her that she is making them late for their dinner reservations). **Emotional effects** relate to how emotional experience impacts communication behavior (Burleson & Planalp, 2000). (When Sophie ran into her friend Alexa at the mall and accidentally called her Deanna, the name of another friend, Sophie was so embarrassed and flustered that she was unable to conduct the rest of the conversation with Alexa without stammering and stuttering).

The first part of this section focuses on the language used in the United States to portray emotion—that is, the metaphors we employ that center on emotion. The second part of this section discusses how we communicate emotion through a variety of verbal and nonverbal cues.

Metaphors for Emotion

As we discussed in Chapter 4, people often employ figurative language, especially metaphors, to talk about abstract ideas like emotion. Further, people use metaphoric language to distinguish among various emotions as well as "the subtle variations in a speaker's emotional state (e.g., *get hot under the collar* refers to . . . [a] less intense state of anger than does *blow your stack*" [Leggitt & Gibbs, 2000, p. 3]). Table 7.4 lists some common metaphors for emotion.

Our figurative language may imply that emotion has a presence independent of the person experiencing it—as in the phrase "she succumbed to depression." Emotions are frequently framed as opponents ("he struggled with his feelings") or as wild animals ("she felt unbridled passion") (Kovecses, 2000). We speak of guilt as something that "haunts" us, fear as something that "grips" us, and anger as something that "overtakes" us (Hochschild, 1983).

Although these phrases are evocative of the feelings that various emotions engender, they leave the impression that people are not responsible for their emotion—that is, that people are acted upon by emotional forces beyond their control. This way of talking about emotion fits in with our earlier discussion of the division between emotion and reason. Such language depicts emotion as something that can make us lose our minds completely as we are overwhelmed by forces beyond our rational control.

How Emotion Is Communicated

As we discussed in Chapters 4 and 5, the tools we have for communicating are verbal and nonverbal cues. In this section, we'll briefly discuss verbal and nonverbal cues that communicate emotion. We'll also discuss how people use combinations of these cues.

Nonverbal Cues

Facial expressions are obviously one of the most important means for communicating emotion. When people view photos of facial expressions for a variety of emotions, they are accurate in their ability to discern one emotion

emotional effects

The ways in which an emotional experience impacts communication behavior.

Table 7.4 Common metaphors and emotions

Anger	
A hot fluid in a container	She is boiling with anger.
A fire	He is doing a slow burn.
Insanity	George was insane with rage.
A burden	Tamara carries her anger around with her.
A natural force	It was a stormy relationship.
A physical annoyance	He's a pain in the neck.

Fear	
A hidden enemy	Fear crept up on him.
A tormentor	My mother was tortured by fears.
A natural force	Mia was engulfed by fear.
An illness	Jeff was sick with fright.

Happiness	
Up	We had to cheer him up.
Being in heaven	That was heaven on earth.
Light	Miguel brightened up at the news.
Warm	Your thoughtfulness warmed my spirits.
An animal that lives well	Tess looks like the cat that ate the canary.
A pleasurable physical sensation	I was tickled pink.

Sadness	
Down	He brought me down with what he said.
Dark	Phil is in a dark mood.
A natural force	Waves of depression swept over Todd.
An illness	Lora was heartsick.
A physical force	The realization was a terrible blow.

Adapted from Kovecses, 2000.

from another (Gosselin, Kirouac, & Dore, 1995). The most researched facial expression is the smile. Smiles usually indicate warmth and friendliness, but, as we mentioned in Chapter 5, smiles can be interpreted to mean something other than positive emotion. For example, Donna's boss, Melanie, often uses a smile as a mocking gesture. Therefore, when Melanie approaches Donna's office with a smile on her face, Donna feels frustration and braces herself for some type of unpleasant interaction.

Although it is not as well researched as the face, the voice is probably equally important in conveying emotion. How loudly people talk, how high-pitched their tone, how fast they talk, how many pauses they take, and so forth give clues to emotion. In addition, "the voice also carries information about whether emotions are positive and negative because, based on vocal cues alone, pride is more likely to be confused with elation, happiness, and interest than it is with the negative emotions" (Planalp, 1999, p. 46). For example, when Jack calls his coworker Theo one morning before work, Theo can tell right away by the way Jack says "hello" that something is wrong. Before Jack explains his problem verbally, Theo is cued by the tone in Jack's voice.

Emotion is "embodied." This means that "people scratch their heads, clench their fists, shake, gesture wildly, hug themselves, pace the floor, lean forward, fidget in their seats, walk heavily, jump up and down, slump, or freeze in their tracks" (Planalp, 1999, pp. 46–47) when they're communicating emotion. However, there isn't a great deal of research on gestures and body movement. Some research has indicated that depressed people gesture less than those who are not depressed (Segrin, 1998).

Some research (Miller, 2007) suggests that caregivers can communicate compassion nonverbally through place and time codes. For example, caregivers stated that they tried to show compassion to patients by being on time to see them and by structuring the environment so that the temperature is comfortable and so forth. One obstetrician in this study said that an environmental concern was organizing appointments so that pregnant women weren't coming to the office at the same time as women struggling with fertility issues.

Verbal Cues

People often fail to state a specific emotion directly (Shimanoff, 1985, 1987). Instead, they use indirect cues. For example, Max infers that Russ is angry with him when Russ calls Max an idiot and tells him that he wants to be alone. Russ doesn't tell Max any direct information about his emotion, but calling him a name and saying that he wants to be by himself are indirect verbal indicators of Russ's emotional state.

We often infer people's emotional states when they use sarcasm or rhetorical questions (Leggitt & Gibbs, 2000). For instance, let's say that Isabella invites Ruth over for dinner, and Ruth shows up an hour late. When Isabella greets Ruth by saying, "Nice of you to show up on time," Ruth gets the idea that Isabella is angry. Ruth would also probably get the same message about Isabella's emotional state if she asked Ruth rhetorically, "Do you ever look at your watch?" In neither case did Isabella say she was angry directly, but her comments were indirect indicators of anger. Later in this chapter, we show you how to use I-messages to verbalize your emotions, which can prevent the confusion that might result from indirect communication.

Combinations of Cues

Although we have discussed these cues separately, people usually communicate emotion through a mixture of cues. People often use verbal and vocal cues while gesturing and smiling. For example, when Dwight surprises Pat with a vacation to Acapulco, Pat tells him that she's happy in a high-pitched voice while grinning and giving him a hug. Sometimes cues are conflicting or incongruent. For example, when Sandy tells her son, Jake, that she is angry that he hasn't put away all his toys, she laughs indulgently. Especially in cases of conflicting cues, people rely on other information to try to discern the meaning. We discuss some of these other influences in the following section.

Influences on Emotional Communication

In this section, we explain a few areas that will help you understand that emotional communication is not a fixed behavior in our conversations with others. Emotional communication is influenced by several factors, including meta-emotions, culture, gender and sex, and context. We briefly discuss each below.

Meta-emotion

How people communicate about emotion is influenced by a related topic: meta-emotion. **Meta-emotion** means emotion about emotion. People who study emotion tend to focus on the process of emotion and specific emotions, but they have not paid much attention to how people feel about expressing certain emotions. For example, in the case of anger, "some people are ashamed or upset about becoming angry, others feel good about their capacity to express anger, and still others think of anger as natural, neither good nor bad" (Gottman, Katz, & Hooven, 1997, p. 7).

Differences in the effects of communicating emotion may result in part because of meta-emotion. For example, compare the emotions of two couples who have been dating for a year: Andrea and José, and Marla and Leo.

meta-emotion

Emotion felt about experiencing another emotion.

REVISITING
CASEINPOINT

1. How does Allison's response to Regina illustrate the concept of meta-emotion?

2. How do you think Allison's meta-emotion will affect how she'll communicate with Regina in the future?

You can answer these questions online under the resources for Chapter 7 at your online Resource Center for Understanding Interpersonal Communication.

Andrea's expression of love for José is accompanied by the meta-emotion pride about her ability to engage in a committed relationship. José feels the same way. On the other hand, when Marla expresses love to Leo, she experiences the meta-emotion shame for becoming so vulnerable in a relationship. Communication transactions between Andrea and José will likely differ significantly from those between Marla and Leo because one couple is proud of their commitment whereas one part of the other couple (that is, Marla) feels shame.

Culture

Remember from our discussion of the biological theory of emotion that Darwin asserted that emotions are primarily universal—that is, people of all cultures respond to the same emotions in the same way. Few people agree with that assertion today. Although some emotional states and expressions—such as joy, anger, and fear—are thought to be universal, the current focus of research is on differences in emotional communication across cultures. As you remember from our discussion in Chapter 3, culture is an important influence on most communication behaviors. The brief review in this section gives you an overview of how different cultures think about emotion and how emotion is communicated in various cultures.

Cultures and Thinking about Emotion

Cultures differ in how much they think and talk about emotion (Planalp & Fitness, 1999). For example, 95 percent of Chinese parents report that their children understand the meaning of shame by age 3, whereas only 10 percent of U.S. parents say their children do. Because of this dif-

Ethics & Choice

Marco Petrillo felt conflicted, and wasn't sure where to turn for help. He had studied hard during his first three years of college to keep his grades up and to make connections so that he could land a choice internship for his senior year. His hard work had paid off; he'd recently begun working for Jones and Markum, one of the best advertising agencies in the city. He was initially overjoyed about the position and had been patting himself on the back for landing it. He thought his advertising classes had prepared him well for this, and he wanted to be successful so he had a chance of being offered a job with the agency after graduation.

Everything seemed to be going well until he was assigned to a group working on a campaign for a video game targeted at kids ages 9 to 13. The game was offensive to Marco because it seemed to glorify violence and was disrespectful of women. In the game, the player received points for beating up people encountered in the street, including a prostitute. The player got double points for picking her up and then throwing her out of the car. Marco had grown up in a pretty rough neighborhood, and he had never found violence fun—he'd seen too much at close range.

(Continues)

ference, it seems that shame plays a more important role in Chinese culture than it does in U.S. culture. Yet, a recent study (Seiter & Bruschke, 2007) found that Chinese respondents suffered less from shame after engaging in deception than did U.S. respondents. This is possibly because deception is more acceptable in a culture like China than it is in the U.S. Thus, it is important to consider not just the emotion but also what triggers the emotion.

Some research (Planalp & Fitness,1999) notes that the Chinese think less about love than do those in the United States. Further, when the Chinese do think of love, they have a cluster of words to describe "sad-love," or love that does not succeed; such words are absent in U.S. culture. Other research (Lazarus, 1991) points to a similar dynamic in Japanese culture. In Japanese stories, when a conflict exists between a couple and the families of the couple, it is resolved in favor of the families, even when that means the couple has to give each other up. In Japan, stories that end with the lovers separating because of family objections are celebrated as showing the triumph of right. In contrast, in the United States and other Western European cultures, many of the stories in books, magazines, and movies end with the couple staying together against the wishes of their families. In these cultures, listeners cheer the lovers on, enjoying the triumph of romantic love.

When Marco reported for the group's first meeting, he was surprised to discover that none of the other group members had a problem with the game. In fact, two of them had come up with what they thought were some great emotional appeals to sell it. They argued that the game should be surrounded with bright colors that kids in the target age group liked, to achieve an immediate nonverbal response. They then proceeded to present a clever series of print ads and television commercials that played on kids' desires and fears. Marco had to give them credit; the ads were good. They pushed a lot of emotional buttons and implied that owning this game would resolve the emotional confusion that the ads themselves created.

What would you advise Marco to do? Should he talk to his advisor at the college? Should he raise his concerns in his work group or with his bosses at the ad agency? Should he quit? Should he stick with it but try to get the group to tone down the emotional appeals? Or should he just keep quiet and go along with the group? What would be the consequences of each of these decisions?

In answering these questions, think about the five ethical systems described in Chapter 1 (categorical imperative, utilitarianism, ethic of care, golden mean, significant choice). Explain how your answers relate to these systems. Do you prefer one course of action over another? Explain.

 Go to your online Resource Center for *Understanding Interpersonal Communication* to access an interactive version of this scenario under the resources for Chapter 7. The interactive version of this scenario allows you to choose an appropriate response to this dilemma and then see what consequences your choice brings about. You can also compare your answers to the questions at the end of the scenario to those provided by the authors and, if requested, email your response to your instructor.

How Emotion Is Communicated across Cultures

People of different cultures express emotion differently (Aune & Aune, 1996). For instance, people from warmer climates have been found to be more emotionally expressive than those from colder climates. In addition, people from collectivistic cultures (like Korea, China, and Japan), which we discussed in Chapter 3, are discouraged from expressing negative feelings for fear of their effect on the overall harmony of the community. Thus, people from these cultures are less inclined to express negative feelings. This does not mean that people from collectivistic cultures do not have negative feelings; it simply means that emotional restraint in communication is a shared cultural value (Nakayama & Martin, 2007). People from individualistic cultures like the

United States have no such cultural value—in fact, emotional openness is valued—so they are more expressive of negative emotions.

Gender and Sex

Gender and sex differences in emotional communication are widely researched. The U.S. culture, which divides many activities according to sex, is interested in the ways in which men and women are presumed to differ. For example, although gender roles are in flux in the United States, parenting is still seen as primarily the responsibility of women, whereas men are expected to work to pay the bills. The two sexes are expected to do different things and have different strengths in the workplace and at home (Buzzanell, Sterk, & Turner, 2004). In this section, we review research that examines emotion and gender stereotypes and then explore research on the expression of emotion and gender.

Emotion and Gender Stereotypes

Of course, the stereotypical view holds that women are more emotional, more emotionally expressive, and more attuned to the emotions of others than are men. Agneta Fischer (2000) wonders why women are thought to be the emotional sex while men are perceived to be unemotional. She asserts:

> As far back as I can remember I have encountered emotional men; indeed, I have met more emotional men than emotional women. My father could not control his nerves while watching our national sports heroes on television (which made watching hardly bearable); my uncle immediately got damp eyes on hearing the first note of the Dutch national anthem; a friend would lock himself in his room for days when angry; a teacher at school once got so furious that he dragged a pupil out of the class room and hung him up by his clothes on a coat-hook; one of the male managers at our institute was only able to prevent having a nervous breakdown by rigidly trying to exercise total control over his environment; and a male colleague's constant embarrassment in public situations forced him to avoid such settings altogether. (p. ix)

Fischer's point is not that men are *more* emotional than women. Rather, she observes that all these examples of men expressing emotion go unnoticed because they do not support the stereotype we have of men as unemotional.

Stephanie Shields (2000) makes a similar point when she argues that emotional expression (or lack of it) defines the essence of femininity and masculinity. She notes that people even use gender stereotypes to make judgments about their own emotions. Shields reports on an earlier study she and her colleagues conducted (Robinson, Johnson, & Shields, 1998, as cited in Shields, 2000), in which participants played a competitive word game. In the study, participants were asked about their emotional experience both immediately after playing and then a week later. The researchers found that the reports about the emotions matched gender stereotypes more closely the longer after the event the reports were recorded. The researchers concluded that when the participants forgot exactly how they felt, they used stereotypes (that is, men are stereotyped as more stoic and women as more emotional) to provide an answer.

Another study also showed the power of gender stereotypes on emotion. This study (Shields & Crowley, 1996) asked college students to read an emotion-provoking scenario and then to answer open-ended questions about the scenario. The scenario was identical for all participants except that in some cases the protagonist was male and in others female. The scenario stated one of the following:

> "Karen was emotional when she found out that her car had been stolen."

> "Brian was emotional when he found out that his car had been stolen."

The researchers found that the respondents judged the word *emotional* in the scenario differently depending on whether they read the Karen version or the Brian version. If participants thought the protagonist was Karen, they attributed the cause of her emotions more to her personality than to her situation, and they imagined her reaction was extreme and hysterical. Respondents who thought Brian's car was stolen downplayed the word *emotional* in the story and described his emotion as what any rational person

How do gender stereotypes influence your perception of how men and women should communicate emotion and how you yourself should communicate emotion? What have been the main social or cultural influences that led you to accept or reject gender stereotypes in regard to emotion: your family, your friends, school, the workplace, the media?

© Michelle D. Bridwell/PhotoEdit

might feel who had worked hard making money to buy the car. The researchers concluded that the respondents used gender stereotypes to answer the questions.

To read more about stereotypes concerning gender and emotion, read the article "Speaking from the Heart: Gender and the Social Meaning of Emotion," available through College Edition. Go to your online Resource Center for *Understanding Interpersonal Communication* to access *InfoTrac College Edition Exercise 7.1: Gender, Emotions, and Stereotypes.*

Emotional Expression and Sex and Gender

Researchers are interested in the differences between men and women in nonverbal expressions of emotion, such as smiling. Four differences are well documented and may be caused by men and women conforming to stereotyped gender roles (Hall, Carter, & Horgan, 2000). Women smile more than men in social situations (Hall et al.). Men and women also differ in nonverbal expressiveness, or facial animation and the liveliness of gestures. Again, women tend to demonstrate their emotional states by using more nonverbal cues than men do (Hall et al.; Jones & Wirtz, 2007). Women are also more accurate than men in figuring out what others' emotional states are based on nonverbal cues (Hall et al.).

Scholars have also investigated sex differences in the verbal expression of emotional support to others. In general men are less likely to give emotional support to a person in distress and when they do provide it, they are less focused on emotion and less person-centered than women (Burleson, Holmstrom, & Gilstrap, 2005). The results of one study (Burleson et al.) suggest that men provide poorer emotional support than women because they see good emotional support as not fitting a masculine gender identity.

"Federal Bureau of Feelings, sir. It seems that last night you neglected to ask your wife how her day was. You have the right to remain silent."

As people age, these gender stereotypes seem to exert less influence on their behaviors. Men tend to become more emotionally expressive, and women become more instrumental or task oriented. A study of 20 married couples over the age of 60 who had been married on average for 42 years shows this change. The researchers interviewing the couples found the men to be expressive about their emotions (saying things like they fell in love with their wives at first sight and reporting how nervous they'd been to meet her parents), whereas wives were more matter-of-fact in their accounts (Dickson & Walker, 2001).

To further explore gender and emotion and how they relate to context, read the article "Gender-Emotion Stereotypes Are Context Specific," available through InfoTrac College Edition. Use your online Resource Center for *Understanding Interpersonal Communication* to access *InfoTrac College Edition Exercise 7.2: Gender, Emotion, and Context*.

REVISITING CASEinPOINT

1. *Do you think the fact that Allison and Regina are both female influenced their interaction and their communication of emotion? Explain your answer.*

2. *Do you think the fact that Allison and Regina are Chinese American affected their interaction? Do you think it played any role in their communication of emotion? Explain.*

Y*ou can answer these questions online under the resources for Chapter 7 at your online Resource Center for* Understanding Interpersonal Communication.

Context

The contexts in which we express emotion are infinite: We express emotion at work, with friends, in our families, at school, over the phone, in person, and so on. We discuss two specific contexts here: historical period and online communication.

Historical Period

The book *American Cool* (Stearns,1994) traces the changes in emotional communication in the United States from the Victorian period (beginning approximately in the 1830s) to the 1960s. The main thesis is that the Victorians were much more emotionally expressive than U.S. citizens of the 1960s. A North American in the 1960s favored "cool" over the emotional excesses of the Victorians. This is the case because culture is governed by **feeling rules**, or "the recommended norms by which people are supposed to shape their emotional expressions and react to the expressions of others" (p. 2) and the feeling rules of U.S. culture changed considerably from the Victorian period to the 1960s.

feeling rules

The cultural norms used to create and react to emotional expressions.

In the 1890s, men in the United States were instructed to express their anger. However, 70 years later, child-rearing experts warned parents not to encourage boys to express anger, arguing that an angry man is possessed by the devil. In the area of romantic love, Victorian men were also encouraged to be expressive, in contrast to the 1960s vision of male love as primarily sexual and silent. A love letter written by a man of the Victorian era illustrates the flowery emotional expression that was the norm:

> "I don't love you and marry you to promote my happiness. To love you, to marry you is a mighty END in itself. . . . I marry you because my own inmost being mingles with your being and is already married to it, both joined in one by God's own voice." (Sterns, 1994, p. 3)

Obviously, a man in Victorian times would be influenced by the feeling rules of his time and would express himself much differently than a man of the 1960s, who would be equally influenced by a very different set of feeling rules. Today, we have different feeling rules as well, although the influence of "cool" is still strong in contemporary U.S. society.

Online Communication

As we discussed in Chapter 1, the channel for a communication transaction influences the communication. Because more and more of our communication time is spent in electronic communication or computer-mediated communication (CMC), online emotional communication is a worthwhile subject of study. You might wonder how email users and frequenters of chat rooms can express emotion without nonverbal cues. As you probably know, the answer to that question is the emoticon. **Emoticons** are icons that can be typed on the keyboard to express emotions. They are used to compensate for the lack of nonverbal cues in CMC.

Emotional communication is obviously vital to online interactions; a preliminary online search yielded more than 100,000 sites in at least five languages that deal with emoticons. Most emoticons look like a face (eyes, nose, and mouth) when rotated 90 degrees clockwise. See Table 7.5 for examples of commonly used emoticons and their translations.

Some research (Rourke, Anderson, Garrison, & Archer, 2001) argues that when people become experienced users of CMC, it is just as rich a communication process as any other, including face to face. Further, CMC doesn't necessarily inhibit emotional expression; one study found that 27 percent of the total message content consisted of emotional communication (Rourke et al., 2001). Yet a *New York Times* article (Williams, 2007), while stating that emoticons are widely used and important to help avoid misunderstandings, also notes that some people are offended when they see the "smileys" or "frownys" appear in a message. One realtor quoted in the article commented that it didn't make her feel any better to see a :(on an email saying she'd lost a deal worth hundreds of thousands of dollars. In fact, she found it highly annoying!

One study investigated emoticon use by males and females (Wolf, 2000). The study showed that when people moved from a same-sex newsgroup to a

emoticon

An icon that can be typed on a keyboard to express emotions; used to compensate for the lack of nonverbal cues in computer-mediated communication.

Table 7.5 Emoticons

:) or :-)	Happiness, sarcasm, or a joke
: (or :-(	Unhappiness
:] or :-]	Jovial happiness
: [or :-[	Despondent unhappiness
:D or :-D	Jovial happiness
: I or :-I	Indifference
:-/ or :-\	Indecision, confusion, or skepticism
:Q or :-Q	Confusion
:S or :-S	Incoherence or loss of words
:@ or :-@	Shock or a scream
:O or :-O	Surprise, a yell, or realization of an error ("uh-oh!")

Common emoticons (n.d.)

mixed-sex newsgroup, men adopted the female standard and began expressing more emotion as evidenced by a greater use of emoticons. We explore the topic of technology and interpersonal communication further in Chapter 11.

The Dark Side of Emotional Communication

As we discussed earlier in this chapter, some classification systems of specific emotions use positive and negative (that is, valence) as a primary dimension for typing those emotions. We are all familiar with the emotions that fall on the dark side: embarrassment, guilt, hurt, jealousy, anger, depression, and loneliness, to name a few. When we discussed the dark side of communication in Chapter 1, we mentioned that hurtful messages are part of the dark side. Indeed, hurtful messages have received recent attention from researchers exploring how this type of emotional communication operates in relationships (for example, Vangelisti & Young, 2000; Young & Bippus, 2001). One study found that if hurtful messages were phrased humorously, they were perceived as less intentionally hurtful and thus caused fewer wounded feelings (Young & Bippus, 2001).

Some dark side emotions are the polar opposites of bright side emotions. For example, empathy, a bright side emotion, is the opposite of the dark side emotion *schadenfreude*. Later in this chapter, we suggest empathy (a skill we discussed in Chapter 6) as a recommended practice for becoming an effective communicator. On the other hand, *schadenfreude* is a German word that, loosely translated, means to take pleasure in another's misfortune. The term is derived from the words *damage* and *joy.* In 2002, some reporters used *schadenfreude* to describe how many people felt when they saw Martha Stewart's image tarnished by her suspected involvement with insider trading (St. John, 2002). Some people might think that the public's fascination with the problems of young stars like Lindsay Lohan and Britney Spears stems from *schadenfreude.*

The fact that *schadenfreude* blends two emotions should come as no surprise. As we mentioned earlier in this chapter, emotions are often experienced in blends, and bright and dark, love and hate, are entangled with one another. Another way that negative emotional communication can have a bright side is that negative expressions of anger can be functional in certain contexts, including the following example (Tavris, 2001):

> A 42-year-old businessman, Jay S., described how his eyes were opened when he overheard his usually even-tempered boss on the phone one afternoon: "I've never heard him so angry. He was enraged. His face was red and the veins were bulging on his neck. I tried to get his attention to calm him down, but he waved me away impatiently. As soon as the call was over, he turned to me and smiled. "There," he said. "That ought to do it." If I were the guy he'd been shouting at, let me tell you, it would have done it, too. (p. 251)

The boss's yelling and showing anger accomplished a goal. There are no simple guidelines specifying when talking is better than yelling because the context, the receiver, the sender, and the social goal all make a difference. It may even be that the categorization of an emotion or even a mode of emotional communication as either dark or bright is problematic because it all depends on whether the context called for the emotion, the sender and the receiver expected the emotion, and the social goals of the situation were accomplished through the emotional communication (Tavris, 2001).

As Tavris (2001) states, "the calm, nonaggressive reporting of your anger (those "I messages" that so many psychologists recommend) is the kindest, most civilized and usually most effective way to express anger, but even this mature method depends on its context" (p. 250).

The Bright Side of Emotional Communication

Communication that offers comfort, social support, warmth, affection, forgiveness, or desire falls on the positive end of the emotional spectrum. However, like the dark side, the bright side of emotional communication does not present a simplistic picture. Some of the research on social support provides a glimpse at the mixture of bright and dark that is expressed simultaneously.

David Spiegel and Rachel Kimerling (2001) introduce an example from a support group for family members of breast cancer patients by saying, "the expression of positive feelings often brackets the expression of painful sadness" (p. 101). Following is the vignette they quote:

> A 20-year-old daughter was tearfully coming to terms with the sudden downhill pre-terminal course of her mother's breast cancer: "I see this black hole opening up in my life. I don't think I will want to live without my Mom. She would stay up at 2 A.M. and talk me through my misery for two hours. She won't be there, but I don't want to make her feel guilty for dying." Her father, also at the family group meeting, held her hand and tried to comfort her, but he clearly was overwhelmed by his own sadness and his lifelong fear of strong emotion and dependency on him by others. The husband of another woman whose breast cancer was progressing rapidly started to comfort her but found his voice choked with emotion: "I am sure you will get through this—there's so much love in your family." "Why are you crying?" the father asked. "I don't know," he replied, and everyone, tearful daughter included, found themselves laughing. (p. 101)

The mix of bright and dark shows a complex tapestry of emotion. Another instance that shows a mixture of bright and dark was reported in the *Annals of Behavioral Medicine* (Ullrich & Lutgendorf, 2002). When college students were asked to write their feelings about a traumatic event as well as their efforts to understand and make sense of it, they became more aware of the benefits of the trauma, such as improved relationships, greater personal strength, spiritual growth, and a greater appreciation of life. The authors concluded that the process of communicating their thoughts and emotion made a negative event seem brighter.

Yet another example of the complexity involved in classifying emotional communication as dark or bright can be seen in the emotional communication of forgiveness. Forgiveness, which is based in numerous religious teachings, represents the bright side because it allows for peace and reconciliation.

Archbishop Desmond Tutu (1999), who wrote a book about reconciliation in South Africa titled *No Future Without Forgiveness,* places a high priority on forgiveness. To stress the importance of reconciliation, he invokes the African concept of *ubuntu,* which means that a person is only a person through other people. Archbishop Tutu chaired South Africa's Truth and Reconciliation Commission, which advocated forgiveness as an alternative to racial hatred. The commission presided over hundreds of hearings in which blacks and whites spoke of past grievances and asked forgiveness for those they had harmed. Archbishop Tutu claims in his book that the commission and the process of forgiveness it supervised spared South Africa from the violence and civil unrest that many expected after years of white-minority rule.

Dean Murphy (2002) writes in the *New York Times* about the power and problematic nature of forgiveness. He cites Roger W. Wilkins, a civil rights

Ethan Miller/Getty Images

When we experience traumatic events as a community, such as the hurricane that hit New Orleans in 2005 or the terrorist attacks of September 11, 2001, we express emotions not only on the negative side of the emotional spectrum but often on the positive side as well. In helping others, receiving assistance, and talking about the experience, we may express gratitude at our ability to stay strong in a crisis, we may experience a greater sense of closeness to our families and friends, and we may feel a heightened appreciation for those things in life that matter to us most.

activist and history professor at George Mason University, who notes that people need to forgive for their own sense of self-preservation. Mr. Wilkins observes,

> After a while you figure it out for yourself: you can't be consumed by this stuff because then your oppressors have won. . . . If you are consumed by rage, even at a terrible wrong, you have been reduced. (Murphy, 2002)

However, Mr. Wilkins recognizes the limits of forgiveness when he reflects on the bombing of the 16th Street Baptist Church in Birmingham, Alabama, in 1963, which killed four young black girls. In 2002, Bobby Frank Cherry was convicted of the bombing deaths and sentenced to life imprisonment. He has not asked for forgiveness and continues to deny his guilt. This makes things complicated because forgiveness requires participation from both sides. In this case, Mr. Wilkins suggests that people can purge hatred from their hearts without actually forgiving.

Murphy (2002) relates another difficult case: Amy Biehl, a Fulbright scholar and California native was stoned and stabbed to death in South Africa

Figure 7.3 The interdependence of the bright and dark sides of emotion

in 1993 and her parents managed to forgive. They quit their jobs to work for racial reconciliation, they testified in favor of political amnesty for the killers, and offered two of them jobs. They said that they found forgiveness liberating.

Forgiveness highlights the bright and dark sides in tandem. To experience the liberation of forgiveness, the Biehls had to suffer the torment of grief. Figure 7.3 illustrates the interdependence of the bright and dark sides of emotional communication.

*R*eflect on your experiences with the dark and bright sides of emotional communication. If you like, you can use your student workbook or your **Understanding Interpersonal Communication** Online Resources to complete this activity.

Choices for Developing Emotional Communication Skills

Competence in expressing emotion and in listening and responding to the emotional communication of others is critical to your success as an interpersonal communicator. Some have called this competence *emotional intelligence*. This concept has received a great deal of attention since the 1995 publication of Daniel Goleman's best-selling book by that title. Goleman notes that communicative skills are central to emotional intelligence (E-IQ) and that E-IQ is required to be successful in contemporary society. To help you develop emotional communication competence, we provide several skills for you to consider: knowing your feelings, analyzing the situation, owning, reframing, and empathizing.

Know Your Feelings

Competence in emotional communication begins with your ability to identify the emotion or mix of emotions you are experiencing at a particular time. This skill requires you to do several things:

1. Recognize the emotion you're feeling.

2. Establish that you are stating an emotion.

3. Create a statement that identifies why you are experiencing the emotion. (You may or may not choose to share this statement with anyone else; it is sufficient that you make the statement to yourself.)

Recognizing Your Emotion

This step requires you to stop for a moment and ask yourself what your emotional state is at the present. In other words, you are to take a time out from the ongoing process and take your emotional temperature. It is important not to skip this step, because it involves making a link between yourself and outer reality. To name your feelings signals how you perceive them and alerts you to what your expectations are. For instance, when you recognize that you are irritable, that cues you that you have less patience than usual, and you may expect others to make allowances for you. The opposite process occurs as well. When you give a feeling a name, you respond to that label, which triggers perceptions and expectations.

This step is difficult for several reasons. First, in the heat of an emotional encounter, you may not be prepared to stop and take a time out. Second, we are often so detached from our feelings that it is difficult to name them. And third, some people are simply less aware than others of their emotional states. If you are "low affective-oriented" (Booth-Butterfield & Booth-Butterfield, 1998), you will be relatively unaware of your own emotional experiences.

You need to practice this skill and work on methods to overcome these obstacles. For example, in a highly charged emotional interaction, you can

Communication Assessment Test
Emotional Intelligence (E-IQ) *(140)*

Although there is no current, valid pencil-and-paper test for your E-IQ that works as reliably as the IQ test, the following test was devised by Daniel Goleman, author of the best-selling 1995 book *Emotional Intelligence*. Answering these questions will give you a rough idea of what your E-IQ might be. You can take this test online. Go to your online Resource Center for *Understanding Interpersonal Communication* and look under the resources for Chapter 7.

C 50

1. You're on an airplane that suddenly hits extremely bad turbulence and begins rocking from side to side. What do you do?
   A. Continue to read your book or magazine, or watch the movie, paying little attention to the turbulence.
   B. Become vigilant for an emergency, carefully monitoring the flight attendant reading the emergency instructions card.

   B 70
   C. A little of both A and B.
   D. Not sure—never noticed.

B

2. You've taken a group of 4-year-olds to the park, and one of them starts crying because the others won't play with her. What do you do?
   A. Stay out of it—let the kids deal with it on their own.
   B. Talk to her and help her figure out ways to get the other kids to play with her.

   C 50
   C. Tell her in a kind voice not to cry.
   D. Try to distract the crying girl by showing her some other things she could play with.

A

3. Assume you're a college student who had hoped to get an A in a course, but you have just found out you got a C– on the midterm. What do you do?
   A. Sketch out a specific plan for ways to improve your grade and resolve to follow through on your plans.
   B. Resolve to do better in the future.
   C. Tell yourself it really doesn't matter how you do in the course, and concentrate instead on other classes where your grades are higher.

   B 0
   D. Go to see the professor and try to talk her into giving you a better grade.

B 0

4. Imagine you're an insurance salesperson calling prospective clients. Fifteen people in a row have hung up on you, and you're getting discouraged. What do you do?
   A. Call it a day and hope you have better luck tomorrow.
   B. Assess qualities in yourself that may be undermining your ability to make a sale.
   C. Try something new in the next call, and keep plugging away.
   D. Consider another line of work.

B 0

5. You're a manager in an organization that is trying to encourage respect for racial and ethnic diversity. You overhear someone telling a racist joke. What do you do?
   A. Ignore it—it's only a joke.
   B. Call the person into your office for a reprimand.
   C. Speak up on the spot, saying that such jokes are inappropriate and will not be tolerated in your organization.
   D. Suggest to the person telling the joke that they go through a diversity training program.

D 50

6. You're trying to calm down a friend who has worked himself up into a fury at a driver in another car who has cut dangerously close in front of him. What do you do?
   A. Tell him to forget it—he's okay now, and it's no big deal.
   B. Put on one of his favorite tapes and try to distract him.
   C. Join him in putting down the other driver as a show of rapport.
   D. Tell him about a time something like this happened to you and how you felt as mad as he does now, but then you saw the other driver was on the way to the hospital emergency room.

(Continues)

7. You and your life partner have gotten into an argument that has escalated into a shouting match; you're both upset and, in the heat of anger, making personal attacks you don't really mean. What's the best thing to do?
   A. Take a 20-minute break and then continue the discussion.
   B. Just stop the argument—go silent, no matter what your partner says.
   C. Say you're sorry and ask your partner to apologize, too.
   D. Stop for a moment, collect your thoughts, then state your side of the case as precisely as you can.

8. You've been assigned to head a working team that is trying to come up with a creative solution to a nagging problem at work. What's the first thing you do?
   A. Draw up an agenda and allot time for discussion of each item so you make the best use of your time together.
   B. Have people take the time to get to know each other better.
   C. Begin by asking each person for ideas about how to solve the problem, while the ideas are fresh.
   D. Start out with a brainstorming session, encouraging everyone to say whatever comes to mind, no matter how wild.

9. Your 3-year-old son is extremely timid and has been hypersensitive about—and a bit fearful of—new places and people virtually since he was born. What do you do?
   A. Accept that he has a shy temperament and think of ways to shelter him from situations that would upset him.
   B. Take him to a child psychiatrist for help.
   C. Purposely expose him to lots of new people and places so he can get over his fear.
   D. Engineer an ongoing series of challenging but manageable experiences that will teach him he can handle new people and places.

10. For years you've been wanting to get back to learning to play a musical instrument you tried in childhood, and now, just for fun, you've finally gotten around to starting. You want to make the most effective use of your time. What do you do?

A. Hold yourself to a strict practice time each day.
B. Choose pieces that stretch your abilities a bit.
C. Practice only when you're really in the mood.
D. Pick pieces that are far beyond your ability, but that you can master with diligent effort.

Scoring

1. Anything but D—that answer reflects a lack of awareness of your habitual responses under stress.
   A = 20, B = 20, C = 20, D = 0

2. B is best. Emotionally intelligent parents use their children's moments of upset as opportunities to act as emotional coaches, helping their children understand what made them upset, what they are feeling, and alternatives the child can try.
   A = 0, B = 20, C = 0, D = 0

3. A. One mark of self-motivation is being able to formulate a plan for overcoming obstacles and frustrations and follow through on it.
   A = 20, B = 0, C = 0, D = 0

4. C. Optimism, a mark of emotional intelligence, leads people to see setbacks as challenges they can learn from, and to persist, trying out new approaches rather than giving up, blaming themselves, or getting demoralized.
   A = 0, B = 0, C = 20, D = 0

5. C. The most effective way to create an atmosphere that welcomes diversity is to make clear in public that the social norms of your organization do not tolerate such expressions. Instead of trying to change prejudices (a much harder task), keep people from acting on them.
   A = 0, B = 0, C = 20, D = 0

6. D. Data on rage and how to calm it show the effectiveness of distracting the angry person from the focus of their rage, empathizing with their feelings and perspective, and suggesting a less anger-provoking way of seeing the situation.
   A = 0, B = 5, C = 5, D = 20

7. A. Take a break of 20 minutes or more. It takes at least that long to clear the body of the physiological arousal

(Continues)

of anger—which distorts your perception and makes you more likely to launch damaging personal attacks. After cooling down, you'll be more likely to have a fruitful discussion.

A = 20, B = 0, C = 0, D = 0

8. B. Creative groups work at their peak when rapport, harmony, and comfort levels are highest—then people are freer to make their best contribution.

A = 0, B = 20, C = 0, D = 0

9. D. Children born with a timid temperament can often become more outgoing if their parents arrange an ongoing series of manageable challenges to their shyness.

A = 0, B = 0, C = 0, D = 20

10. B. By giving yourself moderate challenges, you are most likely to get into the state of flow, which is both pleasurable and where people learn and perform at their best.

A = 0, B = 20, C = 0, D = 0

The highest score is 200, and 100 is average.

repeat a phrase like "it's time to take a time out," or you can make a prior agreement with a relational partner that you will check every half hour to see if a time out is needed. You might want to list emotions in a journal so you can consult the list to remind yourself of the variety of emotion you might be experiencing. You can also monitor your physical changes to check for signals of emotion. As we noted in Table 7.2, emotion is often accompanied by physiological conditions such as a hot flush, a lump in the throat, and so on. And you can monitor your thoughts to see how they might relate to feelings.

Establishing that You Are Stating an Emotion

This step in the process provides a check to see that you are really in touch with emotion language. It isn't enough to simply say "I feel"; you must be sure that what follows really is an emotion. For instance, if you say "I feel like seeing a ball game," you are stating something you want to do, not an emotion you are experiencing. A better phrasing would be: "I feel restless because I have been working on this project all weekend and I'd like to get out and see a game."

Creating a Statement that Identifies Why You Are Feeling the Emotion

This step involves thinking about the antecedent conditions that are contextualizing your feelings. Ask yourself, "Why do I feel this way?" and "What led to this feeling?" Try to put the reasons into words. For example, statements such as the following form reasons for emotion:

- "I am angry because I studied hard and I got the same grade on the exam that I got when I didn't study."
- "I am feeling lonely. All my friends went to spend the weekend upstate and left me alone at home because I couldn't take time off from work."

- "I am feeling really happy, proud, and a little anxious. I finally got the job I wanted, and I worked especially hard to make a good impression at the interview. All the prep work I did paid off. But now I have to actually make good on everything I said I could do!"

- "I'm feeling guilty. I told my boyfriend I couldn't see him tonight because I had to study, but I really just felt like having a night to myself."

Going through this exercise should help you to clarify why you are experiencing a particular emotion or emotional mix. Further, it should point you in a direction to change something if you wish to. For instance, if you wish to reduce your guilt, tell your boyfriend that you need some time to yourself occasionally without having to give him a reason.

Imagine yourself...

...at work

You have been working on an important project with a coworker, Angela. You become angry and upset because you believe that you are not being acknowledged for your contributions on the project. In fact, it seems like Angela is taking credit for work you did. You know you have done a good job and worked very hard, yet you're not getting the appropriate recognition. At the recent progress meeting with your supervisor, Angela wouldn't let you get a word in edgewise and you watched the supervisor nod approvingly when Angela described an idea you originated. Can you think of a way you could own your feelings and communicate them to Angela without causing an argument or being unprofessional?

...at your best friend's apartment

You and your best friend, Talbot, are at his apartment talking about a trip you will be taking this summer. You have been talking for a while when you notice that Talbot hasn't said anything for a long time—not even "hmmm" or "uh-huh." Talbot seems sad, and you aren't sure why. You like Talbot so much and you've had a long and rewarding friendship, but you feel a little resentful that you have to stop thinking about your wonderful, exciting trip plans to deal with Talbot's bad mood. It seems like something is always bothering him, and today you don't really want to get into it. You just want to feel happy. How do you respond in a way that honors Talbot's nonverbal communication as well as your own emotional reactions?

Analyze the Situation

After identifying your emotion, analyze the situation by asking yourself these questions:

1. *Do you wish to share your emotion with others?* As we mentioned previously, some emotional experiences are not ready for communication—that is, you may not completely understand the emotion yet or you may feel that you would quickly slide into conflict if you communicated the emotion. Or, you might decide that you are comfortable with the emotion and that you don't ever need to share it. For example, if you are looking through your high school yearbook and feel nostalgia for the time you spent there, you might enjoy your reminisces and not feel the need to talk about it with anyone. If you wake up early one morning and experience a beautiful sunrise, you may feel joy without needing to tell anyone about it.

2. *Is the time appropriate for sharing?* If you decide you want to communicate an emotion to someone else, an analysis of the situation helps you decide if the time is right. If your partner is under a great deal of stress at work, you might wait until the situation improves before talking

about your unhappiness at how little time you spend together. If you just found out you are pregnant with a wanted baby and your best friend has recently suffered a miscarriage, you also might decide to wait to share your joy.

3. *How should you approach the communication?* Analyzing the situation helps you think about how to share your emotion. If you are angry with your boss, you need to consider if and/or how to express your anger. Obviously, anger at a boss and anger at a partner provide entirely different situational constraints. Because the workplace climate is not conducive to emotional communication, you may decide not to tell your boss how you feel even though you would like to do so.

4. *Is there anything you can do to change the situation if needed?* Your analysis allows you to think about how and whether to change the situation. In the case of a workplace issue, you might consider instituting new norms at work, accepting the way things are, or looking for a new job.

Own Your Feelings

As we discussed in Chapter 4, **Owning** is the skill of verbally taking responsibility for your feelings. Owning is often accomplished by sending **I-messages**, which show that speakers understand that their feelings belong to them and aren't caused by someone else. I-messages take the following form:

"I feel _____ when you _____, and I would like
_____."

For example, let's say that Vanessa is unhappy that her boyfriend, Charles, spends more time with his buddies than with her. Vanessa's I-message would be something like the following:

"I feel unhappy when you spend four nights a week with your friends, and I would like you to spend one of those nights with me."

I-messages differ from you-messages, in which I place the responsibility for my feelings on you. If Vanessa had sent a you-message to Charles, she might have said:

"You are so inconsiderate. All you do is hang out with your friends. I can't believe I am staying with you!"

You can see that Charles's reaction might be more positive to the I-message than to the you-message. Using I-messages does not guarantee that you will get what you ask for. Charles could still tell Vanessa that he wants to spend four nights with his friends. But I-messages help to ensure that Charles hears what Vanessa wants and that he doesn't get sidetracked into a defensive spiral where he argues with her characterization of him as inconsiderate. The I-message focuses on Vanessa's emotion, which is what she wants to talk about with Charles.

owning
Verbally taking responsibility for our own thoughts and feelings.

I-message
A message phrased to show we understand that our feelings belong to us and aren't caused by someone else.

interpersonal explorer

Before you finish reading this chapter, take a moment to review the theories and skills discussed. How do you think the theories discussed in this chapter can help you better understand interpersonal communication and emotion? In what ways can the skills discussed help you interact more effectively with other people in your life?

Theories that relate to emotion

- **Biological theory**
  Emotions are instinctual and universal because they're based in human biology
- **Social theory**
  Emotion is related to biology but it goes beyond that because social interactions and context teach us how to interpret and experience emotion

Practical skills for developing emotional communication skills

- Know your feelings
- Analyze the situation
- Own your feelings
- Reframe when needed
- Empathize

Explore your interpersonal choices

Are you ready to explore your interpersonal choices regarding emotions? Use your online Resource Center for *Understanding Interpersonal Communication* to access an interactive simulation that allows you to view the beginning of an interpersonal scenario regarding emotion, make a choice about how the people in the scenario should proceed with their interaction, consider the consequences of your choice, and then see three possible outcomes to the interaction.

Reframe When Needed

Reframing refers to the ability to change the frame surrounding a situation to put it in a more productive light. When Jane Brody (2002) wrote about suggested methods for reducing hostile tendencies, she alluded to the skill of reframing. Brody quotes Dr. Norman Rosenthal, a psychiatrist in the Washington, DC, area who specializes in depression and anger. Rosenthal comments that a friend often grew angry when waiting in his car at long red lights. The friend's wife reframed for him by reminding him that "the red light doesn't care, so he might as well save his fury" (p. D7). Rosenthal suggests that it is easier for people to reframe their thinking about something than it is to change the world. He goes on to say that after you discover what makes you mad, you can reframe those irritants by changing the messages you give yourself. If you think of other people as rude, that frame may cause hostility. If you change the frame to respecting yourself for being polite, you will feel less anger and hostility.

Carol Tavris (2001) talks about a similar process when she recounts what anger management expert Ray Navaco advises clients who come to him for help in anger management. Navaco points out that "anger is fomented, maintained, and inflamed by the statements we make to ourselves and others when we are provoked—'who does he think he is to treat me like that?' 'What a vile and thoughtless woman she is!'" (p. 252). He teaches his clients to reframe and to substitute other statements, such as "Maybe he's having a tough day" and "She must be very unhappy if she would do such a thing."

For information about how to disclose private information about your health, use your online Resource Center for *Understanding Interpersonal Communication* to access **Interactive Activity 8.1: Disclosing Health Information.**

Self-Disclosure as a Subjective Process

As you've probably noticed, whether information is considered self-disclosure depends on subjective assessments made by the discloser. The degree of risk involved is a personal judgment; what one person considers to be risky might be information that someone else would find easy to tell. Taking this fact into consideration, let's make a distinction between *history* and *story.*

History consists of information that sounds personal to a listener but is relatively easy for a speaker to tell. Disclosures that are classified as history may be told easily because of the teller's temperament, changing times, or simply because the events happened a long time ago and have been told and retold. For instance, Nell was in a serious car accident when she was 19. The story of the accident and its aftermath is a dramatic one, but it doesn't feel risky to tell it because she has told it so many times that it has become routine. In another example, Melanie, who married Jeff in 1970, used to feel nervous about telling people that her husband had been married once before. By 1990, when she and Jeff had been married for 20 years and the divorce rate in the United States had reached almost 50 percent, Melanie stopped being concerned about that disclosure.

In contrast, **story**, or true self-disclosure, exists when the teller *feels* the risk he or she is taking in telling the information. A disclosure should be considered story (or authentic) even if it doesn't seem personal to the average listener. For instance, when Marie told her friend, Fernando, that she had never known a Mexican American person before, Fernando thought that she was simply making a factual observation. However, to Marie, that admission felt very risky. She was afraid that Fernando would think less of her and judge her as provincial because she was unfamiliar with people other than white Anglo-Saxons like herself. Marie was engaging in story even though Fernando heard it as history.

Another way to think about history and story relates to the topic of a disclosure. Some topics seem inherently more or less personal than others. For example, you could share a great deal of information about a topic like sports without seeming to become very personal ("I love the Green Bay Packers," "I think the Bears are the most improved team in the NFL," "I believe that professional athletes make too much money"). However, topics such as sex or money seem intrinsically more personal. Thus, disclosures are typed based on **topical intimacy.** However, a person can reveal an actual disclosure (that is, story) about what seems to be a low-intimacy topic. For instance, Jill might feel she's taking a risk to tell her feminist friends that she's a football fan. The reverse is also true; a person can reveal little personal information

history

Information that may sound personal to another person but that is relatively easy for us to tell.

story

Information we feel we are taking a risk telling another.

topical intimacy

The level of intimacy inherent in a topic.

about a high-intimacy topic. For example, when Mike says he wants to take a course in the sociology of sex, he may not think he's risking much. It all depends on the risk the teller feels while disclosing to a listener.

At this point in our discussion, you may be thinking of self-disclosure as an event in which one person tells another something of consequence. In fact, this is the way many researchers have talked about self-disclosure. However, some people think that disclosures aren't discrete, finite events; rather, they are processes that occur on a continuum. Some research (Dindia, 1998) indicates that gay men saw self-disclosing their sexual identity as an ongoing process. Dindia quotes one of her participants as saying, "I . . . am in the process of coming out. . . . When you say, 'hey, I'm gay.' That's the beginning. Yeah, [first you come] out to yourself and then [you] slowly [come] out to other people as well" (p.87). Self-disclosures are unfinished business because there is always something more or someone else to tell.

Factors Affecting Disclosure

Although our definition of self-disclosure is fairly straightforward, the discussions of history and story, as well as considerations of self-disclosure as a process, show that it is not a simple concept or skill. A complete understanding of self-disclosure requires consideration of many factors, including individual differences, relational issues, cultural values, and gender and sex. We explore each below.

Individual Differences

People have different needs for openness. Whereas Karl has no problem telling his friends all about his personal feelings, Selena saves disclosures of that nature for her family and most intimate friends. Think about your own tendencies to share

---

Ethics & Choice

Theo Henley was on his way to his third interview for a position he really wanted. After making it through the first and second interviews, Theo was feeling good about himself and thought he had a solid chance for an offer. At the previous interviews, he'd gotten along well with everyone and the more he learned about the job and the company, the better he felt. He thought that the job was a perfect fit for him.

However, despite his high hopes, he was worried. He faced the same old dilemma: Should he reveal anything about his disability, multiple sclerosis (MS), to the prospective employers? When he had been diagnosed seven years ago, it had seemed like a death sentence, but he'd learned to live with the disease. His situation was complicated by the fact that he had what his doctors called "invisible symptoms." Although he sometimes suffered because of the MS, no one knew he had it unless he told them. His worst symptom was excessive tiredness.

For the past three years, he'd been experiencing a remission, and his condition was much improved. However, he lived with the knowledge that the symptoms could return any time. The doctors knew little about this unpredictable disease.

Theo knew he could do the job. He was sure he could do it even if the symptoms returned, because he'd held down a job through the seven years of his illness. Occasionally he had called in sick because of the fatigue and disorientation brought on by the MS, but he didn't think he was absent more than anyone else. And he always got good performance reviews.

But he wasn't sure if it was right to keep this information from a prospective employer. Moreover, what if the MS returned and became even worse? If that happened, he would need to ask for some assistance at work. If he hadn't told the company before, he might be in a bad position if he needed help. In addition, he wanted to be honest. But he wasn't sure how this information would be received or if he needed to reveal this personal problem.

What do you think Theo should do? In answering this question, what ethical system of communication informs your decision (categorical imperative, utilitarianism, ethic of care, golden mean, significant choice)?

 Go to your online Resource Center for *Understanding Interpersonal Communication* to access an interactive version of this scenario under the resources for Chapter 8. The interactive version of this scenario allows you to choose an appropriate response to this dilemma and then see what consequences your choice brings about. You can also compare your answers to the questions at the end of the scenario to those provided by the authors and, if requested, email your response to your instructor.

Communication Assessment Test
Exploring Your Approach to Self-Disclosure

Directions: Complete the following sentences about your approach to self-disclosure. There are no right or wrong answers for this assessment, and there is no method of scoring. Rather, simply taking a moment to think about your approach to self-disclosure can help you make thoughtful choices about when and how you self-disclose in future interactions. You can take this test online. Go to your online Resource Center for *Understanding Interpersonal Communication* and look under the resources for Chapter 8.

1. Intimate communication to me means . . .
2. The hard thing about intimate communication is . . .
3. Sometimes I withdraw from intimate communication when . . .
4. When I disclose, I do so because . . .
5. One of the things I'd like people to know about me is . . .
6. When I try to talk about things that are important to me . . .
7. When I try to express intimate feelings . . .
8. If I were more open about expressing my feelings and opinions . . .
9. When people try to talk with me, sometimes I . . .
10. If I weren't concerned about the listener's response . . .
11. Sometimes I become blocked when . . .
12. One of the ways I sometimes make it difficult for people to disclose to me is . . .

Adapted from Michigan State University Counseling Center, 2003.

information with others in your life. Do you believe that some things are better left unsaid, or do you think friends and family should know everything about you?

Even people who have a high need to disclose don't wish to tell everyone everything. Although Deanna might tell her partner, Eric, about the fact that she was sexually abused by her stepfather, she may have no problem keeping that information secret from her friend Trish.

Relational Issues

Self-disclosures wax and wane over the life of a relationship. Telling each other every secret may be important early in the relationship, but in long-term friendships, marriages, or partnerships, self-disclosures account for a much smaller amount of communication time. "Getting to know you" is an important part of developing a new relationship, but as relationships endure and stabilize, the participants need to disclose less because they already know a great deal about one another (Knapp & Vangelisti, 2005).

Researchers suggest that some general patterns of self-disclosure may be related to the life of a relationship (see Figure 8.1). The first pattern pictured represents the general scenario we've described: People meet, get to know each other, begin to tell each other more and more personal information, and then decrease their disclosures as the relationship endures. This pattern shows a gradual increase in self-disclosing that parallels the growth of the relationship until the relationship stabilizes; at that point, self-disclosures decrease. One study (Huston, McHale, & Crouter, 1986) found that after one year of marriage, couples were less self-disclosing than they had been as newlyweds, yet they were still satisfied with their relationships.

The second pattern pictured in Figure 8.1 represents two people who know each other as casual friends for a long time before escalating the relationship with self-disclosures and increasing intimacy. The long-term relationship is characterized by low self-disclosures and then a spike up before a leveling off of openness. Let's look at an example. Steven, an emergency room nurse at a local hospital, has worked for four years on the same shift as Beth, an intern at the hospital. They have spoken to each other a lot about working conditions and emergency health care. Although Steven and Beth don't know each other well, they like each other and respect each other's medical skills and steadiness in an emergency. One night, Steven's father suffers a stroke and is brought into the emergency room. When his dad dies a few hours after being admitted, Steven finds comfort in sharing his feelings with Beth. This tragedy leads to increased disclosures between them. One year later, they refer to each other as best friends. This pattern shows that, as with the first pattern, Beth and Steven's disclosures will eventually decrease over time.

The third pattern, sometimes referred to as "clicking," shows a high incidence of self-disclosing almost immediately in the relationship. Researchers refer to these relationships as ones that just "click" from the start rather than needing a gradual build. For example, Ben and Marcus met twenty years ago as 12-year-olds at football camp. They immediately found each other easy to talk to and enjoyed being together. Now, two decades later, they still enjoy an openness and a deep friendship.

Researchers explain the clicking process by suggesting that people carry around relationship scripts in their heads, and when they find someone who fits the main elements of that script, they begin acting as though all the elements were there (Berg & Clark, 1986). In other words, let's say that Ben expects a friend to have the same interests he has, resemble him physically, be open and attractive, and have a good sense of humor. When he finds all those characteristics in Marcus, he quickly begins acting as though they have a developed friendship. If Marcus has a similar response, we should see the clicking pattern. Again, in this third pattern, we see a leveling off of self-disclosures over time.

In all three patterns in Figure 8.1, self-disclosures eventually level off—and, in many cases, they eventually decrease dramatically if relationships last a long time. However, when new issues arise, even longtime friends or couples

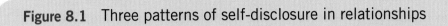

Figure 8.1 Three patterns of self-disclosure in relationships

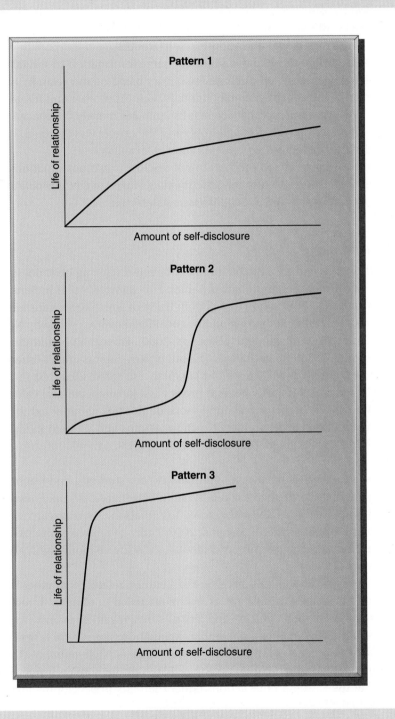

who have been together a long time self-disclose. Another time self-disclosures may increase is when people feel their relationship has fallen into a rut, and they wish to bring back some of its earlier excitement and intensity. Further, if self-disclosures decrease suddenly and radically between people, the decrease may signal that a relationship is in trouble.

Finally, although we may disclose the same information to several people, the way we frame our disclosure may vary based on our relationship with the person involved. For example, Jim tells both his mother and his good friend, Rose, that he has cancer. When Jim tells his mother, he concentrates on how hopeful his doctor is and how early the cancer was detected. When Jim tells Rose, he focuses on his fears and vulnerability.

To assess your own willingness to self-disclose in various situations, use your online Resource Center for *Understanding Interpersonal Communication* to access *Interactive Activity 8.2: Self-Disclosure Assessment*.

Culture

Like all the behaviors we discuss in this text, self-disclosing behavior is moderated by cultural prescriptions and values. For example, Asian Indians' sense of appropriate self-disclosure differs from those of North Americans and Western Europeans. Asian Indians would be considered overly private by North American or Western standards (Hastings, 2000). Parents and children in Pakistan self-disclose to each other less often than parents and children who are native to the United States. Most Japanese also self-disclose less than North Americans, primarily because privacy is a Japanese cultural value. Most Asians believe that successful persons do not talk about or exhibit feelings and emotions, whereas most North Americans and Western Europeans believe that a willingness to disclose feelings is critical to relationship development.

Some researchers have observed that scholars, students, and teachers focus on self-disclosure because of a Western bias that favors openness over privacy and disclosure over withholding information. These researchers (Bochner, 1982; Martin & Nakayama, 2007; Parks, 1982) have criticized the cultural biases that cause Westerners to value disclosure more highly than privacy and secrecy.

Further, the level of self-disclosure of a culture relates to whether it is a high-context or low-context culture. As we discussed in Chapter 3, high-context cultures (such as China and Japan) derive meaning mainly from activity and overall context, not verbal explanation; the reverse is true in low-context cultures (such as the United States). Thus, explicit verbal disclosures are unnecessary in high-context cultures. For example, some research confirms that the Chinese value actions rather than talk in developing relationships (Chen, 1995; Martin & Nakayama, 2007).

Considering the above, it should come as no surprise that North Americans are seen as more disclosive than Asians, yet it is important to recognize that within the United States, different ethnic groups vary in their frequency of disclosure (Klopf, 1998). For instance, European Americans are generally more disclosive than Latinos.

Gender and Sex

Many people believe that gender or sex is a major factor in self-disclosing behaviors. Yet the research is inconclusive on this topic. Some research suggests that in general, in the United States, women seem to self-disclose more than men, and they value self-disclosures more (Ivy & Backlund, 2000; Wood, 2000). This was confirmed in research (Maccoby, 1998) showing that when female friends talked, they usually related emotional disclosures. One study found that even at a young age (second graders), girls talked easily with one another and shared personal stories (Tannen, 1990). Other research shows that men do express closeness through talking, just not as much as women do (Canary & Dindia, 1998). And some researchers have noticed that when the goal in a situation is clear (for example, developing a relationship or impressing a partner who has high status), men can disclose as much or more than women (Derlega, Winstead, Wong, & Hunter, 1985; Shaffer & Ogden, 1986).

Yet an analysis of 205 studies examining sex differences in self-disclosure (Dindia & Allen, 1992) found that the differences between women and men were rather small. And, more recent research (Mathews, Derlega, & Morrow, 2006) found no sex differences in self-disclosures.

Biological sex might not be as important to differences in self-disclosure as other issues such as gender role or the composition of the couple. In terms of gender role, men who are **androgynous** (that is, they embody both masculine and feminine traits) hold the perspective that self-disclosure characterizes close relationships (Jones & Dembo, 1989). Androgynous men desire friends

androgynous

Having both masculine and feminine traits.

© Jason Harris

The common stereotype holds that women disclose a great deal about themselves and men disclose very little. However, research shows that the differences between men and women's self-disclosures are not that dramatic. For example, although men tend to establish close relationships by doing things together more than women tend to, men can disclose as much or more than women do, particularly in certain situations, such as when they are establishing a relationship.

who want to share themselves through talk, and they want to do the same. With reference to sex-composition, male-male pairs seem to disclose the least and female-female pairs the most (Burleson, Holmstrom, & Gilstrap, 2005).

Because the way in which gender or sex influences self-disclosing behavior is complex and uncertain, you might be tempted to fall back on stereotypes depicting disclosing women and silent men. However, most of the research doesn't support such a conclusion. The overall differences between women and men as self-disclosers are relatively small, and they are more likely to be differences of degree rather than kind (Dindia, 2000).

To read an interesting article about how the fear of self-disclosure prevents some people from seeking psychological help, use your online Resource Center for *Understanding Interpersonal Communication* to access *Interactive Activity 8.3: Fear of Self-Disclosure*. And to examine the relationship between what we expect will happen when we disclose personal information and what actually happens, access *InfoTrac College Edition Exercise 8.1: Expected versus Actual Responses* to read the article "Expected versus Actual Responses to Disclosure in Relationships of HIV-Positive African American Adolescent Females."

Principles of Self-Disclosure

From our discussion so far, you should have a picture of the self-disclosure process and how it is affected by factors we've mentioned, such as relational issues, culture, and gender and sex. To focus this picture further, we now examine four principles, or norms, of self-disclosure.

Your turn

*Keep a record of self-disclosures you make and receive for the next two weeks. At the end of that time, see if you can discern a pattern in the disclosures. If you like, you can use your student workbook or your **Understanding Interpersonal Communication** Online Resources to complete this activity.*

We Disclose a Great Deal in Few Interactions

This principle suggests that if we examine our total communication behavior, self-disclosures are somewhat rare. Some researchers estimate that only approximately 2 percent of our communication can be called self-disclosure (Dindia, Fitzpatrick, & Kenny, 1997; Pearce & Sharp, 1973; Rosenfeld, 2000). We generally spend a lot more time in small talk than in the relatively dramatic behavior of self-disclosure.

For instance, think about a typical day some of you may have. Maybe you get up at 7 a.m. and mumble a morning greeting to those you live with as you hurry to get ready for your day. You may grab a fast-food breakfast at a drive-through and then go to your part-time job. At work, you may have to

To Achieve Self-Awareness

Self-disclosures provide us with the means to become more self-aware. We are able to clarify our self-concepts by the feedback we receive from others when we disclose and by the process of hearing ourselves disclose. For example, when Kara discloses to her sister, Martha, that she feels stupid for not learning how to swim till she was an adult, Martha responds by praising Kara for having the courage to tackle a new skill later in life. Martha tells Kara that she is really proud of her and feels that she is setting a good example for their children that it's never too late to learn. Kara is pleased to hear her sister's comments. As she reflects on them, she realizes that persisting with swimming lessons was worthwhile, even though it was more difficult to learn at age 35 than it would have been at age 5. After talking to Martha and thinking about their conversation, Kara feels really good about herself.

In another example, when George discloses to his friend Julia that he is thinking about quitting his job and starting his own business, he surprises himself. Although he had been feeling discontented with work, until he hears himself tell Julia that he wants to start his own business, he hadn't really been sure of this. When he puts that thought into words for Julia, he begins to clarify his feelings for himself. This process is pictured in the Johari Window, which we described earlier; as we listen to ourselves disclose and receive feedback, we increase the side of the window that is known to us.

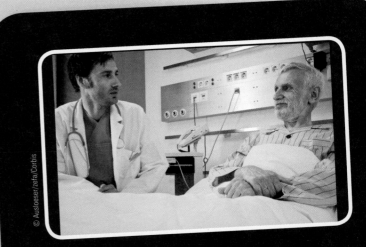

© Ausloeser/zefa/Corbis

IPC in the News

An article in *USA Today* discusses a study examining self-disclosures made by physicians during patient visits. The co-author of the study commented that he thought that self-disclosing to his patients would strengthen his connection with them. For instance, he would tell his older patients about his elderly mother, who was struggling with health issues. However, he found that when he disclosed this information, his patients became distracted, worried about his mother, and possibly even doubtful of his abilities as a doctor because he couldn't help his own parent. The study confirmed that self-disclosures from doctors to patients are inappropriate, noting that "empathy, understanding and compassion work better than self-disclosure" (p. 9D).

Rubin, R. (2007, June 26). Doctors often shift focus from their patients to themselves. *USA Today*, p. 9D.

To Initiate a Relationship

As we discussed previously, disclosers are prompted to tell private information as a way of developing a new relationship with someone who seems interesting. One study (Vittengl & Holt, 2000) supports the idea that self-disclosures help develop new relationships: "Self-disclosure within get-acquainted conversations is accompanied by liking or feelings of social

Self-disclosure is an integral part of initiating a relationship. When we want to get to know someone better, we often also want them to know us better, so we disclose information that we might not disclose to just a casual acquaintance.

© David Lees/Taxi/Getty Images

attraction to conversational partners and by an increase in positive emotions" (p. 63). Here it is important to remember that "social attraction" includes friends, partners, coworkers, and so forth, not simply romantic and/or sexual attraction.

To illustrate these findings, let's examine the case of Anita and Zoe. Anita is a working single mother attending the local community college part time and holding down a part-time job as an administrative assistant at a law firm. Because she's so busy, she hasn't made many friends at school or work. One day when she is rushing to finish a project at the firm, she bumps into Zoe. Anita had met Zoe, who is also a single mother, during her orientation. Zoe works full time at the law firm and mentors new employees.

When they met, Anita had thought that it would be nice to get to know Zoe, but she just hadn't had the time. When they bump into each other, Anita is worrying about her son, Brad, who has been getting into fights at school. Zoe says "hi" in a friendly way and asks if Anita would like to have coffee later. Although Anita really doesn't have the time, she says yes and is surprised when, over coffee, she finds herself telling Zoe some of her concerns about Brad. Zoe listens with empathy and then responds that her son had some behavior problems when he was Brad's age, too, and that she, like Anita, had worried that her work schedule might have been partly to blame. Zoe mentions that she and her son had benefited from some counseling sessions with the school psychologist. When Zoe and Anita part, they both think they have begun a friendship.

To Maintain Existing Relationships

Existing relationships also benefit from self-disclosures. In an interesting study examining why people tell others about their dreams, researchers found that 100 percent of their participants attributed their disclosures to some type of relational goal (Ijams & Miller, 2000). People said they told a relational partner about a dream to enhance closeness, warmth, and trust. The authors quote one of their respondents, who explained why revealing dreams was important:

> "My brother and I have a good sibling relationship. We tell each other everything that goes on in our dreams. Each time we reveal something, the bond between us strengthens. It seems melodramatic, but there is a strong bond between us." (p. 141).

To Satisfy Expectations of What Constitutes a Good Relationship

As we mentioned earlier, the ideology of intimacy dictates that we should be completely open and self-disclosive with people in intimate relationships. If we fail to do so or if we consciously keep secrets from intimate others, we often believe that our relationships are flawed or not as good as we want them to be. Self-disclosing allows us to see our relationships in a positive light.

As an example, in the study referred to in the previous subsection (Ijams and Miller's, 2000), some study participants said they told a partner about their dream because the partner was already close to them, and the participants' expectation was that in a close relationship people tell each other everything, including their dreams. As one of their respondents stated: "'He knows everything about me. I love him and trust him and pretty much share everything with him'" (p. 141).

To Escalate a Relationship

As previously mentioned, self-disclosing provides a way to get to know someone and to allow that person to know you. This process escalates a relationship, often moving it from one stage to another. Casual acquaintances may become close friends after they spend some time telling each other personal information about themselves. For example, when Laurie tells her friend, Javier, that she used to suffer from bulimia and that she still worries every day that she might slip back into her old binge-and-purge habits, Javier feels honored that Laurie trusts him with this information. Her self-disclosure makes him feel closer to her and advances their relationship to a more intense level.

However, as we discussed elsewhere in the text, communication can be used for dark purposes as well as positive goals. Indeed, self-disclosures can be used to manipulate a relational partner. For example, a person can offer a self-disclosure that could be considered history (or inauthentic) to manipulate a relational partner, through the norm of reciprocity, into revealing something truly personal. In this manner, the relationship may escalate faster than it would have otherwise, which might be the devious objective of the first discloser. Or, one person may say "I love you" early in a relationship simply to advance the intimacy of the relationship.

Reasons Not to Self-Disclose

Although opening up to another person provides benefits, there are also compelling reasons to keep our secrets to ourselves. The dialectics model we discussed earlier argues that in any relationship, both desires are extremely important. We want to be open with our partners, but at the same time, we want to maintain our secrets. Although ethical questions arise when we keep something that is critically important from someone else, most of the time, maintaining privacy is ethical. We need to remember that it's our choice as to whether we disclose or not.

Some of the reasons people choose to be silent rather than to disclose are outlined in Table 8.3 and discussed in this section. As you read the examples, think about the ethical implications of choosing to keep silent.

To Avoid Hurt and Rejection

Perhaps the most common reason for keeping a secret is because we believe that the person we reveal it to may use the information to hurt us or may reject us when they know our inner selves. For example, Mick doesn't tell his friend, Marci, that he served time in a juvenile detention center for possession of drugs because he fears that she will be angry, respect him less, or bring it up in a taunting way in an argument. All of these negative outcomes are reasons for keeping a secret private.

If we share a really critical piece of information, even with a sympathetic friend, we have given this friend some potential power over us, and we can't

Table 8.3 Reasons to avoid self-disclosure

- To avoid hurt, rejection, or both
- To avoid conflict, protect a relationship, or both
- To keep one's image intact, maintain individuality, or both
- To reduce or forget about stress

be absolutely sure that our friend would never use this power against us or in a way that we would not like. When Audra confides in Allen that she thinks she's a lesbian, she figures he's a trustworthy confidante because he is a long-time friend who is gay himself. However, she doesn't realize Allen feels strongly that being homosexual is nothing to hide. Allen tells several mutual friends about Audra's disclosure. Although Audra doesn't believe that being a lesbian is shameful, she wasn't ready to tell their friends yet; she was still getting used to the idea herself. She was extremely hurt by what she saw as Allen's betrayal.

To Avoid Conflict and Protect a Relationship

Some secrecy may actually be helpful in a relationship. For example, Lois thinks she doesn't need to tell her friend, Raymond, that she voted Republican in the last election. Lois knows Raymond is a staunch Democrat and she believes the disclosure would cause a conflict that could harm their relationship.

As another example, Marsha does not like her brother's wife. When Marsha chooses not to tell this to her brother, Hal, she figures that her silence keeps the relationship between them more peaceful. Because Marsha knows that Hal is happy with his wife, it seems irrelevant to reveal that she isn't.

"You never tell me anything. Keep up the good work."

Victoria Roberts

This secret does not affect their relationship much, because they live in different cities separated by thousands of miles, and Marsha and Hal keep in touch mainly by email and phone.

As discussed previously, culture influences people's views of self-disclosures and whether they help or harm a relationship. A study of Chinese business people (Hamid, 2000) found that disclosing to one's mother was negative for the relationship because it increased feelings of stress in both parties.

Finally, some research indicates that if you disclose to someone who responds in a negative fashion, you are likely to feel badly about the interaction, the other person, and about your relationship with the other person (Afifi & Guerreo, 2000; Roloff & Ifert, 2000). Some people may believe disclosing isn't worth that risk.

To Keep Your Image Intact and Maintain Individuality

Some people withhold self-disclosures because they're concerned that if they begin disclosing, they will lose control and be unable to stop. Further, these people fear that disclosures will bring with them unrestrained emotionality, perhaps causing them to cry uncontrollably. In a related vein, some people worry that self-disclosing will cause them to lose their sense of mystery and individuality. For instance, Caitlin may fear that if Nolan knows all about her, she won't seem interesting to him any longer. And Gary's fear is that if he tells his friend Lyle all about himself, Gary may become so much a part of this friendship that he'll disappear as a separate individual.

Further, if someone has established a particular role in a relationship, they may fear changing that role and their image. For example, Lucy and Rebecca have been friends for five years. In their relationship, Rebecca often turns to Lucy, who has been married for 15 years, for advice when she has problems with a boyfriend. When Lucy and her husband fight, she doesn't feel comfortable confiding in Rebecca because it seems to negate her identity as a happily married person who gives support but doesn't need to ask for it.

To Reduce Stress

In the previous section, we mentioned that people often engage in self-disclosures to reduce stress. Although this is frequently the case, some evidence indicates that self-disclosures can sometimes increase stress. For instance, Valerian Derlega and his colleagues (1993) give the following example:

> Bill, 20, and Mark, 21, are juniors at a state university. They are flying together to Florida for spring break. Bill is uncomfortable about flying, and he tells Mark about being nervous. Mark, in turn, describes an unpleasant experience when, on another flight, his plane had mechanical problems. As the plane takes off, neither of

them is feeling very good. Somehow, talking about their fears made
them feel worse rather than better. (p. 103)

Similarly, Anita Vangelisti and her colleagues (2001) observe that continuing
to think and talk about stressful issues can result in more stress. They note
that stress is reduced only when the disclosures begin to reflect a positive
outlook.

To explore the possible consequences of choosing not to reveal personal
information, read the article "The High Costs of Hidden Conditions," available through InfoTrac College Edition. Use your online Resource Center for
Understanding Interpersonal Communication to access **InfoTrac College Edition
Exercise 8.4: The Cost of Choosing Not to Disclose.**

Choices for Effective Disclosing

Although we may have good reasons for keeping silent at times, we need to
refine our self-disclosing skills for those times when we wish open up. In this
section, we outline important techniques for building our self-disclosing skills.

Use I-Statements

Owning, or the use of I-statements, which we've discussed in previous chapters, is the most basic verbal skill for self-disclosing. Saying "I think," "I feel,"
"I need," or "I believe" indicates that you accept that what you're saying is
your own perception, based on your own experiences, and affected by your
value system. When you self-disclose using owning, you take responsibility
for your feelings and experiences. In addition, your listener realizes that you
are speaking for yourself and not trying to make a generalization. Let's take a
look at an example of an owned self-disclosure. Edward tells Mike, "I don't
know if I will really be happy going to college in New York. It's so far away
from my family—I know I'll be homesick." This is different from Edward
stating, "It's important to stay near home for college. It's not good to put too
much distance between family members." When Edward uses the latter
phrasing, he doesn't own his feelings; instead, he presents them as a general
rule that all people should consider when deciding where to go to college.

Be Honest

Honesty in self-disclosure refers to being both clear and accurate. If you are too
ambiguous and unclear, your self-disclosures may not be "heard" as real disclosure. Yet, if you and your partner know each other very well, you may be able
to offer disclosures more indirectly (Petronio, 1991). For instance, if you know
your partner is struggling with several deadlines at work, you will be able to
hear a disclosure in your partner's sarcastic comment: "I had a great day at

..... at work

At work, self-disclosures can be difficult and may sometimes seem inappropriate. After all, self-disclosure is about sharing personal information, and the workplace is a public arena. But at times some type of self-disclosure is called for. For instance, let's say that your coworker Tanya asks your opinion about a report she needs to turn in next week. If you think that Tanya can improve the report significantly, you should use specific language to let her know the ways in which you feel it can be strengthened. You don't need to be unkind, but you do need to tell her exactly what you believe the report lacks. If you are not clear, Tanya may leave your conversation not knowing if she needs to change the report or not. Can you identify other instances where self-disclosure might be needed in the workplace?

... with your sister at a vacation hotel

It's spring break, and you and your sister, Ellen, have taken your first vacation together as adults. You're both in graduate school now and are discovering how much you enjoy each other's company. You've just come in from the pool and are sitting on the deck reminiscing about family vacations in the past. Ellen mentions a trip the family took to Florida when she was eight and you were ten. You feel a little chill because you've never told Ellen that you were the one who was responsible for her losing her prized stuffed dog on that trip. The family spent hours looking for Toto, and Ellen sobbed for a whole day when they finally gave up looking for it. You had seen it sitting on the restaurant bench when the family left after a lunch stop, but you were mad at Ellen at the time and didn't bother to let her know she was leaving it behind. Now you wonder—should you tell Ellen this story? Would she be furious or think it was funny? What factors of self-disclosure will influence your decision to tell or not?

work today. What a pleasure palace that job is!" Generally speaking however, you need to be clear and accurate in your disclosures. If you are dishonest or inaccurate while disclosing, you are defeating the purpose of self-disclosure.

Be Consistent with Your Verbal and Nonverbal Communication

Consistency means that your nonverbal communication should reinforce, not contradict, your verbal communication. For example, if Shannon tells Josie that she's really upset about her grades this semester, but she smiles while saying it, Josie may be confused about whether Shannon is upset or not.

Focus Your Nonverbal Communication

Try to focus your nonverbal communication on the issue at hand and provide nonverbal cues that add meaning rather than ones that distract from your message. For instance, if Mia continually taps her pencil against a table while telling her mother that she wants to quit school, her mother may be distracted by the gesture and have trouble concentrating on Mia's disclosure.

Be Sure Your Content Is Relevant

Relevancy to the context refers to an assessment of the appropriateness of the disclosure to the situation itself. For example, if Ron is at a company picnic, he may decide that it isn't the time or place to tell his boss that he is unhappy at work and wants more responsibility. In this chapter's opening Case in Point, Roberta tried to make a good context for her disclosure. She prepared a nice dinner to set the stage for telling Philip her secret.

For example, when Marty thinks of his happiest moments, he usually thinks of the times he has spent with his best friend, Ray. However, Marty's unhappiest time was also associated with Ray. Ray had thought that Marty was flirting with Ray's girlfriend, and Ray had been furious, not speaking to Marty for a week, even when they were at basketball practice and classes together. Marty had felt a lot of pain because he'd thought that their friendship was over. Finally, Ray realized that Marty wasn't really guilty, and they were able to resume their friendship. Marty found it surprising that being around the same friend could sometimes be so much fun and other times feel like torture.

Interdependence is the main reason that conflict is a natural and inevitable part of life. The more we rely on another, the more potential there is for observing differences and being affected by them (Lulofs & Cahn, 2000).

Perception

Perception, as we discussed in Chapter 2, refers to the psychological process involved in sensing meaning. The definition of conflict states that for conflict to exist, the interdependent people have to *perceive* that they have incompatible goals. For example, Carmen wants to go on a family vacation to Florida. She misunderstands a statement that her husband, Dave, makes and jumps to the conclusion that he disagrees with the vacation destination. Even though Carmen and Dave really agree on where to take their vacation, if Carmen believes they disagree, they will come into conflict. This type of conflict persists until the parties come to understand that their goals really are similar.

Some researchers emphasize the importance of perception to the conflict process when they apply a competence model to interpersonal conflict. Competency suggests that people judge themselves and their conversational partners based on how well they communicate and how successful they are in reaching their conversational goals (Spitzberg & Cupach, 1984, 1989). When applying this model to conflict, one study (Canary et al., 2001) found that people's perceptions of competency during the conflict directly affected the relationship. For instance, if Josie and Melissa have an argument about cleaning the apartment, and each perceives that both of them are competent in their conflict, they will be more satisfied and happier with one another than they would be if they'd had the exact same conflict but thought they'd behaved less competently. Therefore, researchers argue that perception of communication competence is an extremely important dimension of interpersonal conflict.

Incompatible Goals

The definition of conflict specifies that friction results when people's goals differ (as in "I want to study, but Jorge wants me to go to a party with him") at the same time that they think others stand in the way of the achievement of personal goals (as in "I want to get promoted at work, but my supervisor wants me to stay in her department"). This feature of the definition implies that conflict is goal oriented—for instance, two cousins, Karla and Meredith, are roommates. One Sunday, Karla wants to go to the ocean and her cousin wants to stay home and have a barbeque. Because Karla's goal isn't compatible with what Meredith wants, they will engage in conflict (Lakey & Canary, 2001) if they are dependent on one another to accomplish their goals. For instance, if Karla needs Meredith to drive her to the ocean and Meredith needs Karla to start the barbeque, they are interdependent and have incompatible goals, which will likely cause conflict between them.

Your turn

Note and evaluate the times you engage in interpersonal conflict during a week. If you like, you can use your student workbook or your **Understanding Interpersonal Communication** Online Resources to complete this activity.

Types of Conflict

Now that we have defined conflict, we can further our understanding by learning about various types of conflict. Understanding these different types helps us gain a better sense of conflict communication.

Image Conflicts

Image conflicts concern self-presentation. For example, if Enid considers herself a competent adult, she may engage in conflict when her mother offers her suggestions about how to manage her career. Enid may feel that her mother isn't respecting her as an adult and, as such, is challenging Enid's image of herself. This type of conflict is especially difficult when two different images are in fact in play. For instance, if Enid's mother does still view Enid as a child, they do have two competing images. A similar problem can exist when a parent pushes a child to grow up faster than the child feels comfortable. In that case, the parent views the child as an adult, whereas the child may still see herself or himself as a child. Sometimes, image conflicts may masquerade as another type of conflict, but at the core of an image conflict is a disagreement about self-definition.

image conflict

A conflict with another about one's sense of oneself.

content conflict

A conflict that revolves around an issue. Also called a substantive conflict.

Content Conflicts

Content conflicts are often called "substantive" because they revolve around an issue. Interdependent people fight about myriad topics. Maeve calls her Internet provider to complain about the service, and the service provider tells her there is no evidence to support her complaint. Nanette likes a tree on her

SIPRESS

"Well, if it doesn't matter who's right and who's wrong, why don't I be right and you be wrong?"

property line, but her neighbor thinks its roots are responsible for cracking his driveway. Matt hates to bowl, and his best friend loves bowling. Ginna wants to spend some savings on a vacation, and her husband, Sean, thinks that would be a waste of money. Penny thinks that the data for her work group's presentation should be rechecked, and the other members of the group think they've been checked sufficiently. Marcus believes that even though he works part time, he should be respected as a member of the company and allowed a say in company policies; however, the full-time workers don't want the part-timers involved in those matters. Although all of these examples involve topics of disagreement, some of these content conflicts have undertones of the other types of conflicts within them. As we discuss the subsequent types, we'll point out this overlap.

Content conflicts can be subdivided (Johnson, 2002; Johnson, Becker, Wigley, Haigh, & Craig, 2007). Some content conflicts focus on **public issues**, or issues outside the relationship. Other content conflicts involve **personal issues** and relate more closely to the relationship. For instance, when Stan and Frank disagree about whether Bill Clinton was a great president, they are debating a public issue. When Stan complains that Frank has no time to hang out with him anymore because he is always spending time with his new girlfriend, they are tackling a private issue. Not surprisingly, research finds that people enjoy arguments about public issues more than conflicts about private issues.

public issue

An issue outside a relationship that can cause a content conflict.

personal issue

An issue related to a relationship that can cause a content conflict.

© David Young-Wolff/PhotoEdit

IPC *in the* News

Siblings engage in some measure of conflict throughout their lives, but according to a recent USA Today/ABC News/Gallup Poll, 30 percent of siblings said that assisting aging parents significantly stressed their sibling relationships. Siblings have varied approaches to splitting up caregiving responsibilities for aging or ailing parents, and each can lead conflict to be manifest in different ways. For example, some siblings mentioned in the article resolved their conflict through a cooperative effort to care for a parent, while negotiations between other siblings deteriorated to caretaking arrangements where one sibling strains to care for a parent while the other sibling drops out of the situation altogether. The article indicates that for many siblings, the level of conflict present when caring for an aging parent mirrors the conflict siblings had when they all lived under the same roof. Conflict is learned and reinforced through the lifetime of a relationship, and practicing healthy conflict habits now could reduce stressful sibling conflict in later life.

Grossman, C. (2008, February 1). Navigating sibling relationships when caring for a parent can be difficult. *USA Today.*

value conflict

A conflict in which the content is specifically about a question of right and wrong.

Value Conflicts

Value conflicts are content conflicts in which the content is specifically a question of right and wrong. The neighbors who are arguing about the tree on their property line may be having a values conflict if they are discussing it in terms of ecosystems and environmental protection. When people disagree about war in Iraq, abortion, or capital punishment, they may be engaging in value conflicts because opinions on these topics largely depend on value judgments made by the participants. For example, arguments about capital punishment often hinge on the value placed on human life and the value placed on punishment and retribution.

Relational Conflicts

Relational conflicts focus on issues concerning the relationship between two people. For example, when Marge argues with Perry, telling him that the way he speaks to her makes her feel disrespected, they are engaging in relational conflict. Couples who argue about how much they should tell their in-laws and how much they should keep private also exemplify relational conflict. In a previous example, Ginna and Sean's fight about whether to spend savings on a vacation would be a relational conflict if it centers on how they make decisions in their relationship. The disagreement would be a values conflict if it underscores a difference in how the two value money.

To read short dialogues that illustrate four of the types of conflict, see Table 9.1. In addition, Figure 9.1 on page 302 presents a dialogue and a picture that show how these conflict types overlap. Even though the types cannot be completely separated, being able to identify what kind of conflict you're having is useful in helping you decide how to manage it.

Table 9.1   Types of conflict

Image conflict	
MARILYN:	Mom, why do you still treat me like a child although I am 22 years old?
MOM:	Marilyn, you are always going to be my little girl.
MARILYN:	That's ridiculous, Mom. You have to let me grow up.

Content conflict	
FRED:	Jeff, I don't think that New York has the largest population of any state in the United States. I am sure I read that it was California.
JEFF:	No, it's New York.
FRED:	Well, we can look it up.

Value conflict	
AMY:	Travis, I can't believe we're so close to getting married, and I am just finding out that you don't want to have kids! To me, that's what marriage is all about.
TRAVIS:	Are you kidding, Amy? I certainly don't believe that marriage is all about having kids. What about love, companionship, and fun? Aren't those the things that marriage is all about?

Relational conflict	
ANGELA:	Marlee, I know this sounds funny to bring up, but I am feeling kind of left out when you and I are together with Justine. You and I used to be best friends, and now it seems like you don't even want to be around me if you have the chance to hang out with Justine.
MARLEE:	That's not exactly true, Angela.
ANGELA:	It sure feels that way to me.
MARLEE:	Maybe I have been spending a lot of time with Justine, but that's just because we have the same major and are in a lot of classes together.

Serial Conflicts

Serial conflict differs from the other four types because it doesn't refer to the subject of the conflict. Instead, it refers to a time frame for the conflict. Up to this point, we've been talking about conflicts as discrete episodes, with specific starting points ("I'm so sick of you using up all the hot water every morning") and specific ending points ("OK, I'll take a quicker shower"). **Serial conflicts** are those that recur over time in people's everyday lives, without a resolution ("Last week you said you take a quicker shower, but you aren't doing that. It's the same thing over and over." "Well, you're always on my back! Leave me alone about the stupid shower."). Researchers (Bevan et al., 2007; Malis & Roloff, 2006) find that these serial conflicts tell us a lot about relational communication. In relationships with a long history (like dating, marriage or

relational conflict

A conflict that focuses on issues concerning the relationship between two people.

serial conflicts

Conflicts that recur over time in people's everyday lives, without a resolution.

Figure 9.1 Overlap in types of conflicts

Conflict Dialogue

Andre: "I am so happy George W. Bush won the 2004 election. He is strong where Kerry would have been weak on terrorism. And besides, he's a born-again Christian, so I know he has good values."

Michael: "Wow, Andre, I thought I knew you and now I am blown away that I knew you so little. Bush is a horrible person who supported the death penalty in Texas and got us into an immoral war. That's hardly good values! I am not sure I can be friends with someone who holds your views."

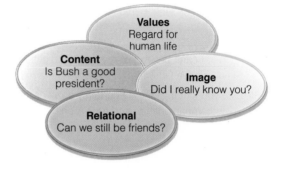

Values
Regard for human life

Content
Is Bush a good president?

Image
Did I really know you?

Relational
Can we still be friends?

REVISITING CASE IN POINT

1. *How would you type the conflict Tamara and Jeff had about the missed coffee date? Is it an image, content, value, relational, or serial conflict? Or is it some combination? Does it have elements of meta-conflict?*

2. *How does typing this conflict help in managing it?*

You can answer these questions online under the resources for Chapter 9 at your online Resource Center for Understanding Interpersonal Communication.

families) partners are likely to have unsettled issues that come up repeatedly whether they want them to or not.

Serial conflicts may also lead to **meta-conflicts**, which are conflicts about the way you conduct conflict! If Jennifer and Dominic argue about something repeatedly, they may also reflect on their conflict process. When Jennifer tells Dominic she hates it when he interrupts her and Dominic replies that he wouldn't do that if she'd get to the point, they are engaging in meta-conflict. Meta-conflicts can happen at any time but they are especially likely during serial conflict.

To read an interesting article about the different styles people use in communicating about conflict, use your online Resource Center for *Understanding Interpersonal Communication* to access *Interactive Activity 9.1: Conflict Styles*.

Myths about Conflict and Communication

As we've stated previously, conflict is a normal part of relational life, but many people find it unpleasant. As a result, people talk a great deal about conflict, which generates myths about it. We'll discuss the very common (but mistaken) beliefs that conflict is just miscommunication, all conflict can be resolved through good communication, and it is always best to talk through conflicts.

Many people believe that all conflict results from miscommunication or unclear communication. However, sometimes people communicate clearly to each other and, they disagree. For instance, if Jim wants to go to Harvard, and his parents tell him they do not want him to go to school so far away from home, Jim and his parents may continue to argue about this topic even though they know exactly what each other's positions are. The problem in this case is not that they haven't been clear; rather, they disagree about whose goal is more important and, possibly, who has the power in their relationship to make such a decision.

The corollary to the myth of miscommunication is the notion that all conflicts can be resolved through good communication. This myth tells us that if we master a certain set of skills for managing conflict, we can resolve all of our conflicts. Although we offer a set of skills later in this chapter, we recognize that some conflicts persist, and partners may have to agree to disagree. For example, no amount of good communication practices will convince Harry to vote Democratic even though his son, Michael, tries to persuade him that the Democrats advocate better policies than the Republicans do. Harry simply states that he has voted Republican his whole life and he is proud to continue to do so.

meta-conflict

A conflict about the way a conflict is conducted.

Communication Assessment Test
Argumentativeness Scale

Argumentativeness may be thought of as contributing to the negative aspects of conflict, but research by Dominic Infante and Andrew Rancer (1982) suggests that this is not always the case. They define argumentativeness as a willingness to argue for your point of view on significant issues. Infante and Rancer distinguish between argumentativeness and verbal aggressiveness, a more negative trait, by saying that whereas argumentativeness focuses on ideas, verbal aggressiveness focuses on winning an argument, even if it means verbally attacking the other person. You can take the following test online. Go to your online Resource Center for *Understanding Interpersonal Communication* and look under the resources for Chapter 9.

Directions:

This questionnaire contains statements about arguing about controversial issues. Indicate whether a statement describes you according to the following scale:

almost never true = 1 rarely true = 2 occasionally true = 3 often true = 4 almost always true = 5

_____ 1. While in an argument, I worry that the person I am arguing with will form a negative impression of me.

_____ 2. Arguing over controversial issues improves my intelligence.

_____ 3. I enjoy avoiding arguments.

_____ 4. I am energetic and enthusiastic when I argue.

_____ 5. After I finish an argument, I promise myself that I will not get into another.

_____ 6. Arguing with a person creates more problems for me than it solves.

_____ 7. I have a pleasant, good feeling when I win a point in an argument.

_____ 8. When I finish arguing with someone, I feel nervous and upset.

_____ 9. I enjoy a good argument over a controversial issue.

_____ 10. I get an unpleasant feeling when I realize I am about to get into an argument.

_____ 11. I enjoy defending my point of view on an issue.

_____ 12. I am happy when I keep an argument from happening.

_____ 13. I do not like to miss the opportunity to argue a controversial issue.

_____ 14. I prefer being with people who rarely disagree with me.

_____ 15. I consider an argument an exciting intellectual challenge.

_____ 16. I find myself unable to think of effective points during an argument.

_____ 17. I feel refreshed and satisfied after an argument on a controversial issue.

_____ 18. I have the ability to do well in an argument.

_____ 19. I try to avoid getting into arguments.

_____ 20. I feel excitement when I expect that a conversation I am in is leading to an argument.

Scoring

1. Add your scores for questions 2, 4, 7, 9, 11, 13, 15, 17, 18, and 20. These questions represent your willingness to engage in arguments.
2. Add 60 to this total.
3. Add your scores for questions 1, 3, 5, 6, 8, 10, 12, 14, 16, and 19. These questions represent your tendency to avoid arguments. Subtract this total from the total you obtained in the first two steps. This number represents your argumentativeness score.

(Continues)

Use the following guidelines for interpreting your score:

73–100 High argumentativeness
56–72 Moderate argumentativeness
20–55 Low argumentativeness

Remember, moderation is probably the most skillful position. Does the score you received seem to reflect how you operate in discussions of controversial issues? If your score is not in the moderate category, what do you think you can do to compensate for the problems you might face in conflict?

From D. A. Infante and A. S. Rancer, "A conceptualization and measure of argumentativeness," *Journal of Personality Assessment* 46: 72–80, 1982. Reprinted by permission.

Underlying these two myths is the idea that it's always best to talk about conflicts.

Relational partners often believe that they simply need to communicate more to reach a mutually satisfying solution to their conflicts. However, many scholars believe that this myth obscures the benefits of avoiding certain topics rather than talking about them in great detail (see for example, Baxter & Wilmot, 1985; Guerrero & Afifi, 1995; Petronio, 2002). Sometimes continuing to talk about a point of disagreement just exaggerates and prolongs the problem. Some arguments are not that important and if you ignore them, they really will go away. For instance, when Mel broke the rain gauge in their backyard, Tina was angry. However, because she realized that it was just a $10.00 item and that getting into a big discussion about it wouldn't be productive for their relationship, she didn't say anything.

Although we acknowledge that many people subscribe to these myths about conflict, they are not accurate. Not all conflicts are based on misunderstandings, are resolvable, or are best dealt with by talking. Remember that communication is an important part of managing interpersonal conflict, but conflict management isn't just about communicating well.

Factors Influencing Interpersonal Conflict

In this section, we briefly discuss two factors that affect conflict interaction: gender and sex, and culture. Although we review them separately, these variables most often act in concert to affect conflicts. For example, a German American man and a Chinese American woman who work together in a small software company may have a disagreement over how to invest their limited research and development budget. In this case, there are cultural forces and gendered messages interacting to influence their conflict. All conflicts take place between people who are gendered and who come from a specific cultural background.

Gender and Sex

As we discussed in Chapter 2, when we talk about gender, we are referring to gender socialization. Men and women are not inherently different in their orientations to conflict or in their conflict behaviors; rather, they have been taught a set of responsibilities and norms that affect their conflict interactions. Further, not all men or all women are socialized to the same degree (Bem, 1993). Thus, we see great variety in how women and men enact gendered social norms.

Because women are taught to be keepers of relational life and men are socialized to pay attention to public life (Sullivan & Turner, 1996), women often want to talk about relationship issues, and men do not. This imbalance may cause conflict within relationships. For example, when Moira tells Jack that she wants to talk about their relationship, Jack may perceive her statement as an indication that their relationship is in trouble and, as a result, try to avoid the problem. Moira may not have intended to imply that she wanted to discuss a specific problem; she just wanted to connect with Jack about the topic of their life together.

Some research suggests that women are more collaborative and men are more competitive in conflict interactions. However, recent studies call this generalization into question. A relatively recent study examining college students found that women were more likely than men to report that they used both cooperative and competitive conflict strategies (Rudawsky, Lundgren, & Grasha, 1999). Another study (Messman & Mikesell, 2000) found that women and men in romantic relationships did not differ in their use of competition as a conflict strategy.

One study (Shuter & Turner, 1997) found that European American women as a group were evaluated by African American women and by themselves as highly conflict avoidant. However, when the researchers asked individual women from both groups to talk about their own approaches to conflict, the responses did not differ significantly. The study concluded that people are affected by stereotypes when asked to talk about a group, but that they see themselves as not necessarily representative of the group to which they belong.

Some evidence does point to more enduring differences between women and men in conflict. For instance, Levenson and Gottman (1985) showed that men and women react differently to the stress of relational conflict. Whereas women seemed to be able to tolerate high levels of the physiological arousal found in conflict with a partner, men were more bothered by this arousal and sought to avoid it. In a more recent test of that conclusion, a study conducted in Belgium (Buysse, De Clercq, Verhofstadt, Heene, Roeyers, & Van Oost, 2000) found that men desired to avoid marital conflict more than women.

For more about gender and conflict, check out the study "Gender-Related Effects in Emotional Responding to Resolved and Unresolved Interpersonal Conflict," available through InfoTrac College Edition. Use your online

source—they felt their marriages were headed for divorce when they and their husbands stopped talking to one another. Yet, both women and men attributed their dissatisfaction to the same overarching reason—they no longer felt cherished in the relationship. Thus, both sexes desired the feeling of being cherished, but men tended to feel that way when their wives did concrete favors for them, whereas women felt most cherished when they experienced good communication with their husbands.

REVISITING CASEINPOINT

1. How does Randy and Hope's relationship illustrate relational scripts?

2. What metaphor might Hope and Randy use for their relationship?

You can answer these questions online under the resources for Chapter 10 at your online Resource Center for Understanding Interpersonal Communication.

Some evidence exists that men and women possess a different relational awareness (Honeycutt, Cantrill, Kelly, & Lambkin,1998). Men are more reticent in communicating and monitoring their relationships, and women are more tuned in to relational goals. However, this difference was slight, and it seems easily explained by social teaching, which categorizes women as relational experts.

Although women and men differ in what they have learned about, what they expect from, and what they experience within close relationships, popular writers like John Gray (who wrote *Men are from Mars, Women are from Venus* in 1992) have taken our cultural interest in sex differences to an extreme. They construct some differences where none really exist, overestimate the differences that do appear, and fail to talk about the cultural context framing these differences.

To read an interesting study about communication in same-sex versus other-sex relationships, particularly self-disclosure and emotional intimacy, check out the article "Close Emotional Relationships with Women versus Men," available through InfoTrac College Edition. Use your online Resource Center for *Understanding Interpersonal Communication* to access **InfoTrac College Edition Exercise 10.1: Who Are You Closer to Emotionally?** under the resources for Chapter 10.

Now that we have discussed several ways of defining close relationships, we turn our attention to communication in three specific types of close relationships: friendships, romantic relationships, and families.

To check out an interesting website that may help you learn more about your own close relationships, use your online Resource Center for *Understanding Interpersonal Communication* to access **Interactive Activity 10.2: Assessing Close Relationships.**

relational culture

The notion that relational partners collaborate and experience shared understandings, roles, and rituals that are unique to their relationship.

Types of Close Relationships

There are three primary types of close relationships: friendships, romantic relationships, and families.

Friendship

Unlike most family relationships, friendship is voluntary, There aren't any religious ceremonies to sanction friendships, or any legal bonds to make dissolving them difficult. This quality makes friendship a somewhat fragile close relationship. Friends may be sacrificed for family in the belief that family relationships are more primary. For instance, Maggie had to exclude her best friend, Leah, from her son's wedding rehearsal because only family members were invited. Friends may come and go based on situational factors. Randi found it hard to stay friends with Marlene after she got married and moved to California while Randi remained single in Chicago. She wanted to stay friends with Marlene, but the long distance and their different circumstances doomed the friendship.

Despite this fragility, friendship is a significant close relationship. Research indicates that friendships provide social support, companionship, and validation. African American men reported that they valued their friendships with women because of their positive qualities and the fact that they communicated strong emotional bonds within them (White, 2006). In a different study African American women said they depended on friendships with other African American women for opportunities to communicate a shared history and identity (Hughes & Heuman, 2006). Other research notes how daily conversation about routine activities like shopping, for instance, creates a deep sense of connection for friends, especially female friends (Braithwaite & Kellas, 2006; Metts, 2006).

Recently, some attention has been paid to the downsides of friendships. Psychologists have examined unhealthy friendships (Lerner, 2001; Parker, Low, Walker, & Gamm, 2005; Yager, 2002) characterized by jealousy, envy, anger, and a whole host of difficulties. There might be as many as twenty-one types of bad friendships, including those that lead you into antisocial or illegal activities (for example, when Sam convinces his friend, Craig, to steal a car with him), as well as those with people who insult, abuse, meddle, and lie.

Research has conceptualized friendship as either highly positive or toxic. But some researchers speculate that communication in friendship has both negative and positive potential (Rose, Carlson, & Waller, 2007). One study examining children's and adolescents' same-sex friendships, found that girls who engaged in what the researchers called *co-rumination,* or excessive discussion of personal problems, had simultaneous positive and negative outcomes. On the positive side, co-rumination increased the girls' feelings of closeness. However, it also increased the girls' depression and anxiety. Boys in the study did not experience depression and anxiety from co-rumination, but did develop increased feelings of closeness with their friend.

Sometimes positive outcomes in relationships are accomplished by communicating in traditionally frowned-upon ways. For instance, gossip may be seen as both aversive and bonding (Bergmann, 1993). Gossip is associated with relational ruin when it's negative and communicated to strangers, but acts as "social glue" when it's positive, communicated to friends, or both (Turner, Mazur, Wendel, & Winslow, 2003). Although gossip has a dark side, it may also be a way to establish intimacy. Sharing secrets together is a way to advance a relationship and to build cohesion and emotional ties (Rosnow, 2001).

The same claim has been made about swearing (Hughes & Heuman, 2006; Winters & Duck, 2001). If Rusty and Kim swear a lot around each other, they may be signaling that they have a friendship that defies social conventions. In general our society considers swearing an undesirable behavior. But when it performs this bonding function, swearing is a positive behavior for friendships.

Friendships, then, are close relationships in which communication plays an important role. Friends communicate social support, solidarity, and positive affect, as well as engage in other daily interactions that can intensify feelings of connection. But not all communication in friendship is positive; some communication behaviors may have both bad and good results. We now turn to communication in another important type of close relationship: the romantic relationship.

Romantic Relationships

A great deal of research interest centers on the romantic relationships of dating and marriage. These relationships are similar to friendships in that they are voluntary, but they differ because they involve sexual and romantic feelings and because they are not assumed to be as fragile as friendships.

Although we know that couples break up and divorce, romantic partners are supposed to exhibit commitment. Heterosexual romantic partners can demonstrate this commitment through the social, legal, or religious institution of marriage. Because same-sex marriage is not legal in most states, this option is not available to some gay and lesbian partners. Many of these couples display their intention to have a permanent relationship through a commitment ceremony.

As we discussed earlier, relational scripts influence communication in romantic relationships. Some research (e.g. Guerrero & Bachman, 2006; Knobloch, Miller, Bond, & Mannone, 2007; Levine, Aune, & Park, 2006) also suggests that individual differences affect how we communicate in romantic relationships. For example, one set of researchers found that an individual's love style—passionate, stable, playful, other-centered, logical, or obsessive—made a difference in three communication practices during three stages of a

© Colin Young-Wolff/PhotoEdit

IPC *in the* News

A recent article in the *Richmond Times-Dispatch* cautions daters of the Internet age not to skip through the age-old courtship steps that are meant to get couples off to the right start. Specifically, online meeting and dating moves quickly, and people can establish a false sense of intimacy early in relationships. Additionally, many dating sites encourage users to narrow their partner choices through specific sets of criteria, allowing people to "meet" only a limited number of people and eliminating the possibility of compatible but unexpected coupling. Although the articles mentions that online dating is still frowned upon by some, the relational experts cited in the article don't recommend ceasing the practice, just slowing it down. Says director of the Family Institute of Virginia Dr. Joan Winter, daters should consider meeting and courting online a precursor to a traditional meeting and courtship, not a replacement for going through the steps of courting in person.

Kapsidelis, K. (2008, January 27). Surfing for love. *Richmond Times-Dispatch*.

relationship: opening lines for picking up someone as a potential partner, intensification strategies for moving a relationship along to greater intimacy, and secret tests for checking on the state of a developing relationship. For example, if Pablo believes love is playful, he'll use cute, flippant pick up lines like "God must be a thief. He stole the stars from the skies and put them in your eyes" (Levine et al., p. 478) to initiate a relationship, sexual intimacy to intensify it, and indirect secret tests like joking and hinting to check the state of a romance. If Pablo is in a relationship with Adele, who has a logical love style, his pick up lines, intensification strategies, and secret tests may not be successful because Adele will have different communication preferences.

Other researchers (Guerrero & Bachman, 2006) found that how secure a person is affects how they communicate to maintain their romantic relationships. People who are more secure tend to use more positive or prosocial behaviors. For example, if Amina is a secure person who's not anxious about relationships, she'll be likely to try to maintain her relationship with Jerome by saying "I love you," touching Jerome affectionately, complimenting him, and being open in her conversations with him. A different group of researchers (Knobloch et al.) made a similar finding that married people who are uncertain about their marriages tend to interpret conversations pessimistically, whereas those who are more confident in their marriages draw more favorable conclusions.

One type of romantic relationship to receive research attention is the long distance dating relationship (LDDR), or a couple who continues to maintain a romantic relationship while separated geographically. While it would seem that being apart would strain LDDRs, some research has found that LDDRs are more stable than dating couples who are geographically close. This finding is explained by the fact that people in LDDRs engage in more romantic idealization of one another and their relationship ("he's the best boyfriend;" "we have a relationship that can stand anything") than couples who live near each other (Stafford & Merolla, 2007). This study also found that although LDDRs are more stable while the couple is apart, they often end when the couple becomes geographically close again.

Although the vast majority of research on romantic relationships has studied white heterosexual couples, some research focuses on gay and lesbian couples (Suter, Bergen, Dass, & Durham, 2006) and interracial couples (Thompson & Collier, 2006). Although many communication issues are the same across all romantic relationships, these relationships must also contend with issues of discrimination and identity. In both gay and interracial relationships, the partners are aware of social disapproval. In some instances, they are alienated from friends and families. They are required to consider social and historical forces concerning race and sexual identity in ways that other couples are not. Their communication behaviors reflect these concerns. Danica (a Black woman) tells her partner Brad (a White man) that they need to be vigilant when they're visiting his hometown because many of the people there are racist. Brad responds with some strategies they can use to combat any racist comments they might get on the visit.

Romantic relationships and the communication that occurs within them vary widely. Cultural scripts guide how people conduct conversations in romantic relationships, but, other factors influence communication in these relationships, too. These factors include individual differences like love style, and the degree of security or certainty about the relationship, as well as contextual considerations like geographic distance and social sanctions. We now address communication in families.

Families

Families are unique close relationships for many reasons. First, their ties can be voluntary or involuntary. Some families consist of people who come together of their own free will, such as married partners, communes, or *intentional families* who band together by choice rather than by blood relationships. But many family members have relationships with others they did not choose, such as parents, grandparents, aunts, uncles, siblings, and so forth.

Families are also distinctive because for many members the close relationship is life-long. Some research (Serewicz, Dickson, Morrison, & Poole, 2007) indicates that even though we expect children to leave the nest as they reach adulthood, continuity of relationships with family members is just as important as increasing autonomy. Finally, unlike friendship or dating relationships, family is a close relationship that receives social, cultural, and legal sanctions through, for example, marriage, adoption, and inheritance.

There is some controversy in the research (see for example, Galvin, 2006; Floyd, Mikkelson, & Judd, 2006) concerning how to define a family. Some researchers (e.g., Floyd et al.) advocate the definition of family as a "socially, legally, and genetically oriented relationship" (p. 37). Others (e.g., Galvin) argue for allowing functions like communication to define the family. In other words, if a group of people function like a family by sharing affection and resources, and refer to themselves as a family, then they are a family. We agree with the more inclusive, communication-based definition.

One communication practice that's been examined as unique to families is storytelling. **Family stories**, or those bits of lore about family members and activities that are told and retold, have been seen as a way for members to construct a sense of family identity and meaning (Kellas, 2005). Some researchers argue that families don't just tell stories, but that storytelling is a way of creating a family (Langellier & Peterson, 2006). When Marie brings her new friend, Danielle, home to meet her parents, the stories that are told to Danielle are a way to bring the family alive for her and to integrate Danielle into the family fold.

Family stories are often pleasurable and entertaining, but they can sometimes serve as cautionary tales about family members who went astray in some way. Phil recalls hearing the story about his great-Uncle Thomas who lost the family fortune by gambling. Phil always got the impression that the story was told repeatedly to warn his generation to keep working hard and avoid developing bad habits.

Another important family communication practice is the **ritual**, or a repeated patterned communication event in a family's life. Rituals can take three forms: *everyday interactions* (for example, the Gilbert family always says grace before eating dinner together), *traditions* (for instance, Rollie and Elizabeth mark their anniversary each year by eating dinner at McDonald's because they met when they both worked there together), and *celebrations* (for example, Meyer and Scott ask their children to each say one thing that they're thankful for every year at Thanksgiving dinner). Celebrations differ from traditions because they involve holidays that are shared throughout a culture as opposed to traditions, which are practices that evolve in a specific family.

We now turn our attention to ways researchers have tried to explain communication in close relationships.

Explaining Communication in Close Relationships

Given the importance of communication in close relationships, it's understandable that research provides many theories to explain it. In fact, trying to explain communication and our relationships is something everyone spends a lot of time doing. We're "naïve psychologists" (Heider, 1958) engaging in "implicit theory making." We often ask why relationships develop the way they do and why some communication helps relationship woes and other communication makes them worse. In this section, we review the basic tenets of four major theories advanced by researchers.

Systems Theory

Systems theory (von Bertalanffy, 1968) compares relationships to living systems (like cells or the body), which have six important properties:

family stories

Bits of lore about family members and activities that are told and retold as a way for family members to construct a sense of family identity and meaning.

ritual

A repeated patterned communication event in a family's life.

- Wholeness
- Interdependence
- Hierarchy
- Boundaries or openness
- Calibration or feedback
- Equifinality

Systems researchers find that understanding how each of these six properties operates allows them to understand how communication in relationships works. Let's consider each of the properties.

Wholeness means that you can't understand a system by taking it apart and understanding each of its parts in isolation from one another. Wholeness indicates that knowing Bert and Ernie separately is not the same as knowing about the relationship between Bert and Ernie. The relationship between people is like a third entity that extends beyond each of the people individually. If you think of a specific relationship that you are in, the concept of wholeness becomes quite clear. The way you act and communicate in that relationship is probably different from the way you act and communicate in other relationships. The other person's reactions, contributions, and perceptions of you make a difference in how you behave, and vice versa. Further, the way you perceive the relationship between the two of you matters. If you are longtime friends with someone, you don't have to explain things to them the same way you might to someone who is a newer friend of yours. Wholeness tells us that just because Karen knows Cara and Susie individually doesn't mean she knows them *in relationship* to each other.

Interdependence builds on the notion of wholeness by asserting that members of systems depend on each other and are affected by one another. If Kyle's sister is injured in a car accident, his life is affected because of his relationship with her. When you talk to the people in your close relationships, you monitor their behavior and respond to it—you are affected by their shifts in mood and tone, and your communication shifts accordingly.

Hierarchy states that these shifts and accommodations don't exist in a vacuum. Kyle's relationship with his sister is embedded in the larger system of his family (all of the members of which are interdependent), and his family is embedded in the larger system of his extended family, his neighborhood, his culture, and so forth. Lower-level systems are called **subsystems**, and higher-levels are called **suprasystems**. Kyle and his sister form a subsystem of his family. Kyle's neighborhood is a suprasystem around his family. (See Figure 10.2 on page 344.)

Boundaries or openness refers to the fact that hierarchy is formed by creating boundaries around each separate system (Kyle and his sister, the family as a whole, and so forth). However, human systems are inherently open, and information passes through these boundaries. (Therefore, some researchers call this element "openness," and some call it "boundaries.") For example, Marsha and Hal are best friends who have a very close relationship, and they

wholeness

A principle that states that we can't fully understand a system by simply picking it apart and understanding each of its parts in isolation from one another.

hierarchy

A principle that states that all relationships are embedded within larger systems.

subsystems

Lower-level systems of relationship, such as a sibling relationship within a family.

suprasystems

Higher-level systems of relationship, such as a neighborhood consisting of several families.

boundaries or openness

A systems principle referring to the fact that hierarchy is formed by creating boundaries around each separate system (e.g., a brother and sister, the family as a whole, and so forth). However, human systems are inherently open, which means that information passes through these boundaries. Therefore, some researchers call this principle "openness," and some call it "boundaries."

Figure 10.2 Hierarchy as a systems principle

Kyle's country

Kyle's state

Kyle's neighborhood

Kyle's family

Kyle and his sister

Kyle

tell each other things that they don't tell their families. This closeness forms the boundary around their relationship. Yet if Marsha confides something to Hal that he finds disturbing, like that she is abusing drugs or feeling suicidal, Hal might ask members of his family or other friends for help. In so doing, Hal would expand the boundaries of their subsystem. Boundaries exist to keep information in the subsystem, but they also act to keep some information out of the subsystem. For instance, if Terry's mother doesn't like her boyfriend, Ron, Terry might work to keep that information away from the subsystem she and Ron create.

Calibration centers on how systems set their parameters, check on themselves, and self-correct. For example, Maggie and her grandmother have a close relationship, and the two of them form a subsystem of Maggie's extended family. When Maggie was 10, she and her grandmother calibrated their system by setting a weekly lunch date. As Maggie got older, she found it harder to meet her grandmother every Saturday for lunch because she wanted to do more activities with friends. She expressed this to her grandmother, and they **recalibrated** (or reset the rules of their system) by changing their lunch date to once a month. When systems experience such a change, it's a result of **positive feedback** (or feedback that's change producing). If they stay the same, the feedback is judged as **negative feedback** (or feedback that maintains the status quo).

Table 10.2 System properties and communication

Property	Communication outcome
Wholeness	The Thompson family is considered outgoing and funny. Ella Thompson is quiet and shy.
Interdependence	I can't talk to you when you act like that!
Hierarchy	Jake talks to his son, Marcus, about how his problems at work are making it hard for him to spend time with Marcus.
Boundaries or openness	Frieda tells a secret to her sister, Laya, and trusts her not to tell the rest of the family.
Calibration	Hap tells Miles they can't play basketball every Wednesday because he needs to spend more time with his son.
Equifinality	Laura and Roy are happily married, and they tell each other everything. Nadine and Bob are happily married, and they keep many things private and don't confide in each other as much.

Equifinality means the ability to achieve the same goals (or ends) by a variety of means. For instance, you may have some friends with whom you spend a lot of time and other friends with whom you spend less time. Some of your friends may be people you play tennis with, and others may be those you like to go to movies with. Each of these friendships may be close, but you become close (and maintain your closeness) in different ways.

Table 10.2 illustrates how each of the six properties of systems theory relates to communication behaviors. Systems theory doesn't explain all communication with our relational partners; it isn't specific enough to give us answers to questions like why some couples argue more than others or why some communication in friendships is more satisfying than others. However, it does give us an overall impression of how relationships work and how communication behaviors function within relationships.

Dialectics Theory

A different explanation for communication in close relationships comes from dialectics theory, which we discussed in Chapter 8. Dialectics focuses on the tensions relational partners feel as a result of desiring two opposing things at once. Dialectic thinking rejects "either–or" approaches in favor of "both–and." In Chapter 8 we talked about one specific tension or dialectic: openness

equifinality

The ability to achieve the same goals (or ends) by a variety of means.

How's this sound? "Man of steel seeks woman of Teflon for non-stick relationship. No women of silicone, please."

© DAN PIRARO. BIZARRO.COM 8.24.04 Dist. by King Features

(disclosing) and protection (keeping silent). Now we'll discuss other tensions that people experience in close relationships.

Along with openness and protection, the most common tensions in relationships are autonomy and connection, and novelty and predictability. The contradiction between **autonomy and connection** centers on our desire to be independent or autonomous while simultaneously wanting to feel a connection with our partner. For example, this tension is apparent when Desiree wants to be with her own friends while also wanting to spend time with her boyfriend, Shane. The tension between **novelty and predictability** manifests in our simultaneous desires for excitement and stability. For example, Malcolm feels bored with the everyday routines he's established in his relationship with Tom, but he also feels comforted and reassured by them. It's scary to leave familiar routines, even when you might find them tedious. These three basic contradictions or dialectics are all seen as dynamic. This means that the interplay between the two opposites permeates the life of a relationship and is never fully resolved.

In addition to these, some other dialectics are found specifically in friendships (Rawlins, 1992). They include the following:

- Judgment and acceptance
- Affection and instrumentality
- Public and private
- Ideal and real

The tension between **judgment and acceptance** involves criticizing a friend as opposed to accepting them. People are often torn between offering (unwanted) advice and accepting a friend's behavior. For instance, if Maria has a friend, Josh, who is dating someone Maria thinks is wrong for him, or someone who is dishonest or untrustworthy, should she offer her opinion or simply accept Josh's choice? Most people want both things simultaneously; they want to be able to make and hear judgments, but they also want unconditional acceptance. The next dialectic, **affection and instrumentality**, poses a tension between framing your friendship with someone as an end in itself (affection) or seeing it as a means to another end (instrumentality). This dialectic

---

autonomy and connection dialectic

The tension between our desire to be independent or autonomous while simultaneously wanting to feel a connection with our partner.

novelty and predictability dialectic

Our simultaneous, opposing desires for excitement and stability in our relationships.

judgment and acceptance dialectic

Our desire to criticize a friend as opposed to accepting a friend for who he or she is.

affection and instrumentality dialectic

The tension between framing a friendship with someone as an end in itself (affection) or seeing it as a means to another end (instrumentality).

Table 10.4 Knapp's model of relationship development

Coming together	
Stage	**Sample communication**
Initiating	"Hi, how are you?"
Experimenting	"Do you like water polo?"
Intensifying	"Let's take a vacation together this summer. We can play water polo!"
Integrating	"You are the best friend I could ever have!"
Bonding	"Let's wear our team shirts to the party. I want everyone to know we're on the same team!"

Coming apart	
Stage	**Sample communication**
Differentiating	"I am surprised that you supported a Republican. I am a longtime Democrat."
Circumscribing	"Maybe we'd be better off if we didn't talk about politics."
Stagnating	"Wow, I could have predicted you'd say that!"
Avoiding	"I have too much homework to meet you for coffee."
Terminating	"I think we shouldn't hang out together anymore. It's just not fun now."

The model answers the following questions: "Are there regular and systematic patterns of communication that suggest stages on the road to a more intimate relationship? Are there similar patterns and stages that characterize the deterioration of relationships?" (Knapp & Vangelisti, 2000, p. 36). The model provides five stages of coming together and five stages of coming apart. See Table 10.4 for a summary of the model.

The model is useful for all kinds of relationships because it provides for relationships that end after only a couple of stages as well as relationships that do not move beyond an early stage (Knapp & Vangelisti, 2005). In addition, the model explains the movement of friendships as well as love relationships. As you read about the stages, try to imagine how they work in a variety of relationships.

Some people have criticized all stage models for presenting a linear picture of relationship development. These critics note that relational development doesn't happen neatly in stages and that the model doesn't clarify what happens when one partner moves to a new stage and the other doesn't. For example, one partner may want to terminate the relationship while the other resists. One study (Buchanan, O'Hair, & Becker, 2006) examines what strategies married partners tried to resist termination, including negativity, pointing out ways they're bonded, expressing commitment, and using violence in some way. All of these strategies proved unsuccessful—all of the respondents were divorced.

Stage models simplify a complicated process. Each stage may contain some behavior from other, earlier stages, and people sometimes slide back and forth between stages as they interact in their relationship. Thus, stage models give us a snapshot of the process of relationship development, but they don't tell the entire story. In the following sections, we briefly discuss each of the stages in the model.

Initiating

This stage is where a relationship begins. In the **initiating stage**, two people notice one another and indicate to each other that they are interested in making contact: "I notice you, and I think you're noticing me, too. Let's talk and see where it goes." Initiation depends on attraction, which can be seen as either short-term or long-term.

Short-term attraction, a judgment of relationship potential, propels us into the initiation stage. **Long-term attraction**, which makes you want to continue a relationship and move through the subsequent stages, sustains and maintains relationships. Sometimes the things that attract you to someone in the short term may be the things that turn you off in the long term. For example, Marge may have initially struck up a friendship with Anita because she saw Anita as outgoing and friendly. However, later in their relationship, Marge may come to resent how much Anita talks to others because it means less time for the two of them to interact.

Both types of attraction are based on several elements, such as physical attractiveness, charisma, physical closeness, similarity, complementary needs, positive outcomes, and reciprocation. People are attracted to others who fit their cultural ideal of attractiveness, but they are more likely to initiate relationships with others who tend to match their own level of attractiveness (Cash & Derlega, 1978; Hinsz, 1989; White, 1980). In other words, we feel more comfortable talking with people who are about as physically attractive as we see ourselves to be. We also like people who are confident and exude charisma. Furthermore, it's more likely that we'll be attracted to those who are in physical proximity to us than to those who are more distant, because it's more difficult to enter the initiating stage with someone who is far away.

We are also motivated to initiate conversations with those who share some of our own attributes, values, and opinions. A study investigating why people are attracted to one another, found that a "likes-attract" rule was much stronger than an "opposites-attract" rule for heterosexual couples in Western cultures (Buston & Emlen, 2003). Yet, too much similarity can be boring, so we may seek a partner with some attributes that complement ours as well. For example, if Chris is quiet and Glenn is talkative, they may want to initiate a conversation because they complement each other. Finally, we are attracted to others who seem attracted to us, or who reciprocate our inter-

initiating stage

The first stage in the coming together part of Knapp's model of relationship development, in which two people notice each other and indicate to each other that they are interested in making contact.

short-term attraction

A judgment of relationship potential that propels us into initiating a relationship.

long-term attraction

Judgment of a relationship that makes us want to continue a relationship after initiating it. This attraction sustains and maintains relationships.

est. For instance, when Renny smiles at Natalie at a party and she doesn't smile back, Renny probably won't go any further with the relationship.

Some of our relationships stay in the initiating stage. You may see the same person often in a place you frequent, such as a supermarket, bookstore, or coffee shop. Each time you see this person, you might exchange smiles and pleasantries. You may have short, ritualized conversations about the weather or other topics but never move on to any of the other stages in the model. Thus, you could have a long-term relationship that never moves out of initiating.

Experimenting

In the second stage, **experimenting**, people become acquainted by gathering information about one another. They engage in **small talk**—interactions that are relaxed, pleasant, uncritical, and casual. Through small talk, people learn about one another, reduce their uncertainties, find topics that they might wish to spend more time discussing, "test the waters" to see if they want to develop the relationship further, and maintain a sense of community.

Many of our relationships stay in the experimenting stage (Knapp & Vangelisti, 2005). We have many friends whom we know through small talk but not at a deeper level. If you see a friend in the coffee shop and go beyond "Hi, it sure is nice to see sunshine today" to small talk, you have deepened the relationship some, but you still have kept it at a low level of commitment. Further, even people in close relationships spend time in this stage, perhaps in an effort to understand their partner more, to pass the time, or to avoid uncomfortable feelings stirred up by a more intense conversation.

Intensifying

This stage begins to move the relationship to a closeness not seen in the previous stages. **Intensifying** refers to the deepening of intimacy in the relationship. During this stage, partners self-disclose, forms of address become more informal, and people may use nicknames or terms of endearment to address one another ("Hi, honey"). Relational partners begin to speak of a "we" or "us," as in "We like to go to the basketball games" or "It'll be nice for us to get a break from studying and go for a walk."

In this stage, people begin to develop their own language based on private symbols for past experiences or knowledge of each other's habits, desires, and beliefs. For instance, Missy and her mother still say "hmmm" to each other, because that's what Missy said when she was little to mean "I want more." And Neil says, "It's just like walking on a rocky path" when he wants Ana to do something because when they first became friends, he made Ana take a walk along a path scattered with rocks when Ana wanted to go the movies instead.

Further, this stage is marked by more direct statements of commitment— "I have never had a better friend than you," or "I am so happy being with you." Often these statements are met with reciprocal comments—"Me neither," or "Same here." In intensifying, the partners become more sophisticated nonverbally. They are able to read each other's nonverbal cues, may

experimenting stage

A stage in the coming together part of Knapp's model of relationship development in which two people become acquainted by gathering information about each other.

small talk

Conversational interactions that are relaxed, pleasant, uncritical, and casual.

intensifying stage

A stage in the coming together part of Knapp's model of relationship development in which the intimacy between the partners intensifies.

replace some verbalizations with a touch, and may mirror one another's non-verbal cues—how they stand, gesture, dress, and so forth may become more similar. One way Candi intensified her friendship with Tricia was to stop dressing like her old friends and to start wearing clothes and makeup that made her look like her new friend.

Integrating

In this fourth stage, the partners seem to coalesce. **Integrating** has also been called "coupling" (Davis, 1973) because it represents the two people forming a clear identity as a couple. This coupling is often acknowledged by the pair's social circles; they cultivate friends together, and are treated as a unit by their friends. They are invited to places together, and information shared with one is expected to be shared with the other.

Sometimes the partners designate common property. They may pick a song to be "our song," open a joint bank account, buy a dog, or move into an apartment together. In our case as authors of this book, coauthoring a series of books together has created a couple identity for us. We are often referred to together, and if people ask one of us to do something (such as make a presentation at a convention), they usually assume that the other will come along as well.

Bonding

The final stage in the coming together part of the model is **bonding**, which refers to a public commitment of the relationship. Bonding is easier in some types of relationships than in others. For heterosexual couples, the marriage ceremony is a traditional bonding ritual. Having a bonding ritual provides a certain social sanction for the relationship.

Other relationships don't have a well-recognized ritual to gain social sanction or public recognition. However, because bonding is important to many people, some have worked to create ceremonies. Examples include commitment ceremonies for gay and lesbian couples, naming ceremonies for new babies to welcome them to the family, and initiation ceremonies to welcome new "sisters" or "brothers" to sororities and fraternities.

integrating stage

A stage in the coming together part of Knapp's model of relationship development in which two partners form a clear identity as a couple.

bonding stage

The final stage in the coming together part of Knapp's model of relationship development, in which partners make a public commitment to their relationship.

Differentiating

The first stage in the coming apart section of the model, **differentiating** refers to beginning to notice ways in which the partners differ. In this stage, individuality is highlighted. This is unlike the coming together stages, which featured the partners' similarities. The most dramatic episodes of differentiating involve conflict, discussed in Chapter 9. However, people can differentiate without engaging in conflict. For example, the following seemingly inconsequential comment exemplifies differentiation: "Oh, you like that sweater? I never would have thought you'd wear sweaters with Christmas trees on them. I guess our taste in clothes is more different than I thought."

People switch from "we" to "I" in this stage and talk more about themselves as individuals than as part of a couple. According to the model, this stage is the beginning of the relationship's unraveling process. However, we know that relationships can oscillate between differentiation and some of the coming together stages, like intensifying. No two people can remain in a coming together stage such as intensifying, integrating, or bonding without experiencing some differentiating.

Circumscribing

The next stage, **circumscribing**, refers to restraining communication behaviors so fewer topics are raised (for fear of conflict) and more issues are out of bounds. The couple interacts less. This stage is characterized by silences and comments like "I don't want to talk about that anymore," "Let's not go there," and "It's none of your business." Again, relationships in all stages of the model may experience some taboo topics or behaviors that are typical of circumscribing. But when relationships enter circumscribing (in other words, if the biggest proportion of their communication is of this type), that is a sign of a decaying relationship. If measures aren't taken to repair the situation—sitting down and talking about why there's a problem, going to counseling, taking a vacation, or some other remedy—the model shows that people enter the next stage.

Stagnating

The third stage of coming apart, **stagnating**, consists of extending circumscribing so far that the couple no longer talks much. They express the feeling that there is no use to talk because they already know what the other will say. "There's no point in bringing this up—I know she won't like the idea" is a common theme during this stage. People feel "stuck," and their communication is draining, awkward, stylized, and unsatisfying.

Each partner may engage in **imagined conversations** (Honeycutt, 2003), where one partner plays the parts of both partners in a mental rehearsal of the negative communication that characterizes this stage. Me: "I want to go visit my parents." Me in Role of Partner: "Well, I'm too busy to go with you." Me: "You never want to do stuff with my family." Me in Role of Partner: "That may be true, but you certainly can't stand my family!" After this

differentiating stage

The first stage in the coming apart section of Knapp's model of relationship development, in which two people begin to notice ways in which they differ.

circumscribing stage

A stage in the coming apart section of Knapp's model of relationship development in which two people's communication behaviors are restrained so that fewer topics are raised (for fear of conflict), more issues are out of bounds, and they interact less.

stagnating stage

A stage in the coming apart section of Knapp's model of relationship development in which circumscribing is extended so far that a couple no longer talks much except in the most routinized ways.

imagined conversation

A conversation with oneself in which one partner plays the parts of both partners in a mental rehearsal.

rehearsal, people usually decide it's not worth the effort to engage in the conversation for real.

Avoiding

If a relationship stagnates for too long, the partners may decide that the relationship is unpleasant. As a result, they move to **avoiding**, a stage where partners try to stay out of the same physical environment. Partners make excuses for why they can't see one another ("Sorry, I have too much work to go out tonight;" "I'll be busy all week;" or "I've got to go home for the weekend"). They may vary their habits so that they do not run into their partner as they used to. For example, if people used to meet at a particular restaurant or a certain spot on campus, they change their routines and no longer stop by these places.

Sometimes it isn't possible to physically avoid a partner. If a couple is married and unable to afford two residences, or if siblings still live in their parents' home, it's difficult for the partners to be completely separate. In such cases, partners in the avoiding stage simply ignore one another or make a tacit agreement to segregate their living quarters as much as possible. For example, the married couple may sleep in separate rooms, and the siblings may come into the den at different times of day. When partners in the avoiding stage accidentally run into one another, they turn away without speaking.

Terminating

This stage comes after the relational partners have decided, either jointly or individually, to part permanently. **Terminating** refers to the process of ending a relationship. Some relationships enter terminating almost immediately: You meet someone at a party, go through initiating and experimenting, and then decide you don't want to see them anymore, so you move to terminating. Other relationships go through all or most of the stages before terminating. Some relationships endure in one stage or another and never go through terminating. And other relationships go through terminating and then begin again (people remarry and estranged friends reunite). Further, some relationships terminate in one form and then begin again in a redefined way. For

avoiding stage

A stage in the coming apart section of Knapp's model of relationship development in which two partners stay away from each other because they feel that being together is unpleasant.

terminating stage

The last stage in the coming apart section of Knapp's model of relationship development, in which a relationship is ending.

example, when Scott and Virginia get divorced, they end their relationship as married partners. However, because they have two children, they redefine their relationship and become friends.

Terminating a relationship can be simple ("We have to end this") or complicated (involving lots of discussion and even the intervention of third parties like counselors, mediators, and attorneys). It may happen suddenly or drag out over a long time. It can be accomplished with a lot of talk that reflects on the life of the relationship and the reasons for terminating it, or it can be accomplished with relatively little or no discussion.

For more about Knapp's relational stages model and information about strategies for terminating relationships, use your online Resource Center for *Understanding Interpersonal Communication* to access **Interactive Activity 10.3: Knapp's Relational Stages Model** under the resources for Chapter 10.

Choices in Communicating in Close Relationships

This section presents several ways to improve communication in close relationships. Because many factors affect relationship development, we are necessarily broad in offering these suggestions. As we have emphasized in this chapter, communicating with people in close relationships is our source of greatest pleasure and greatest grief.

Communication Skills for Beginning Relationships

Beginning a relationship requires a fair amount of skill, although you may not

Ethics & Choice

Connie and Paul Miller had been married for four years, and were very happy. They wanted children, but after trying unsuccessfully to conceive for almost a year, they were discouraged. They finally consulted a fertility expert, who told them the sad news that they'd never be able to conceive because Paul's sperm count was too low. However, the doctor did offer one intriguing possibility to the couple—a sperm donor. If they chose this option, Connie could carry the baby and give birth. They went home to think about it.

After they'd talked about it endlessly, they still weren't sure what to do. They decided to ask their family and friends what they thought of such a method of conception. They were a little afraid that they'd be seen as strange or freakish if they had a child using this technology. They knew that the procedure was common, but they didn't personally know anyone who had used a sperm donor, and the idea still seemed like science fiction to them.

At a family gathering one evening, Connie and Paul made seemingly offhand comments about how a friend was considering conception via sperm donor, and they were happy to find that no one seemed to consider the prospect too weird. The day after the family dinner, Paul got a call at work from his brother, Lucas. Lucas told Paul that he wondered if Paul and Connie were thinking about using a sperm donor to conceive. Paul was actually relieved that Lucas knew the truth, and by the end of their conversation, Lucas had volunteered to be the donor.

Connie and Paul accepted Lucas's offer gratefully, and soon Connie was carrying a child who was born healthy and perfect. The baby, whom they named Hannah, was a pure delight, and the Millers were completely happy. Yet, as Hannah got older, Connie began to wonder whether they should tell her that half of her genetic makeup was contributed by her uncle, not Paul. At first, they hadn't planned to tell her. Lucas hadn't asked them to do so, and he was very comfortable in his role as Hannah's uncle. Because Lucas and Paul were brothers, Hannah resembled her father, and there didn't seem to be any obvious reasons to make the disclosure.

However, lately Connie had been wondering if keeping a secret so big might cause some problems down the road for her family. She thought that Hannah had a right to know how she came into the world. Yet, Connie worried about how telling Hannah the truth might change the relationships among herself, Hannah, Paul, and Lucas, not to mention Paul's parents, who hadn't been told. Things seemed to be going so well, and Connie didn't want to disrupt her family's harmony.

(Continues)

think about developing these skills. Most people meet new people fairly frequently, and they don't consciously think about how they go about striking up conversations and cultivating new friends. One study (Douglas, 1987) examined the skills needed to initiate relationships; these techniques are described below.

Paul was very proud of his daughter, and Connie definitely didn't want to change how they regarded each other. Wrestling with this decision was keeping her up at night. What do you think Connie should do in this situation? How should she broach the subject with Paul, Lucas, and her in-laws? What are the implications of keeping family secrets? Do you agree that keeping secrets creates a toxic situation that erodes trust and ultimately damages relationships? Is it ethical to tell something that you know will hurt someone else, at least in the short run? In answering these questions, what ethical system of communication informs your decision (categorical imperative, utilitarianism, ethic of care, golden mean, significant choice)?

 Go to your online Resource Center for *Understanding Interpersonal Communication* to access an interactive version of this scenario under the resources for Chapter 10. The interactive version of this scenario allows you to choose an appropriate response to this dilemma and then see what consequences your choice brings about. You can also compare your answers to the questions at the end of the scenario to those provided by the authors and, if requested, email your response to your instructor.

networking

In relational development, finding out information about a person from a third party.

offering

Putting ourselves in a good position for another to approach us in a social situation.

approaching

Providing nonverbal signals that indicate we'd like to initiate contact with another person, such as going up to a person or smiling in that person's direction.

Networking

Networking means finding out information about the person from a third party. Easing into a relationship with the help of a third person means that you're behaving efficiently and in a socially acceptable fashion.

Offering

Offering means putting yourself in a good position for another to approach you. If you sit near a person you'd like to get to know better, or walk along the same route that they do, you're putting proximity to work for you.

Approaching

Approaching means actually going up to a person or smiling in that person's direction to give a signal that you would like to initiate contact. Approaching allows the relationship to begin, with both parties involved in some interaction.

Sustaining

Sustaining means behaving in a way that keeps the initial conversation going. Asking appropriate questions is a way to employ sustaining.

Affinity Seeking

Affinity seeking means emphasizing the commonalities you think you share with the other person. Sometimes affinity seeking goes hand in hand with asking appropriate questions; you first ask questions to determine areas of common interest or experience, and then you comment on them. "Do you like reality shows?" "No kidding? I'm a big fan, too." According to research, people use a variety of affinity-seeking strategies to get others to like them (Bell & Daly, 1984) (see Table 10.5 for a summary of their strategies).

CASEinPOINT

Matthew Leone had loved computers for as long as he could remember. When he was little, he'd had a Game Boy.

As he'd gotten older, his father had let him use his office computer so Matthew could download pictures of antique cars. Throughout college, Matthew not only emailed nearly everyone in his life, but also had a MySpace page where he uploaded pictures of such diverse events as his sister's wedding and his dog's birthday party. It was clear that Matthew loved computers, and as a cell phone junkie, iPod user, and DVD collector, he was also a lover of technology in general.

Matthew was graduating in the spring, so he spent the month of February working on his résumé and applying for jobs. He knew that his degree in economics and his 3.4 GPA would help him secure a good job, and he felt especially confident about his prospects after reading a glowing recommendation letter from one of his professors. Although Matthew's credentials were outstanding, he couldn't figure out why he wasn't being contacted for interviews. He sent his résumé and cover letter to all sorts of companies—large and small, public and private—but never scored even one interview.

He was confused and concerned, and it wasn't long before he emailed his best friend, Anna, to ask her what she thought.

Anna wrote that she was also surprised that Matthew hadn't been contacted for any interviews. As she rambled on in her email, she made one observation that stopped Matthew in his tracks. She told Matthew that she'd read a newspaper article about how "controversial" material on MySpace had prevented a man in Florida from getting a job. Apparently, the company the man had applied to had seen some damning pictures of him in a neo-Nazi jacket. Matthew immediately thought of the pictures he'd put on his website of his spring break vacation in Cancun, Mexico. He didn't finish reading the rest of Anna's email. He went immediately to his MySpace page and saw that, indeed, there were several provocative pictures of him drinking. In one picture taken in a bar, his friend Damien poured beer down Matthew's throat. Matthew sat motionless in front of his computer. Certainly, he thought, plenty of potential employers have been drunk and

Use your online Resource Center for *Understanding Interpersonal Communication* to watch a video clip of Matthew.

> Access the resources for Chapter 11 and select "Matthew" to watch the video (it takes a minute for the video to load). > As you watch the video, think about Matthew's situation. In what ways could he modify his online presence to make him look more attractive to potential employers? > You can respond to this and other analysis questions, and then click "Done" to compare your answers with those provided by the authors.

must know that these pictures were taken for fun. Still, he no longer wondered why he wasn't being called for interviews. Over his lifetime, Matthew Leone had loved technology. But now this technology was influencing his life in ways he had never imagined or considered.

We have been using technology to communicate for more than 100 years. One technology, among many, seems to have ridden the technological wave for centuries now: the telephone. The invention of the telephone in 1875 allowed people to talk to a next-door neighbor or a distant cousin. It was a major invention at the time and today, the phone has undergone a transformation that even its inventor, Alexander Graham Bell, could never have imagined. Although "land lines" are a still a popular option for many households, it's likely that most people you know no longer have to untangle a telephone cord, use a rotary dial, or figure out if the phone is a "wall mount." Indeed, the telephone of yesteryear has largely been supplanted by the cell phone, which nearly 140 million people use daily in the United States (http://www.epa.gov/epaoswer/education/pdfs/life-cell.pdf). As Michael Bugeja (2004) notes, "cell phones remind us that we dwell in more than one place at most times, splitting consciousness in parks, cars, schools, restaurants, and malls" (p. B5).

Clearly, the phone—in all of its incarnations—has a rich past and continues to have a vibrant present and future. However, this chapter is about more than the phone. It is about all types of technology. Web feeds, virtual worlds, web conferencing, palm organizers, pagers, beepers, Zunes, instant messaging, and email, are, to name just a few, technological options available to us in our personal and professional lives. The effect that this technology has on our communication with others forms the basis of this chapter.

Just a few years ago, a chapter such as this was not found in an interpersonal communication textbook. But, we believe this topic merits serious consideration in our text now. We cannot ignore the influence that technology has on our conversations and relationships with others. What were once "ground rules" in meeting and conversing with others have changed.

To be sure, with the advent of content aggregation, our technological world will keep changing. **Content aggregation** has been called "information architecture" by some (http://www.usabilitysciences.com/services/field-studies-and-focus-groups/content-aggregation/). David King (www.daweed

content aggregation

The process of collecting online data from different and multiple sources to suit a particular need, such as populating a search engine or preparing digital slides for a presentation.

.blogspot.com) on his blog notes that content aggregation happens in two stages. First, someone writes text or records some audio or video clip and makes that available to the public. Secondly, someone else ends up subscribing to the content and then decides to absorb, study, scan, or delete the content and he or she aggregates (or collates) the content for a particular reason. In a sense, then, when you aggregate content, you are collecting data from different and multiple sources to suit your needs. In its broadest sense, content aggregation occurs when large search engines (e.g. Google, Yahoo!, etc.) aggregate content from other websites, which, interestingly, gives rise to complaints of copyright infringement. On a smaller scale, you might aggregate information from a video, website news stream, and podcast for a classroom presentation on diversity. The notion of content aggregation has been applied to advertising, computer technology, and marketing. As you read the chapter, you will soon see content aggregation as it applies to interpersonal communication.

It appears that many in the United States can't acquire technology fast enough. Our society seems to constantly crave the next level of innovation. We're ready to understand the next version of Windows, the newest Mac upgrade, or the latest video game software. Even toys for the youngest children, such as "Webkinz" (stuffed animals that serve as virtual pets) are linked with technology. We have also come to demand new technology that can be used in conjunction with our current technology. Responding to that need, Steven Jones (1998) comments that "technologies continue to converge" (p. xiv). **Convergence** is the integration of various technologies. We are living in a time where many technologies are morphing and interacting with other technologies. Think about voice-activated computers or cell phones that take pictures. Or, consider the evolution of the phone-fax-answering machine. More

convergence

The integration of various technologies, such as online radio or cell phones with cameras.

Photodisc/Getty Images

Since the advent of the personal computer and the mobile phone in the 1980s, the use of communication technology has exploded. Everywhere you look, someone is accessing email via a wireless connection, texting on a cell phone, or recording an appointment on a handheld organizer. What technologies do you use to communicate with your family, friends, and coworkers?

recently, the convergence of a digital camera, MP3 player, voice recorder, and camcorder resulted in a mobile phone. Finally, some of you may be familiar with PlayStation 2, which converges a CD player, DVD player, and the Internet.

As a society, we have grown accustomed to convergence. We tend to expect technologies to evolve so that they are more efficient and less cumbersome. Many people cannot afford a new technology when it first comes out, so they wait for prices to decrease. For example, when the plasma television came on the market in the 1990s, it cost more than $10,000. In recent years, the price has dropped by almost 80 percent. The lower the cost, the more affordable technology becomes. The more affordable, the more people will own it. And, the more people own it, the more they will tend to use it. And, as affordability occurs, people will use the technology and this same technology finds itself immersed in our conversations and interpersonal relationships.

Once people begin to use technology, that technology not only becomes part of our vocabulary (think of iPod or PlayStation, for instance), but also can affect the relationships we have with others and even our professional lives. In our opening story, Matthew Leone, who grew up with technology, now finds himself being negatively affected by the same technology he embraced so passionately. Although he never envisioned that a MySpace picture could influence his job prospects, technology has now given others the ability to view his (recent) past. Given that potentially millions of people post questionable words and images on social networking sites like MySpace, Matthew will likely not be the only person facing this difficult dilemma. We return to social networking sites later in this chapter.

Technology has the potential to affect who we are, what we do, and how we interact with others. For some, technology serves as a bonding mechanism. Consider the words of Alcestis Oberg (2003), who comments that families who use technology are more likely to remain close:

> My children and I all have moved together into cyberspace. It no longer matters anymore where we are physically. If home is where the heart is, then our hearts have moved into the invisible realm of mobile and wireless communications, and into the ethereal hometown called the Internet. There, we can be—and always will be—together. (p. 11A)

computer-mediated communication (CMC)

The use of various technologies to facilitate communication with others.

technological determinism

A theory that states that technology is irreversible, inevitable, and inescapable.

This chapter examines the role that technology plays in our interpersonal communication. Specifically, we focus on **computer-mediated communication (CMC)**, which refers to the use of various technologies to facilitate communication with others. A valuable theoretical framework to consider as you read this chapter is **technological determinism**, which suggests that technology is irreversible, inevitable, and inescapable (McLuhan & McLuhan, 1988). In other words, it's hard to ignore the impact that communication technologies have had upon us—and, according to technological determinists, we have no choice but to deal with that impact

As pervasive as technology is in our society, we need to remember that people have different technological fields of experience. We cannot operate

"Would you mind talking to me for a while? I forgot my cell phone."

under the assumption that everyone has the same background and technological access. Some of you grew up with a full awareness of, and expertise in, technology. You had at least one computer at home, you know how to set a VCR, you have a contract for a personal cell phone, you've created a blog, subscribed to a web feed, and are comfortable using almost any technology. For others of you, figuring out how to change the message on a telephone answering machine is a challenge. Because you and your classmates probably have various levels of experience and exposure to technology, we want to ensure that we all have the same foundation of knowledge in this area. Therefore, we begin with a discussion of the characteristics of communication technology.

Characteristics of Communication Technology

We need to understand the essential characteristics of technology so we are better prepared to make effective choices when using it. We consider three characteristics of technology: It is pervasive, paradoxical, and powerful.

When we state that technology is pervasive, we are saying that it is everywhere. We cannot escape or ignore technology in our lives. We wake with an alarm clock. We make telephone calls to our family. We fax reports at work. We take digital pictures on our vacations. We are beeped by our children, who ask what's for dinner. These same children sit down in front of the television to play video games. We text message our friends to ask them what time they want to meet. And some of us try to organize all of these activities on our BlackBerry or Sidekick.

Because technology is everywhere, we rely on it as a matter of course. Consider, for instance, how you would make it through the day without technology. Most of us would feel overwhelmed if we were deprived of the convenience that technology offers us. While some may lament the influence of technology on our lives, others embrace the fact that our lives are made easier because of technology. As communication and culture scholar Siva Vaidhyanathan (quoted by Neil Swidey, 2003), said, "It's the collapse of inconvenience. It turns out inconvenience was a really important part of our lives and we didn't realize it" (p. 11).

Technology is also paradoxical, meaning that it is conflicting, inconsistent, and ironic. To understand this concept, consider what communication theorist Marshall McLuhan (1964) called the **global village**. McLuhan coined this term to describe how communication technology ties the world into one political, economical, social, and cultural system. Although the phrase *global village* is almost a cliché these days, McLuhan is the one who, more than 40 years ago, expressed the idea that technology has the ability to bring people together. McLuhan stated that "the globe is no more than a village" (p. 5). The paradox is evident; the term *global* suggests an expansive view of the world, whereas the term *village* suggests a small community. The idea that technological devices, which mediate relationships in so many ways, can actually bring people together seems paradoxical.

When we say that technology is powerful, we mean that it influences people, events, and entire cultures. Technology can affect how people think, what

global village

The concept that communication technology ties the world into one political, economic, social, and cultural system.

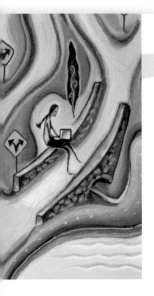

REVISITING
CASEINPOINT

1. *Apply the relevancy of the phrase* global village *to Matthew Leone's situation.*

2. *Apply all three characteristics of communication technology to Matthew's experiences.*

Y*ou can answer these questions online under the resources for Chapter 11 at your online Resource Center for* Understanding Interpersonal Communication.

they think about, when they develop relationships, and how they process their emotions with others (Turkle, 2007). For instance, let's say that Jana is a student who decides to skip a group presentation. She emails some group members to let them know about an unplanned doctor's appointment. She sends a text message to other group members complaining about her lack of time to get things done. In this case, because Jana uses technology to inform her group members of her dilemmas and because technology does not allow for nonverbal communication to be present, it is likely that the group members will read her emails and text messages and reach different conclusions about her not being at the presentation. As we noted in Chapter 5, nonverbal communication influences meaning between and among people. In its absence, some may think Jana is lazy, others may view her as self-serving, and others may decide not to waste energy worrying about her motivations. Technology has the power to cause others to make judgments, even though the communicators are not face-to-face.

Thus far, we have addressed the overall importance of communication technology in our lives and identified its primary characteristics. We will now discuss technology's accessibility and various uses.

The Accessibility of Communication Technology

Accessibility refers to the availability of technology to everyone. Accessibility helps eliminate the technological gap that exists between people and between cultural communities. Some have called this gap the "digital divide" while others have called it a battle between the information "haves and have-nots." Some writers contend that there is no battle and that even the poorest of the poor have access to technology, specifically the Internet (Ghostman, 2007).

Of the approximately 6 billion people who populate the globe, more than 1 billion use the Internet (www.internetstats.com). Over 73 percent of people in the United States go online, according to the Pew Foundation (http://www.pewtrusts.org/news_room_ektid23772.aspx). Technology reporter Mike Wendland (2002) argues that if you live in a suburb, make lots of money, and are highly educated, you most likely have no problem understanding the Internet. If you dwell in a large city, have a low income, and possess a limited education, you're probably not connected to or benefiting from the Internet. Some racial and geographic differences concerning Internet use suggest a digital divide. The Pew Foundation's study of Internet use and race, for example, found that among the major racial groups, more than half of white people (58 percent) have used the Internet, as compared with 43 percent of African Americans, and 50 percent of Hispanics (http://www.pewtrusts.org/news_room_ektid23772.aspx). In studying rural and urban use of the Internet, Sandra Guy (2004) finds that "rural residents go online [for instance] for information and to seek support groups, sports leagues, and civic groups—communities they cannot find in their neighborhoods."

The Pew Foundation has discovered some trends in technology usage and grouped people into three categories: elite users, middle-of-the-road users, and those with few technological assets. Table 11.1 describes these groups and shows the pervasiveness of technology across the U.S. population.

Table 11.1   Groups of U.S. users of information and communication technology

	Group name	% of adult population	Their characteristics
Elite tech users (31% of American adults)	Omnivores	8%	They have the most information gadgets and services, which they use voraciously to participate in cyberspace, express themselves online, and do a range of Web 2.0 activities such as blogging or managing their own web pages.
	Connectors	7%	Between feature-packed cell phones and frequent online use, they connect to people and manage digital content using information and communication technologies (ICTs)—all with high levels of satisfaction about how ICTs let them work with community groups and pursue hobbies.
	Lackluster veterans	8%	They are frequent users of the Internet and less avid about cell phones. They are not thrilled with ICT-enabled connectivity.
	Productivity enhancers	8%	They have strongly positive views about how technology lets them keep up with others, do their jobs, and learn new things.
Middle-of-the-road tech users (20%)	Mobile centrics	10%	They fully embrace the functionality of their cell phones. They use the Internet, but not often, and like how ICTs connect them to others.
	Connected but hassled	10%	They have invested in a lot of technology, but they find the connectivity intrusive and information somewhat of a burden.
Few tech assets (49%)	Inexperienced experimenters	8%	They occasionally take advantage of interactivity, but if they had more experience, they might do more with ICTs.
	Light but satisfied	15%	They have some technology, but it does not play a central role in their daily lives. They are satisfied with what ICTs do for them.
	Indifferents	11%	Despite having either cell phones or online access, these users use ICTs intermittently and find connectivity annoying.
	Off the network	15%	Those with neither cell phones nor Internet connectivity tend to be older adults who are content with old media.

Adapted from Pew Internet & American Life Project (2007), *A Typology of Information and Communication Technology Users.*

The digital divide is evident with nearly all communication technology. And nowhere is the divide more apparent than in our telephone ownership and usage. Even telephones—one of the most ubiquitous of technologies—vary in their accessibility. The National Telecommunications and Information Administration (NTIA) (http://www.ntia.doc.gov/ntiahome/net2/falling .html), for example, notes that there is a significant divide among racial communities. The national survey showed that overall, households headed by white individuals have a higher telephone availability and usage (95 percent) than African American households (85.4 percent) and households headed by Hispanic individuals (84.6 percent). With respect to income, the NTIA notes that as the household income falls, so does telephone ownership. For instance, in households where income was between $5,000–9,999, over 15 percent of these homes did not have a telephone. In homes with less than $5,000 of income, that number soars to nearly 25 percent! And, be cautious in believing that these homes have a cell phone and not a land line; the fees, monthly costs of long-distance calls, among other expenses prohibit any phone accessibility for the very poor among us. Each of us, then, has to be thoughtful and sensitive in our assumptions about technology and the availability of technology.

For an alternate look at the current state of the digital divide in the United States, use your online Resource Center for *Understanding Interpersonal Communication* to access **Interactive Activity 11.1: What Digital Divide?** under the resources for Chapter 11.

What does accessibility to communication technology have to do with interpersonal communication? If everyone does not have an understanding of and access to the same technologies, problems with meaning will likely occur. It will be difficult for us to achieve meaning in our conversations if others cannot understand us when we talk about "video streaming," "mobile networking," or our "MP3 players." What many of you may take for granted (for example, a telephone call, a text message, an instant message, and so forth) may not be universally accepted or understood because of accessibility issues. Remember not to assume that a classmate has a certain technology available to them.

Accessibility to communication technology has many benefits for interpersonal communication: It increases safety, creates a sense of play, and improves psychological well-being between and among people. Making phone calls in case of emergencies seems instinctive to most of us. Playing chess on the computer or having a conversation with other dog owners in an online discussion group helps increase the element of play. We explore how technology can improve psychological well-being when we discuss the bright side of technology a bit later in this chapter.

To this point, we have been discussing the Internet as if each of us has the same understanding of it. To make sure we share a common understanding, let's talk about the background of the Internet as well as its dark and bright sides.

The Internet: Connecting Now

Imagine being on the streets of New York City. All the streets, from the major arteries to the small alleys, comprise a complex network. Now, imagine you are in the office of the city's Director of Streets and Sanitation looking at a lighted grid of every street in Manhattan. The grid encompasses the 22.4 square miles of the island.

This image should help you understand what the Internet is. The Internet has been called a "network of networks" because of its embedded connections and because it "has changed the way people work, learn, play, and communicate" (Barnes, 2003, p. 3). Although many people use the terms Internet and the World Wide Web ("the web") interchangeably, the distinction between the terms needs to be noted. The Internet connects computers together and the information that travels from one computer to another computer does so through various technological "languages." The web is just one of the ways that information is shared over the Internet. The web uses a language called *HTTP* to transmit data. In other words, the web is part of the Internet and is not synonymous with the Internet. In this chapter, we will focus primarily on the web. The Internet and the web promise to be an important presence in communication technology for years to come. We will begin by discussing how the web has changed since its inception. We will then discuss several cautionary tales and points of opportunity associated with the Internet.

Web 1.0 and Web 2.0

Web 1.0

The earliest incarnation of the World Wide Web, which was used primarily as a storehouse of online information and tools that could be accessed to achieve an end, such as finding a website, emailing a friend, or purchasing a product.

Web 2.0

The latest incarnation of the World Wide Web, which is increasingly used as a means of interactivity and personal expression; establishing online communities, sharing files, and blogging exemplify Web 2.0.

Scholars now refer to the web as it first appeared in the late 1970s as Web 1.0. **Web 1.0** provided a technological means to achieve an end. That is, recalling the linear model we discussed in Chapter 1, Web 1.0 enabled a user to accomplish an immediate goal (e.g., access a website, email a friend, etc.). The label Web 2.0 has been used to describe the web in the past several years, as it has become more expansive, more democratic, and more interactive. Blogger Paul Graham (www.paulgraham.com/web20.html) states that **Web 2.0** is "using the web the way it is meant to be used."

Former president of software giant *Oracle,* Ray Lane, believes Web 2.0 reflects development from "the bottom up" (http://www.businessweek.com/technology/content/jun2006/tc20060605_641388.htm). That is, an amateur can have as wide an audience as a professional. With Web 1.0, news was still largely controlled by major networks and news organizations. Web 2.0 offers a much broader range of perspectives through blogs, podcasts, and access to news sources worldwide. These changes have affected both the availability of news, as well as our perceptions of what is considered newsworthy.

According to Tim O'Reilly, one of the pioneers in thinking about Web 2.0, Yahoo!, Amazon.com, and eBay are all examples of Web 2.0. Each of these companies had its origins in Web 1.0, but were able to transition to

Table 11.2   Differences between Web 1.0 and Web 2.0

Web 1.0	Web 2.0
Britannica (Encyclopedia) Online	Wikipedia
Page views	Cost per click
Publishing	Participation
Personal websites	Blogging
Content management systems	Wikis
Evites	upcoming.org
Netscape	Google

Web 2.0 by incorporating "user engagement"—that is, each began to encourage interactivity. For instance, Amazon became more than a "bookseller" by engaging prospective customers with opportunities to review and, as O'Reilly notes, "invitations to participate in varied ways on virtually every page." Table 11.2 provides additional examples of differences that O'Reilly sees between Web 1.0 and Web 2.0. (http://www.oreilly.com/pub/a/oreilly/tim/news/2005/09/30/what-is-web-20.html).

The Dark Side of the Internet: Proceed with Caution

Communication technologies such as the Internet should be approached cautiously. Like nearly any technology, there is always the opportunity for something to go wrong. There are more than 108 million websites in the world (http://news.netcraft.com/archives/web_server_survey.html), with an average of 4–5 million sites added each month. The sheer volume makes it impossible to control web content. Anyone can put up a website, and no one has to verify its accuracy. In fact, as Verlyn Klinkenborg (2004) writes in the *New York Times,* "Make no mistake. The web is still a place where you find every kind of fraud, deceit, obscenity, and insanity—more of it than ever" (p. A24). In other words, a lot of stranger danger lurks on the Internet. Let's examine four significant issues to consider as you use the Internet: accountability, hate, flaming, and a sacrifice of privacy. (See Table 11.3 on page 378 for examples of each of these dangers.)

Little Accountability

It's easy to develop a web page. All you have to do is figure out a possible web address, find out if the domain name has been taken, and post the content

Table 11.3   The dark side of internet usage

Little accountability	*Example:* Chad decides to go online to a website that promotes itself as "the only website for single men who wish to meet accountants." After logging in, Chad meets a woman who claims to be an accountant for a large firm in the Midwest. After several email exchanges, he is favorably impressed and decides to give her his cell phone number. The problem is that Chad's online conversational partner is not an accountant; rather, she is an advertiser who wants to find out what sorts of hair care products he uses. The website was created by a large advertising company who specializes in men's cosmetics.
Fostering of hate	*Example:* Lena is assigned to examine various websites on "spiritual values" for her modern history class. When she types that phrase into a search engine, thousands of websites match that description. However, one website, called "Spiritual Values for the New Century," catches her attention. As appealing as that title sounds, Lena soon figures out that the website is filled with hate. The home page of the website states that "abortionists will burn in hell" if they don't "repent." Further, some links on the site allow Lena to read essays with such titles as "Why Abortionists Should Die," "What God said about the Abortion Doctors," and "Killing the Fetus Slowly." Lena soon discovers that the website promotes the execution of doctors who perform abortions.
Flaming	*Example:* David can't believe what he is reading. As a new parent, he had wanted to learn a bit more about temper tantrums. But, as his experience in a chat room on parenting is teaching him, people can be awfully vicious in their attacks. First, he reads the comments of one participant, who has no children, that every parent is a "selfish b**tard" and that "kids just boost egos!" A parent responds by telling the childless participant, "too bad your mom didn't fall down the steps carrying u!" David sits sadly by. He wants to jump in, but knows that he would probably just provoke even more incendiary remarks. He can't believe that people would discuss a topic such as parenting with such hostile and aggressive comments.
Sacrifice of privacy	*Example:* Cassandra loves her dad, but she is now disgusted with what she discovered about him. Using a special software package, Cassandra's dad discovered a way to find out what websites she surfs, what keyboard strokes she makes, and even passwords that she uses while online and using the family's computer. Cassandra is appalled that as a 14-year-old, she has nothing that is private. Years ago, she thought, a lot of parents found the key to a diary and tried to read the entries. Today, however, Cassandra finds the invasion of her privacy by her own parent more manipulative and intrusive.

on your site. There is no accountability for this information. Robert Danford (1999) writes,

> Users of the Web must approach the plethora of Web sites with the skills of a good consumer to see if the product offered is indeed what it purports to be, to see if the site will fulfill the user's need, to see which of the sites is available is the "best" in a given situation so that the user will be able to count on the information or services offered. (p. xiii)

hate speech

Extremely offensive language that is directed toward a particular group of people.

In other words, we shouldn't accept any information we find on the web at face value. We should always think critically about it. If we don't make ourselves accountable for determining a website's credibility, we have the potential to be misguided, misinformed, and manipulated.

For example, suppose Damian is interested in trying online dating. He has had little luck meeting interesting people in person and has heard success stories from his roommate, so Damian decides to go to the Internet. Although Damian may be inclined to start surfing the web for dating sites, he should first ask himself a few questions. What criterion is he using to locate a particular website? What evidence shows that the site he accesses is legitimate? Does the site have a sponsor? Will Damian have to pay fees, or does the site's revenue come from advertisements? What protections are in place to ensure his privacy? How do others looking for dates contact you? Is there a way of verifying the credentials of potential dates? What sorts of ads appear on the website? Are they sexually explicit or professional? Are there restrictions for downloading pictures or personal information? What is the site's record for successful matches?

Some progress has been made in helping people evaluate websites. For instance, software programs that provide Internet filters to weed out potentially objectionable sites are now available. But you must still take responsibility for assessing web content yourself. Doing anything less may result in communication consequences that you did not expect.

© Reuters/Corbis

In the weeks following the terrorist attacks of September 11, 2001, many anti-Arab sites went up on the Internet, erroneously labeling some prominent Arab Americans as Islamic terrorists. The harmful effects of the misinformation spread by these sites illustrate the need for accountability on the Internet—not only were innocent people unfairly targeted, but many Internet providers spent time and money deleting these sites.

Fostering Hate

Certainly, websites have the potential to positively affect your conversations and relationships with others. Yet, the dark side of communication technologies suggests that hate on the Internet is alive and proliferating. **Hate speech** can be defined as extremely offensive language that is directed toward a particular group of people. Although hate speech is protected by First Amendment rights, such extremist communication has the potential to negatively affect another's communication.

Websites that use hate speech have proliferated over the years. They cover the spectrum, focusing on everything from anti-abortion sites that promote the death of abortion providers to websites denying that the Holocaust occurred. The Internet has fueled intolerance, hatred, and incivility to the extent that some hate groups now have an immediate referent point in their antagonistic pursuits. Because offensive points of view are protected by First Amendment free-speech rights, hate speech on the Internet is probably here to stay. Websites that promote gay bashing, anti-Semitic views, the reinstitution of slavery, and so forth will continue. One way to combat this hatred is to visit sites that are dedicated to wiping out cultural hate. For example, the Southern Poverty Law Center (www.splcenter.org) promotes the development of community coalitions to combat hate. And a relational step you can take to combat hate is to speak up to others to educate them about why their biases are misplaced.

Flaming

At times, relationships with others online can get tense. **Flaming** occurs when people exchange malicious, hostile, or insulting comments. Flamers using the Internet often suffer from some sort of social or psychological instability since many would not engage in this hostility in face-to-face interactions; the possibility for altercations and embarrassment are too strong. This lack of civility is like electronic road rage—it has the capacity to escalate. Janet Kornblum of *USA Today* (2007, July 31) notes that "the Internet has always had an anything-goes atmosphere where flame wars and harsh language are common" (p. 1A). Flaming may simply be an exercise of control over others or a bold attempt at aggression. Regardless of how long you may have known the flamer, flaming is best dealt with by disengaging and using more subtle ways of communicating. Avoiding capital letters, extreme punctuation (such as exclamation marks or ellipses), and accusatory language may help prevent further incivility. Consider the difference between the following two examples in a chat room of gay men:

Situation 1

Flamer:	U F*GS R GONNA BURN IN HELL!:))))))))
Participant 1:	UR the freakn @-hole!
Flamer:	STAY 2UNED. . .MORE>>ONS!!
Participant 2:	And we're afraid of what? A PIG ^ O ^ like you?
Flamer:	DIE F*GS!

Situation 2

Flamer:	U F*GS R GONNA BURN IN HELL!
Participant 1:	Get LOST!!!!!!
Flamer:	CAN'T TAKE IT? FEEL THE HEAT?
Participant 2:	Taking off Come back L8R.

flaming

Exchanging malicious, hostile, or insulting comments over the Internet.

Choosing disengagement and not becoming personally antagonistic, which is the strategy shown by Participant 2 in the second situation, should help you remove yourself from flaming and the flamer.

Consider how this interaction might have differed if it had happened in person instead of online. Some people find it easier to be uncivil in electronic than in face-to-face settings. Perhaps technological interactions provide a higher comfort level because a hateful person can be anonymous while cowardly hiding behind a computer screen. Remember the wizard in *The Wizard of Oz?* He lost all of his composure, aggressiveness, and anger when the curtain was literally pulled open. Would cyberhate be limited if individuals were required to communicate in person?

Privacy Sacrificed

In Fall 2007, *Parade* magazine, one of the largest supplements in national newspapers, asked the following question on its cover: "Is Anything Private Anymore?" Clearly, with advances in communication technology, the answer to that question is a resounding "no." In the article, author Sean Flynn notes that "in today's world, maintaining a cocoon of privacy simply isn't practical" (p. 4). With people giving names, addresses, social security numbers, among other things, in order to get car loans, mortgage approvals, grocery store discounts, tollbooth easy lane passes, credit cards, and drivers licenses, we have to forfeit a great deal of private information.

The issuance of private information to others has resulted in an onslaught of privacy concerns, particularly pertaining to the Internet. Because we are citizens, consumers, and investors, according to one expert, our privacy has been sacrificed (Nehf, 2007). Our online activities with others are consequential, to be sure. When we choose to email others and disclose our personal thoughts or life experiences, for instance, as we noted in Chapter 8, we become more vulnerable. At one point or another in our lives, we have and will disclose something on the Internet. When we disclose on the Internet, we allow others a chance to frame our words in any manner they see fit. Unwittingly, we may be sacrificing our privacy further. In some cases, our personal emails have been intercepted and handed over to government investigators, client information has been sold to telemarketing companies, and credit records have been "misplaced" by unscrupulous lenders.

Some privacy experts (Tavani, 2000) suggest that search engines are able to "discover" personal information about you and for some, once they "google" their name, for instance, all of the information that they thought was private now is public. It is no wonder that some writers (e.g., Nehf, 2007) argue that despite privacy policies on various websites, most people do not take the time to read them nor do they "shop" for privacy among websites. It appears Janet Kornblum (2007, October 23) has it right when discussing the Internet, she states: "Privacy? That's so old-school" (p. 1D).

The Bright Side of the Internet: New Opportunities

Although the Internet certainly has its dark side, it also offers us unique opportunities. Generally speaking, we can communicate with people we might not have been able to communicate with otherwise. Further, such communication is quick and seamless, and even those with little technological know-how can quickly learn to communicate via the web. Let's look at

Table 11.4 The bright side of internet usage

Widen your social network	**Example:** As a newcomer to Chicago, Ramona isn't prepared to deal with the millions of people in the city. Her hometown has only 300 people, and although her previous job had taken her to the Windy City, she has never felt so alone in her life. Ramona isn't in the habit of going out; when she isn't at work, she usually stays home and watches television or emails her sister. However, one night Ramona decides to surf the Internet. She soon finds herself in a local chat room reading messages about one of her favorite topics, Hispanic history. She particularly likes reading about the history of mask making in Mexico. After several weeks in the chat room (during which she interacts with some of the other participants, sharing some of her thoughts on the topic), Ramona decides to meet several people from her chat room at a local museum that is featuring Aztecan masks. One person in particular catches Ramona's eye, they hit it off, and she soon thinks Chicago is one of the best cities in the world!
Enhance your educational accessibility	**Example:** Morgan stands in his dining room looking at pictures of his wife. She has been dead for nearly a year now, and he still finds himself crying all the time. He decides that he can either cry every day or make something out of the rest of his life. Not wanting to let his emotions control him, Morgan decides to do something he has been wanting to do for many years but had been reluctant to tackle because he was uncertain how to proceed—he decides to start his own handyman business. So, he goes to the Internet and types "starting a business" in his search engine. Morgan soon begins to learn about self-employment tax, state regulations, and other matters small business owners need to know. He trusts the government's Small Business Administration website and downloads all of the information he can digest in one sitting. Morgan is excited about finding an opportunity to learn about an area he had never thought he would understand.

two areas of Internet opportunities. First, the Internet has afforded us chances to widen our social network and second, it has enhanced our educational opportunities. (See Table 11.4 for examples of each of these benefits.)

Widening Your Social Network

With the Internet, and the web in particular, you can widen your social circles tremendously in a short period of time—something you can't do with face-to-face communication. Overall, computer-mediated communication (CMC) allows individuals to seek out information and to develop their relationships. Although we address social networks a bit later in this chapter, a few points merit attention.

First, in many ways, the Internet serves as a vehicle to secure information. Among the areas most sought out are chat rooms. Chat rooms are excellent venues to discover information about a particular subject—for example, the qualifications of political candidates, how to start a small business, or where to go on a cruise. In addition, information-seeking web users can facilitate online discussions with professionals who have credentials in a particular area. For example, let's say Marcie was recently diagnosed with diabetes and has no idea what the disease is all about. Marcie's first step will probably be to go to the Internet to find information using a search engine. After she discovers that there are literally hundreds of websites available on the topic, she has to decide which one to visit first. Inevitably, she will discover some chat rooms where physicians who specialize in the disease are able to answer her questions or respond to her concerns. However, keep in mind the important information about accountability that we discussed a bit earlier. Marcie should not be misled by those who are not qualified to offer suggestions in this area. Yet, along the way, Marcie is likely going to encounter a site where she and others with diabetes are able to communicate about their challenges and high-points.

In addition to getting relevant information, Barnes (2003) also noted that CMC can aid in the maintenance and expansion of our relationships, both romantic and professional. In fact, CMC is "redefining how people engage of relationships of all types" (Pauley & Emmers-Sommer, 2007, p. 411).

How can our relationships be maintained via electronic means? First, we live in a mobile society, with people transferring jobs or working across the miles; communication technology can bridge the geographic divide. Whether moving across town or across the country, migration usually requires adaptation to new surroundings and maintenance of existing relationships. Past friends and current family members, for example, will likely expect ongoing communication, and email can facilitate keeping in touch.

A second way in which our relationships are maintained via technology pertains to supporting others. In fact, some research indicates that entire communities are built and maintained online. For instance, Elena Larsen (2004) notes that faith communities in particular are flourishing and individuals are using the Internet to show their support for each other and each other's religious identity. Larsen concludes that "more than 90 percent of online congregations reported that their members email each other for fellowship purposes" (p. 47). Individuals can seek out others for prayer requests, spiritual assistance and advice, and even facilitate spiritual relationships that were previously nonexistent. With technology, individuals who were once strangers can become linked in ways unimagined prior to the Internet.

Enhancing Your Educational Accessibility

Earlier in this chapter, we talked about how the digital divide cuts across various racial groups. Another type of divide exists as well—a division between younger and older generations in terms of their Internet usage. Simply put, those who are younger (say, under the age of 60) tend to use the web (in particular) much more frequently than those who are older (say, those over 60 years old). Why is this the case? Karen Riggs (2004) believes that ageism may be at play. Many people—from employers to physicians—maintain stereotypes of older adults, including the belief that they are unable to adapt to new technology. Yet, Riggs argues that with some training and enough tenacity, older adults are able to rapidly and competently deal with any technological challenge.

Just because older adults may not go online as frequently as younger adults does not mean that this group remains technologically ignorant. Many will derive benefits from using technology. For example, when older adults do go online, research shows that they are less likely to report health-related problems and identify with stronger feelings of independence (Stark-Wroblewski, Edelbaum, & Ryan, 2007). Consider, for example, Jackson, a 55-year-old father of two, who decides to use the Internet to obtain information about employment discrimination. Or, Leo, a 70-year-old father of five, a diligent parent who browses the web for volunteer jobs. Cassandra, a 59-year-old single woman, goes online to find out about her recent diagnosis of ovarian cancer. And Rodney, a 65-year-old single man, seeks out potential mates on a website for single senior citizens. The new economy requires a host of technological experiences and expertise. People of all ages are an integral part of that technology.

Now that you better understand the characteristics of technology and the dark and bright sides of the web, we turn our attention to how people present themselves online and then to more specific forms of communication technology and how they affect interpersonal communication.

The Presentation of Self Online

In Chapter 2, we emphasized the role of the self in interpersonal communication. In this section, we describe the way individuals present themselves online. Sherry Turkle (1995) reminds us that people online develop a "cyber-self" and that in "virtual reality, we self-fashion and self-create" (p. 180). The following story reported by Alexandra Alter (2007, August 10) in the *Wall Street Journal* illustrates this point:

> On a scorching July afternoon, as the temperature creeps toward 118 degrees in a quiet suburb east of Phoenix, Rick Hoogestraat sits at his computer with the blinds drawn, smoking a cigarette. While his wife, Sue, watches television in the other room, Mr. Hoogestraat chats online with what appears on the screen to be a tall, slim redhead (p. W1).

Rick is part of a growing virtual world called Second Life, which, according to Alter, is a fantasyland in which a synthetic identity plays itself out in intriguing ways. Mr. Hoogestraat has become so entranced with Janet Spielman, the "redhead" with whom he has a "second life," that he has asked her to become his virtual wife. Alter writes that "The woman he's legally wed to is not amused" (p. W1).

avatar

A digital fictional and fantasy representation of a user in a virtual world.

This story underscores the growing presence of **avatars**, a digital fictional and fantasy representation of a user in a virtual world. Avatars have become dynamic interjections into people's relational lives. Alter (2007) quotes Edward Castronova, a telecommunications expert, who encapsulates the

Avatars allow you to communicate with others online in a visual and highly interactive way. These Second Life avatars have shrunk to the size of mice to interact with tiny aliens in a Second Life environment. Notice how idealized the human avatars are. The women are big-breasted supermodels and the man is a tall, stylish hunk. What do you think the real people who created these avatars are trying to communicate about themselves by creating such sexy online representations?

concern of many people in relationships with avatar-obsessed partners: "There's a fuzziness that's emerging between the virtual world and the real world" (p. W8).

We will begin with a brief examination of a few assumptions associated with the way identities are managed online, and then we sort out some of the identity markers available to those in electronic relationships. As you review this section of the chapter, keep in mind that much of it can be framed by **signaling theory**, which proposes that people have qualities that they wish to present to others. Your participation on an online site may be accompanied with technical expertise, particular language, and/or "bells and whistles." For instance, as Marcia places a personal ad on a dating website in order to attract a college-educated mate, she may use language that is clear and precise and have a personal biography of her accomplishments. Further, she may not want a great deal of flashy or twinkling icons, instead choosing to be more professional in her approach. In this way, Marcia is signaling her desire for a particular "type" of person. If she were looking for a "drinking buddy," Marcia would likely use a much different approach.

Assumptions of Online Presentations of the Self

Understanding a few assumptions of how individuals present themselves online will expand your thinking about the self and its relationship to technology. With each of the assumptions we describe, we draw comparisons to face-to-face (FtF) encounters.

signaling theory

A theory that proposes that people have qualities they wish to present to others.

Ethics & Choice

Bernadette Amarosa sat staring blankly at her computer screen. She had just done something she rarely did: She had lied. She hadn't meant to, she thought to herself, but she had gotten carried away with her online conversation with Michael and had typed in the lie before she thought it through.

As a divorced woman, Bernadette was not in the habit of going online to seek out a relationship. As a matter of fact, she laughed at her close friends—all of whom are married—when they encouraged her to visit some online dating websites. She thought that guys who placed personal ads online were rather desperate, and she certainly didn't want to date a desperate man! Yet, for some reason on this hot summer evening, Bernadette had decided to search for a website that specialized in dating. She had soon found herself entering some personal information, including her screen name ("Dot") and some other details, such as her dating preferences, including sex ("man"), age ("25–40"), profession ("be employed"), and location ("southeastern United States").

As she searched the personal ads, Bernadette was attracted to a profile of a man named Michael. She read his "stats" and felt something in common with him. She also thought that Michael, smiling with his baseball cap on backward in the picture, was cute. Bernadette finally worked up the nerve to email Michael. After a few minutes, he responded and said he was happy she connected. He said he had looked at her picture and profile and found her attractive.

(Continues)

Assumption 1: The Computer Screen Can Deceive

When people are online, they often pretend to be someone or something they are not. Online dialogues can lead to deceitful presentations. Men can become women who want to talk to other women. Convicted felons can pose as young girls or boys interested in Miley Cyrus or Zac Efron. The unemployed can become corporate CEOs, and CEOs can present themselves as unemployed. . .or someone else. For example, several years ago, John Mackey, the CEO of Whole Foods, disguised himself as another person and wrote anonymous attacks online against his company's biggest competitor. Under the name "Rahodeb" (an anagram based on his wife, Deborah's name), Mackey predicted bankruptcy for Wild Oats, and stated that its stock was overpriced. Eventually, Whole Foods received government permission to buy Wild Oats, but this episode remains a cloud over the company.

In face-to-face encounters, being deceitful to such an extent is usually much tougher. We can't lie about our biological sex, and we can't claim to be a tall and toned person when we are short and stocky. Our conversations with others are in the present; they are not delayed or responded to later, as are our online dialogues. If we ask a question, we expect a response. If we don't get a response, we may walk away from the encounter.

Although chat rooms are in "real time," people can choose when they'd like to respond. Researchers have referred to the "real time" communication as **synchronous communication**, or communication between the sender and receiver taking place at the same time. If the sender and receiver do not have to synchronize before and after each communication exchange, they are engaged in **asynchronous communication**.

Assumption 2: Online Discussions Often Prompt Introspection

Imagine that Bob and Shelly email each other about what they thought of the midterm exam. Shelly tells Bob that she thought it was pretty easy, but Bob thought it was pretty tough. As Bob reads Shelly's email, he starts to think about why he and Shelly each had different perceptions. They had studied together, after all. Before responding to the email, Bob starts to think about the material he didn't understand. "Yeah," he thinks, "there was some stuff I just didn't get." Email, in this situation, inspired Bob to think about

synchronous communication

Communication between a sender and a receiver that takes place at the same time, as in face-to-face communication.

asynchronous communication

Communication that doesn't require a sender and a receiver to have an exchange at the same time, as in online communication.

his own study habits, an introspective behavior that may not have occurred without his friend's prompting.

Not every email elicits this self-assessment. Yet, when we do email someone, we frequently engage in something similar to an internal dialogue. Think about when a supervisor emails an employee requesting a meeting as soon as possible but offers no specifics. Or, consider a time when a partner sends you an email wanting to break up, yet fails to explain why. These instances provoke us to reflect on both the message and our response to that message.

With FtF communication, this same introspection and self-dialogue is not as apparent. First, we often don't take the time to think about the words of another *while they are being stated*. Stopping to think about what another person was saying in the middle of a conversation would likely bring the conversation to a halt. We are not trained or conditioned to pause or stop conversations in this way. Instead, we typically mentally replay and analyze conversations once they are over. Most of our interpersonal encounters move rather freely from one point to another, with little reflection time.

Soon the two started emailing each other. Bernadette was not entirely truthful in her emails—for example, she didn't tell Michael that she was divorced and that she had two adult sons. Further, although she told Michael that she was in her 40s, she really was 53. As time went on, Bernadette grew more nervous about her deception. She thought she might have gotten herself in way too deep with her lies.

Bernadette faces a number of options in this technological predicament. She could tell Michael her real age and the fact that she has two children. Or, she could reveal part of this information to him. Or, she could choose to continue to conceal her true age and her children's existence. Are there other alternatives? What ethical issues are inherent in this circumstance? Reflecting on the five ethical system of communication we identified in Chapter 1 (categorical imperative, utilitarianism, ethic of care, golden mean, significant choice), explain your response with these frameworks in mind. Is one system more relevant than another? Explain.

 Go to your online Resource Center for *Understanding Interpersonal Communication* to access an interactive version of this scenario under the resources for Chapter 11. The interactive version of this scenario allows you to choose an appropriate response to this dilemma and then see what consequences your choice brings about. You can also compare your answers to the questions at the end of the scenario to those provided by the authors and, if requested, email your response to your instructor.

Assumption 3: Online Discussions Promote Self-Orientation

In Chapter 3, we discussed individualism, which is a cultural orientation that favors the self over the group. When communicating online, we tend to value our way of doing things. Working on and with the computer is essentially a personal endeavor. We search out people, websites, and chat rooms in which we are interested. If others wish to contact us, we make a choice whether or not we want to respond to their overture. In electronic relationships, keep in mind that one or both individuals may either choose to reply or not to reply. Because we have no physical proximity, we are not compelled to interact. People communicate at their own convenience.

We typically must be collaborative in our conversations while FtF. Although we can choose to say nothing, our silence—as we learned in Chapter 7—can communicate a great deal. In addition, when we are speaking in person, there is give and take, questions require answers, and our answers usually result in further dialogue. People cannot avoid the ongoing and

transactional nature of communication in face-to-face conversations. And like FtF conversations, our conversations vis-à-vis CMC are transactional.

Assumption 4: *Self-Disclosure Occurs Online*

The process of revealing aspects of yourself to another is not confined to face-to-face conversations. Research shows that self-disclosure occurs online and that some people reveal quite a bit through electronic communication (Miura, 2007). Particularly with blogs, self-disclosure is at a premium. As we learned in Chapter 8, when people self-disclose, they are inclined to give people important pieces of information about themselves. Further, we know that self-disclosure tends to increase intimacy.

Some people feel comfortable disclosing online because they don't have to deal with immediate reactions of disgust, disappointment, or confusion. Individuals may find it easier to reveal emotionally laden information in a technological medium. The problem, according to Susan Barnes (2003), is that **postcyberdisclosure panic (PCDP)** can set in. PCDP is a situation in which someone discloses personal information in an email message or on a message board only to experience significant anxiety later because the discloser begins to think about the number of people who could have access to that message. For instance, if Fran emails a coworker about her past problems with alcohol, that information has the potential to be passed (even inadvertently) to others, both in and out of the workplace. Interestingly, people may reveal information about themselves online that they would never reveal while face to face, perhaps because the computer screen is an impersonal object that doesn't have the capacity to show emotion.

The self-disclosive conversations we have with people while FtF can be dramatically different from those we engage in via email. In face-to-face interactions, we have to contend with facial reactions. We are often asked to clar-

postcyberdisclosure panic (PCDP)

A situation in which we disclose personal information in an email message only to experience significant anxiety later because we begin to think about the number of people who could have access to that message.

ify our thoughts or disclosures, and we may find it difficult to simply leave. We can't "turn off" another person as easily as we can turn off our computer screen. Self-disclosure in person generally causes an immediate reaction, which is something we don't necessarily have to deal with while online. To read an interesting article that discusses self-disclosure on the Internet and how some people fared moving from online to face-to-face relationships, check out "Relationship Formation on the Internet: What's the Big Attraction?" available through InfoTrac College Edition. Use your online Resource Center for *Understanding Interpersonal Communication* to access *InfoTrac College Edition Exercise 11.1: Self-Disclosure Online* under the resources for Chapter 11. To read another article, "Can You See the Real Me?" which discusses the presentation of the true self online, access *InfoTrac College Edition Exercise 11.2: Can You See the Real Me—Online?*

Identity Markers on the Internet

On the Internet, individuals typically communicate who they are through identity markers. An **identity marker** is an electronic extension of who someone is. In other words, an identity marker is an expansion of the self. Two primary identity markers exist on the Internet: screen names and personal home pages.

Screen Names

As in face-to-face relationships, online relationships inevitably require introductions. Yet, unlike in interpersonal relationships, we can introduce ourselves online by using names that are odd, silly, fun, editorial, or outright offensive. These screen names are nicknames and often serve to communicate the uniqueness of the sender of a message. Many screen names function as a way for communicators to protect their identities from others until more familiarity and comfort develops.

People use a wide variety of screen names. Some are shaped by fiction (>madhatter< or >hobbit<), others by popular culture (>AmIdol< or >TRUMPthis<), and still others by a desire to reinforce personal values (>WARRingOUT<). Haya Bechar-Israeli (1996) observes that many people place a great deal of importance on their screen names and nicknames and that they invest a great deal of thought in their creation. According to Bechar-Israeli, "References to collective cultural, ethnic, and religious themes in nicknames might indicate that the individual belongs to a certain social group." (p. 12) Her research shows that rather than frequently changing their names, people tend to keep their names for a period of time, which underscores the fact that they commit themselves to a screen identity.

At first glance, screen names may seem unimportant in building an electronic discussion and relationship. However, unlike your name (which was probably given to you at birth), screen names are created by the individual and reflect some degree of creativity, a value that others may consider important when encountering people online. And despite the relative stability of

identity marker

An electronic extension that communicates a person's identity, such as a screen name or a personal home page.

screen names, people can change their names much more easily in virtual life than in real life. If you encounter someone who is verbally offensive online, you can leave a chat room, establish a different name, and reenter the chat room under an entirely different alias (remember our earlier story of the CEO of Whole Foods). Even wigs and cosmetic surgery can't achieve such a transformation so quickly! Finally, most of our given names at birth (for example, Joe, Luisa, Natalie) communicate little to others. On the other hand, screen names give others insight into people's interests or values. A screen name such as >STALKU< can tell others a lot. As we noted in our Chapter 6 discussion of email addresses, screen names that are appropriate for some aspects of our life may be inappropriate for others.

Your turn Examine and evaluate different types of identity markers by surfing some chat rooms. If you like, you can use your student workbook or your **Understanding Interpersonal Communication** Online Resources to complete this activity.

Personal Home Pages

If an individual wants to communicate a great deal of personal information, a personal home page may be the first step. Personal home pages, sometimes called web pages, present a number of features that depict who the person is, such as information on personal hobbies and genealogy; photographs of the person and his or her family members, friends, pets, and home; and links to groups with advocacy causes or contacts.

Communicating one's identity via a personal home page is often enlightening to others. Personal websites can contain information that may be deliberate or accidental. First, as is the case with personal interactions, people may strategically present themselves in a certain way on their personal web pages. Digital photos, slick graphics, funky fonts, interesting links, and creative screen names may communicate a sense of organization, creativity, insight, and invitation. These sorts of intentional markers may be consciously presented on web pages so that others have a comprehensive understanding of who the person is and can find out a bit about his or her attitudes, beliefs, and values. The message is clear: "I'm a person you want to meet. I've got it together online. You can imagine how together I will have it when you meet me." However, some personal home page designers would do well to remember a corollary of Murphy's law: If nothing can go wrong, it will anyway! Someone may have the best intentions of communicating clarity and authenticity, but they go awry. Consider the following greeting on a personal home page: "Welcome to my home page. I hoop you get a kick out of reading the different stories me." Or, what about the web page that had inadvertently been linked to a pornographic website? And then there are personal home pages that have so much personal information on them that it feels like an episode of Dr. Phil. When people encounter spelling errors, accidental links to websites, and over-disclosing, they may skip over a home page rather than engage it. As in face-to-face encounters, although we mean well, the words (and pictures and links) sometimes come out wrong.

Screen names and home pages are just two ways that individuals communicate their identity on the Internet. By now, you should have a clear sense of how the Internet functions in online dating and how the self influences the process of electronic relationships. We now explore the interplay between communication technology and our interactions with others.

REVISITING CASEINPOINT

1. *Discuss what sorts of identity markers or other technology Matthew Leone might use in his communication with a potential employer during an interview.*

2. *What cautions would you provide to Matthew as he works toward eliminating his prior actions on the Internet?*

You can answer these questions online under the resources for Chapter 11 at your online Resource Center for Understanding Interpersonal Communication.

Communication Technology and Relational Maintenance

Communication between and among individuals is forever changed because of technology. People are now able to initiate, maintain, and terminate relationships through technological means. Years ago, to get a date with someone, you had to meet in a common place, such as a laundromat, church, grocery store, bar, or classroom. Today, if you're *wired* with the right *hardware*, a *mouse* will help you *google* a date on *cupid.com*. The effects of technology on our interpersonal relationships are unprecedented, unpredictable, and unstoppable. We begin this section by discussing the interplay between online and "traditional" relationships, and then discuss some online communication approaches. Finally, we look at social networking and the phenomenal rise of MySpace and Facebook.

Our interpersonal communication and our relationships with others are influenced by online technology. Indeed, communication technology is changing the way we look at relationships. In that spirit, we first explain the role that online relationships play in our lives, and then look at how people develop their virtual relationships into face-to-face relationships.

The Electronic and Face-to-Face Relationship

Researchers have examined the association between electronic and interpersonal communication (e.g., Pauley & Emmer-Sommers, 2007). This scholarship has helped to differentiate between online relationships and traditional relationships. Succinctly noting why online dating is a good idea, Judith Silverstein and Michael Lasky (2004) observe that "traditional dating is fundamentally random" (p. 10). What they mean is that during the dating stage, people tend to "stumble" onto others at a social gathering. You might find yourself in the right place at the right time and meet the right person. Or, you might not. Regardless, this way of meeting people involves a lot of luck.

However, developing an online relationship is not as random; online dating "reverses the standard rules of dating" (Shin, 2003, p. D2). Silverstein and Lasky (2004) note a number of advantages to meeting someone online:

- Many people online are available and seeking companionship.
- Before you exchange personal information, you have the power to secure a profile of the other person.
- You know something about how the other person thinks and writes.
- You know how to contact him or her.
- You have the chance to exchange email and talk on the phone without ever revealing your identity.
- You can do all of this for less than what it might cost for a typical first date, like dinner at a moderately priced restaurant.

In addition, many online dating services help match people who have similar qualities, interests, and relationship goals, increasing the chances that you will meet someone with whom you are compatible. Let's look at an example to explain how an online relationship might develop. After a breakup with his partner, Willy decides to post a personal ad and photograph with an online dating service. In a few days, he receives more than twenty inquiries from women all over the state. One woman in particular, Lena, is especially appealing to Willy. He emails Lena, she emails back, and he soon discovers that she shares one of his interests—she, too, is an amateur skier. After an ongoing exchange of email (in which they communicate their dating history, feelings about family, and other personal details), they swap phone numbers. Soon, they are talking every night. After several weeks of phone calls, Willy and Lena decide to set up a time to meet. Meeting strangers online and forming the sort of virtual relationship that Willy and Lena have formed is what Warren St. John (2001) calls "**hyperdating**," which is the development of an online relationship at "lightning speed" (p. D1).

At what point do we move from an online relationship to a face-to-face relationship? First, the all-important telephone call begins the process of moving from the computer screen to a live voice. The wise use of the phone is critical. As Silverstein and Lasky (2004) conclude, "The phone can hurt you or help you in online dating" (p. 237). As with all communication technology, the effectiveness and usefulness of the telephone can vary. Necessary cautions such as caller ID blocking and not disclosing personal details about one's self are essential. Ensuring that another person is not lying to you is also paramount. Remember, all communication has the potential to have a dark side.

hyperdating

The highly accelerated development of an online relationship.

The "Language" of Online Relationships

We observed in Chapter 6 that language is the primary way that people communicate with each other. We also concluded that the language of the Internet is unique. When we put that language in the context of interpersonal relationships, we have a recipe for an interesting electronic relationship. We capture some of this uniqueness here by exploring abbreviated language, graphic accents, and blogging.

Abbreviated Language

Because technology is often used while people are on the go, it makes sense to use **abbreviated language** for efficiency in online relationships. People commonly use abbreviations such as ASL (age/sex/location), AFK (away from keyboard), PAW (parents are watching), HAND (have a nice day), S^ (s'up—what's up?), A3 (anyplace, anytime, anywhere), SETE (smiling ear to ear), and one of our favorites, FMTYEWTK (far more than you ever wanted to know). One challenge with abbreviated language is that both the sender and the receiver have to understand the abbreviations. An additional challenge is that abbreviated language does not often lead to shared meaning. If you don't understand an acronym, will you ask its meaning? How do you go about getting clarification? Abbreviated language occurs quite a bit in text messages and its usage suggests the texter's familiarity with the person he's texting. If that familiarity is not there, this abbreviated wording may prevent meaning from being communicated.

Graphic Accents

Some writers talk about CMC as a "lean" medium for interaction. Users try to compensate for this spareness by using graphic accents. In Chapter 4, we mentioned that emoticons, such as smiley faces, are used to communicate emotions. An **articon** is a picture used in an electronic message; it can be downloaded from a website or created with keyboard characters. Researchers have discovered that using graphic icons can elaborate on the words being used. For example, Diane Witmer and Mary Lee Katzman (1997) discovered that emoticons and articons helped clarify for the reader the meaning of the written word. They also concluded that both men and women use graphic accents sparingly. Perhaps they feel that their words and abbreviations are sufficient. The use of emoticons and articons will become more frequent as computer graphic programs become more sophisticated and Internet users continue to download websites filled with faces, bodies, and objects depicting various emotions. In fact, on the horizon is an ever-growing list of artwork that, unlike most emoticons, does not require you to tilt your head, but rather allows you to look at the icon straight on:

(::[ ]::)	@(*0*)@	=^.^=
Band-Aid for comfort	koala for playfulness/cute	cat for frisky

These kinds of graphic accents show creativity and, when used by both communicators, allow for shared meaning. Although it may be easier for some to

abbreviated language

Shorthand used for efficient communication in online relationships.

articon

A graphic image used in an electronic message that can be downloaded from a website or compiled from keyboard characters. An articon may or may not be used to communicate emotion.

express their feelings via technological displays, eventually two people have to meet before they can facilitate an intimate bond.

Blogging

In our electronic relationships with others, we may also keep or read blogs. As many of you already know, a blog is a running commentary—a journal on the Internet—that usually includes personal thoughts and feelings about a particular topic or individual. Blogs detail everything, including information about family, work, and personal heartaches. Andrew Sullivan (2002) notes that blogs are "imbued with the temper of the writer." Blogging is a techno-logical intrapersonal and interpersonal experience. It is intrapersonal in nature because the authors are communicating something about themselves every time they write something for others to read. Blogging is also an inter-personal experience because others may comment on what is written or may be directed to Internet links relevant to the conversation taking place.

Especially given Web 2.0, writing your thoughts and feelings for public consumption should be done cautiously. For example, blogging about work colleagues (also known as gossip!) can come back to haunt you (Armour, 2007). Imagine, for instance, blogging about a coworker's decision to elope or chatting about his mental illness. Further, as a result of search engines, remember that the original blog is often quickly placed on the Internet. Finally, keep in mind one fundamental tenet of this course: Communication is irreversible. Once you blog, that information is available and regret, remorse, or anxiety will not take back the words you post. Clearly, there are ethical considerations associated with such disclosures.

Social Networking: Beyond the Keyboard

No discussion on technology and interpersonal communication can be com-plete without some discussion of social networking. **Social networking**, in its broadest sense, refers to linking individuals and communities of people who share common interests, activities, and ideas. Most social networks allow users a vast array of means by which to electronically communicate with others: email, instant messaging, file sharing, blogs, and so forth. A person is able to place a personal profile online at a social networking site, "allow" others to post their comments, and subsequently, decide to develop an online relationship. Social networking allows users to connect from one profile to another, ultimately establishing a personal network. According to danah boyd and Nicole Ellision (2007), technology historians, what makes social networks unique is "not that they allow individuals to meet strangers, but that they enable users to articulate and make visible their social networks" (http://jcmc.indiana.edu/vol13/issue1/boyd.ellison.html).

The first social network appeared in 1997. Researchers boyd and Ellison (2007) note that from 1997–2003, 13 social network sites (SNSs) appeared, the most notable being Friendster. Because Friendster eventually became a fee-based site, its users began to post messages encouraging them to join a

social networking

Linking individuals and communities who share common interests, activities, and ideas through such online websites as Facebook or MySpace.

Communication Assessment Test
A Chat Self-Test

Internet users in chat rooms frequently create personal identities. To get a sense of whether you engage in identity management, answer the questions below. Make sure you respond spontaneously and select an honest reaction; try not to think too much about a question before answering it. Use the scale to respond to the statements. You can take this test online. Go to your online Resource Center for *Understanding Interpersonal Communication* and look under the resources for Chapter 11.

YES   yes   ?   no   NO

_____ 1. It's important for me to make sure people know my real name while I communicate with them online.

_____ 2. If chat room participants refuse to reveal their real names, they have something to hide.

_____ 3. I believe "cutesy" or "childish" screen names say a lot about a person.

_____ 4. When people start to make fun of others in a chat room, they are really creating a sense of play.

_____ 5. Using screen names creates an expressive connection.

_____ 6. Using emoticons or articons is an effective way to provide others some insight into who you are.

_____ 7. Chat rooms and other e-groups generally draw those who have nothing else to do with their time.

_____ 8. The typical person in a chat room tries to create a false identity of who he or she is.

_____ 9. All email in chat rooms should be archived and available to anyone.

_____ 10. There should be explicit rules of behavior for chat room participants.

Interpretation of Results

If you found yourself answering YES or NO to any of these questions, look at the individual statements. What guided your thinking for each? What online experiences have you had in chat rooms that would have influenced your responses? If you responded with a "?" to any of the statements, think about why you are not sure about your response. Does identity management play a role in your decisions? If so, in what capacity? Be sure to reflect on the importance of online identity in your response.

new free site: MySpace. It was then, according to boyd and Ellison, that MySpace "was able to grow rapidly by capitalizing on Friendster's alienation of its early adopters." A few years later in 2006, seeking to capture a niche in the college community, a site that required its users to have a college address was born. This site, Facebook, and MySpace soon became the two most popular SNSs on the Internet.

Over the past decade, social networking has proliferated. In fact, over 55 percent of all children who are 12–17 claim to have visited an SNS (Lenhart & Madden, 2007). A quick search will show that there are hundreds of millions of profiles contained on MySpace and Facebook with enormous opportunity for interpersonal commentary. In one month, in the United States alone, over 80 million people visited MySpace and Facebook, and the

Social and professional networking sites, like MySpace and LinkedIn, provide us with almost unlimited opportunities to connect with others. What types of interactions do you have on networking sites? Do your interactions on these sites differ in significant ways from the face-to-face interactions you have with people in your immediate social and professional circles?

© Colin Young-Wolff/PhotoEdit

two sites have an annual combined profit of about $300 million (Hamilton, 2007). We will now provide you with a brief introduction to each site.

I Need MySpace

Browsing, searching, inviting, filming, and mailing are just a few of the options available to users of the largest social networking site in the world: MySpace. By some estimates, there are over 115 million users of MySpace worldwide (Spencer, 2007) and its growth is approximately 50 percent per year. According to one expert, 5 percent of all global Internet traffic is on MySpace (Hicks, 2007). The site works like this: You join the site, create a profile with all sorts of options (e.g., favorite dog's name, most interesting place you've visited, favorite books and movies, etc.), and then invite your friends to join. You also "mine" the site to see if you already have friends on that site who become part of your "friend space," or your social network. When people choose what information to share in their profile, they communicate with their online social network—about themselves, their values, their beliefs, and their attitudes.

Let's Face(book) It

Founded by a Harvard University student, Facebook was originally available only to college students. Today, the site is open to everyone over the age of 13. It is ranked as the most popular site for the 18–24 age bracket; women are twice as likely as men to use it (Bulik, 2007). Facebook's 72 million users (Hamilton, 2007), like MySpace users, create a profile and establish an online network of friends. Facebook users can upload photos, write notes or develop a blog, get the latest news from other friends, post videos, and join a network in a particular region of the country or affiliated with a particular high school or college.

Once you've set up a profile in Facebook, there are several ways to interact with your online network. First, you can "poke" someone to say hello. A **poke** is an electronic invitation to another person to communicate with you. However, if he/she does not poke back, a user's face may be threatened, a topic we examined in Chapter 2. Mini-feeds are also available. Depending on your point of view, the feature is either a creepy invasion of privacy or an opportunity to "innocently stalk" someone (Prowse, 2006). **Mini-feeds** are streaming bulletins that announce almost all of the activities of your Facebook friends. For instance, a mini-feed might note: "1:10 p.m.-Sasha added the Dave Matthews Band to her Favorite Music" or "9:30 a.m.-Nicky deleted *Citizen Kane* from her Favorite Movies." These mini-feeds provide uninterrupted insights into your behaviors, which makes it challenging to be incremental in your self-disclosures. Finally, Facebook users can post and view comments on "the Wall." Andrew Hampp (2007) describes the Wall as follows: "Think of it as a yearbook you can sign 24/7. Friends can use it to recap the previous night's events ("OMG! I still have your keys from Amanda's party! LOL!"), schedule get-togethers ("Lunch with the crew on Saturday? Hit me up!"), or carry on entire conversations that would normally be conducted through phones, email or, at the very least, text messages" (p. 32). "Poking," mini-feeds, and "the Wall" represent new and unique ways of conducting interpersonal communication online.

As we noted, not all online discussions evolve into interpersonal relationships, and you should always err on the side of caution when communicating with others online, especially on such sites as MySpace and Facebook. Some people may be feigning interest in you and your profile, manipulating you to gain information, or simply having a good time at your expense. For a list of safety tips and warnings of potential dangers when meeting and communicating with potential friends or romantic partners online, use your online Resource Center for *Understanding Interpersonal Communication* to access *Interactive Activity 11.2: Safe Online Relationships* under the resources for Chapter 11. And for a good reminder that we are responsible for and can control our own safety on- and offline, access *InfoTrac College Edition Exercise 11.3: Finding Love Online the Safe Way* to check out the article "Finding Love Online—How to Be Safe and Secure," available through InfoTrac College Edition.

We close the chapter with specific skills to remember when communicating online.

Choices for Improving Online Communication Skills

Your ability to function effectively in social and professional settings depends a great deal on your ability to be competent with communication technology. As we have seen, individuals utilize technology to cultivate online relationships.

poke

On a social networking website, an electronic invitation to another person to communicate with you.

mini-feed

Streaming bulletins that announce the activities of a Facebook user's friends.

We close our discussion by exploring several skills to consider as both a sender and a receiver of electronic communication. We begin with the sender of electronic messages, move to the receiver, and then—following our transactional model of interpersonal communication, explained in Chapter 1—we expand our discussion to both sender and receiver.

Sender Skills for Electronic Messages

The following sender skills apply to the source of an electronic message. If you are an avid consumer of communication technology, you might try to identify additional skills that are not explained here.

Be Succinct When Necessary

You have probably written or received an email that goes on and on and on. This stream-of-consciousness writing is easy to do because the sender doesn't have to organize his or her thoughts before sending a message. For example, if you want to email another person about your likes and dislikes, your hobbies, and what you do in your spare time, your message could continue for several pages! Learn to abbreviate your thoughts. The longer the message, the more the receiver will be inclined to emphasize parts of your message that may not deserve such attention. Stay on point. Consider the following example:

> Hi. I'm really not all that excited about writing U. I waz nervous the first time we "talked" online. Of course, I realize that we weren't really talking, but it's strange anyway. So, HOW RU? I'm OK! So much 2 tell u. DAH! I should SU so U can talk!!!

The sender appears to be babbling aimlessly, which communicates some nervousness on the sender's part. The receiver may read far more into this stream-of-consciousness writing than the message warrants. Now, look at an alternate, more succinct opening:

> Hi. this online stuff is new to me, so help me out if i mess up. i hope you're OK. being online keeps me thinking. . . what am i gonna say next?

This is a much more concise way of opening up the dialogue and letting the receiver know that you're new to electronic discussions.

Write Literally

Regardless of whether communication is electronic or face to face, we must be precise in our wording to others. Using concrete and precise language avoids ambiguous and convoluted thoughts. Because a sender of an electronic message isn't privy to the recipient's facial reactions, body movements, and eye expressions, it is important to be as clear as possible when sending a message so that it is less likely to be misinterpreted.

Senders of email messages need to be especially careful in communicating feelings; an emoticon or articon isn't always sufficient. In fact, if you use one during a challenging discussion, the receiver might view it negatively. For example, sticking in a frowning face while talking about a family mem-

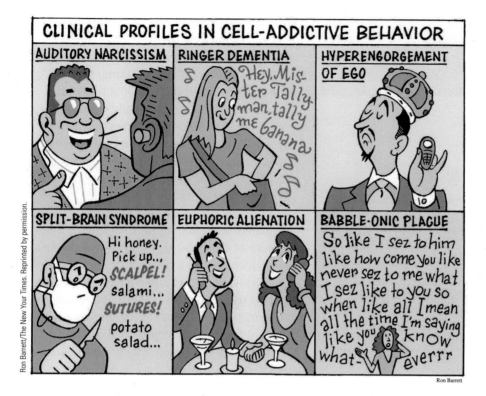

Ron Barrett/The New Your Times. Reprinted by permission.

Ron Barrett

ber's illness may be viewed by the receiver as flippant, which is probably a different message than what the sender intended.

Stay Polite

Although it's easy for us to suggest politeness, it's frequently difficult to practice. As in face-to-face conversations, when someone communicating online is passionate about a topic, he or she may blunder and be offensive. Keep in mind the permanency of the written word and the fact that communication is irreversible; after we write something mean or offensive, we can't take it back.

Let's look at an example. Breanna is mad that she didn't get the Friday night off from work that she requested, so when her boss emails her asking if she can work a double shift on Wednesday, Breanna sends the following message: "Sorry, can't do. I have to rest from being required to work Friday night!" Breanna's boss will surely perceive her message to be impolite. Now, consider an alternative response from Breanna: "I need to get back to you. Let me check it out, and I'll talk to you on Tuesday when I work." Courtesy and deference when communicating online are far more constructive than rudeness. Also, Breanna asks for a face-to-face conversation so that she can fully explain herself. Doing so will likely result in less misinterpretation than an email exchange would.

We are not suggesting that you simply roll with the punches all the time and avoid sticking up for yourself when matters become heated. At times, you do have to be direct in your email communication. Yet, we suggest that you temper your eagerness to make a point by recalling the power of words and their lasting effect upon both senders and receivers.

... on an online dating site

As you scroll through the personal ads on the dating website, you begin to wonder why you even placed an ad in the first place. Nearly all of those whom the website administrator identified as a "match" had ads that indicated that they were "in transition" with jobs, divorced, or "very willing." Disgusted with the options, you decide to utilize a different dating site and create a different personal ad to attract the sort of companion you seek. After receiving nearly a dozen replies to your ad, it's now time to respond to those who have taken the time to email you with their interests. What steps do you take as you construct messages to your senders? What cautions do you exercise as you send and receive electronic messages with potential partners?

Take a Deep Breath

This suggestion is both literal and figurative. When you inhale and release your breath, you reduce stress. Figuratively speaking, taking a deep break means thinking about what you want to write before you actually write it and press "Send." Reflect on your message. Reread it. In electronic discussions, we always recommend taking a deep breath before responding too quickly or taking action without first thinking about the ramifications.

Consider the following examples. Neil sent an email at work and forgot to delete the original draft of the email at the bottom of the message, which blasted a colleague for not responding quickly enough to a previous message. Marla, a student who received a poor grade on a midterm, wrote an email to the professor telling him that his questions didn't make sense and that the exam was way too long. And Tavo disclosed his entire life story in one email to a potential future partner online, unaware that his disclosure revealed that his ex-wife was the best friend of the woman he was dating! We can't urge you enough to take a deep breath before any online dialogue begins.

Receiver Skills for Electronic Messages

The receiver of information must also be savvy in the ways of online communication. Here, we explore receiver skills of online dialogues. As with the sender skills, think about additional receiver skills that may be needed.

Check In with the Sender

The receiver should always make sure that what he or she is responding to is what the sender intended. Checking in may be as simple as asking the sender to clarify. Or, a receiver may simply want to send out a brief **electronic trial balloon**, which is an overture that briefly responds to a sender's message. For example, when asked what she "does for fun" from someone responding to an online personal ad, Kia responds this way: "If U mean, what do I do in my spare time, I love animals. I volunteer at an animal shelter. What DID U mean?"

What Kia offered was an electronic trial balloon. She briefly responded to the question but then asked for more clarification. Checking in is an efficient form of communication because the receiver can avoid responding with unnecessary or irrelevant information. Checking in saves time and allows for clarity.

electronic trial balloon

An online overture that briefly responds to a sender's message in order to clarify the sender's intended message.

Show Empathy When Possible

When we discussed listening in Chapter 5, we addressed the need to be empathic. Empathy, as you recall, means to put yourself in another's position. In face-to-face conversations, empathy may take the form of hugging another when he's down and out or giving a "high-five" and shouting "yeah!" when a friend tells you she just got engaged. In our online discussions, we don't have the benefit of showing empathy in such ways. However, we can still show empathy for someone even though we aren't sharing the same physical space.

Being empathic online can take various forms. You might use articons (sparingly) to express how you feel about the situation in conjunction with words that show how you feel. For example, when Keith gets laid off from his job, Lee's written response should show some level of comfort: "We've all been there, buddy. You'll pull through this one (::()::) I know you will." Lee's words accompanied by the symbol of comfort (a Band-Aid) provide some degree of empathy that Keith will likely appreciate.

Listen beyond the Words

Listening applies to electronic conversations as well as those we conduct in person. When you listen to others online, you need to read between the lines to figure out the intention, emotion, and intuition. Yet, we need to be careful since we may be attributing too much detail to words, and we may come to an inaccurate conclusion. That's why we need to check in with the sender, a skill we noted previously.

Listening beyond the words is difficult. Recall Chapter 5 where we stated that listening is easier said than done, particularly on topics about which we have strong beliefs or opinions. Further, during our online conversations, we may have more distractions than during our face-to-face interactions. For example, while online, you may choose to answer the door, make breakfast,

© Ahmad Al-Rubaye/AFP/Getty Images

New technologies allow us to communicate with loved ones more quickly and more efficiently than ever before. For example, parents can take pictures of their new baby with a digital camera and email them the same day to anyone in the family who has access to email—no photo developing or scanning required. And friends and family can easily email empathy and support to people in places where mail delivery is slow.

talk to a roommate, pay your bills, clean your bedroom, change a light bulb, or do a number of other things that you feel need attention. Of course, your online partner doesn't necessarily know you are doing anything else except communicating with him or her.

Sender and Receiver Skills for Electronic Messages

In Chapter 1, we introduced the transactional model of communication, which suggests that a sender and receiver simultaneously engage in the communication process. Like face-to-face interactions, online conversations are transactional in nature. Let's explore a few skills needed by both sender and receiver while online with each other.

Take Responsibility for Your Own Words

Many people tend to forget that they "own" the words they choose to use. That is, whether we are in front of a person or a computer screen, we need to take responsibility for what we say or write. When communicating with someone online, this language ownership becomes important when we consider that the written word has the power to be permanent; it's not available to only you for future use—it's available to virtually anyone!

We recommend that you adopt a mantra that places responsibility for what is written solely within yourself, regardless of whether you are a sender or a receiver. Consider an earlier skill we identified that encouraged you to reflect before writing anything. And if you write something you didn't mean to write, try to reframe the situation by placing your words in context. Try not to cast blame on another for the words you chose to use.

Build Your Dialogue

We can think of a face-to-face conversation as a play. The scene may need to be set up, the characters have to be notified about their parts, and the setting should be clear to the audience. In online relationships, a similar metaphor seems reasonable. Plays don't begin in the middle. You don't expect a cast member to know what happens next unless you give some sort of background. You present ideas and concerns as a process, not as an ultimatum.

Building a dialogue online ensures that topics and ideas are arranged in order of importance. Subordinate ideas should be given less attention than primary ideas. For instance, if Tess is concerned that her online conversation is taking a turn to the highly intimate with J. C., she might inform J. C. about her feelings first and then proceed to explain why she is concerned. Perhaps Tess feels that too much personal information is being shared early in the development of the electronic conversation. If so, she needs to clearly state her belief.

To read an article that discusses building a dialogue online by asking questions that can help you reduce your uncertainty of others, check out "Interrogative Strategies and Information Exchange in Computer-Mediated Communication," available through InfoTrac College Edition. Use your

Student Workbook

Understanding Interpersonal Communication:
Making Choices in Changing Times

ENHANCED SECOND EDITION

Richard West
Emerson College

Lynn H. Turner
Marquette University

Workbook prepared by Deborah London, Merrimack College

Table of Contents

Chapter 1: Introduction to Interpersonal Communication

Chapter Goals
- Explain three prevailing models of human communication.
- Describe the impersonal-interpersonal communication continuum.
- Define and interpret interpersonal communication
- Understand the principles of interpersonal communication.
- Demystify stereotypes associated with interpersonal communication.
- Explain how ethical awareness relates to interpersonal encounters.

Outline
I. Communication apprehension
    A. Legitimate life experience that usually negatively affects our communication with others. (See communication assessment test).
    B. This book is about improving your ability to interact with other people.
II. We engage in interpersonal communication daily.
    A. Scholars have identified six kinds of situations in which human communication exists.
III. Models of Communication—visual, simplified representations of complex relationships in the communication process.
    A. Linear model of communication (Shannon & Weaver, 1949), see figure 1.1.
    B. Four types of noise can interrupt a message:
    C. The linear view suggests that communication takes place in a context, which is multidimensional, or the environment in which a message is sent.
    D. Although the linear model was highly regarded when it was first conceptualized, the linear approach has been criticized because it presumes that communication has a definable beginning and ending.
    E. Feedback and the Interaction Model (see figure 1.2).
    F. Like the linear model, the interactional model has been criticized for its view of senders and receivers.
    G. Shared meaning and the Transactional Model (see figure 1.3).
    H. Many interpersonal communication scholars embrace the transactional process in their research; such as, Julia Wood (1998, p. 6) who believes that human communication "is always tied to what came before and always anticipates what may come later."
    I. Our notion of communication models is continually evolving.

IV. The Nature of Interpersonal Communication
   A. The interpersonal communication continuum.

   B. There are three important issues when determining the extent to which an encounter is impersonal, interpersonal, or in between: relational history, relational rules, and relational uniqueness.

   C. Defining Interpersonal Communication is the process of message transaction between people to create and sustain shared meaning.

V. The Value of Interpersonal Communication

   A. A variety of sources report that interpersonal skills top the list of skills employers are looking for in new hires.

   B. A number of recent conclusions by both academic and medical   communities show the value of communication and relationships and how they affect our lives physically, emotionally, and psychologically.

VI. Principles of Interpersonal Communication

   A. Interpersonal communication is unavoidable (Watzlawick, Beavin, & Jackson).

   B. Interpersonal communication is irreversible.

   C. Interpersonal communication involves symbol exchange.

   D. Interpersonal communication is rule-governed.

   E. Interpersonal communication is learned.

   F. Interpersonal communication has both content and relationship information.

VII. Myths of Interpersonal Communication

   A. Interpersonal communication solves all problems.

   B. Interpersonal communication is always a good thing.

   C. Interpersonal communication is common sense.

   D. Interpersonal communication is synonymous with interpersonal relationships.

   E.   Interpersonal communication is always face-to-face.

VIII. Interpersonal Communication Ethics

   A. Five ethical systems of communication are categorical imperative, utilitarianism, the golden mean, ethic of care, and significant choice.

   B. Understanding ethics and our own values.

Terms for Review

Categorical imperative
Channel
Historical context
Interactional Model of Communication
Internal feedback
Process
Psychological noise
Receiver
Relational history
Relational rules
Relational uniqueness
Relationship information
Self-actualization
Semantic noise
Sender
Significant choice

Student Activities

1. **Directions:** Read each passage and identify which principle of Interpersonal Communication is best illustrated.

A.   Now that Brian has graduated from college, his friend Tom's parents keep telling him he should use their first names. This is awkward for Brian because his parents always told him to address adults using their last names and a title.

Interpersonal Communication _____

B.   Danielle asked her roommate, Jane, if she borrowed her new pink sweater because it smelled like Jane's perfume. Jane didn't say anything and continued reading her book, refusing to look at Danielle. Danielle knew Jane heard her and she got her answer even though Jane never said anything.

Interpersonal Communication _____

C.   When Chris came home, Terry said in an accusing tone of voice, "I thought you were going to take out the garbage this morning. That's the third week in a row you forgot."

Interpersonal Communication _____

D.   In Renee's family they were not allowed to sing at the dinner table and always took turns telling about their day while they had dinner.

Interpersonal Communication _____

E.   Javier and Maria always teased each other, so when Javier told Maria he loved her she misunderstood his feelings and thought he was joking.

Interpersonal Communication _____

Answers: A. learned, B. unavoidable, C. content and relationship dimensions, D. rule-governed, E. symbol of exchange

2. Directions: Look at ten different want ads for jobs in the newspaper or online. How many of them list communication or interpersonal skills as part of the job description? Compare your results with another student.

3. Directions: Review the communication models discussed in the chapter. What would you include in your own model of communication? Is there anything you would omit? Draw and label your own model below. Share and compare your model with another student.

4. Directions: Write down 4 or 5 adjectives that you think describe the following based on stereotypes. Do you believe these are accurate? Why or why not?

Athlete_____

_____

_____

Cheerleader_____

_____

_____

Secretary_____

_____

_____

Doctor_____

_____

_____

Muslim_____

_____

_____

Christian_____

_____

_____

Jew_____

_____

_____

Interactive Activities

1.1 Interactive Models of Communication

http://pirate.shu.edu/—yatesdan/model.html

Check out Seton Hall University professor Daniel Yates' active view of the linear, interactive, and transactional models of communication. (Click on the "Next" link to move from model to model.) Notice the development of the models from the early linear model to the more advanced transactional model.

1. What elements are consistent? What elements are changed or added?

2. Can you think of a communication experience in your own life where the interaction was similar to that shown in the linear model? In this interaction, you may have been the sender or receiver with little or no feedback. However, most communication situations are better represented with the transactional model, in which the participants are engaged in real dialogue.

1.2 Communication in Emergency Situations

http://envstudies.brown.edu/oldsite/Thesis/2003/Jessica_Galante/pages/commemerICS.html

The communication roles illustrated by communication models vary depending on the situation. Brown University student Jessica Galante's research indicates a changing model of communication for environmental science and in the case of emergencies. For example, in an emergency, there may be time only for a very brief message with little feedback.

1. Read Galante's web page "Communication in Emergencies."
2. After reading this page, click on the link "Emergencies" at left. Think back to a time when you were experiencing great emotional stress or in an emergency situation. How did you communicate during that situation? How did the various elements in the communication model change?

3. At the bottom of this page, click on "How does communication work in emergencies in time of urgency and direction?" What happened to the transactional model of communication? In this case, does the linear model seem most appropriate? Why or why not?

1.3 Technical versus Interpersonal Skills

http://envstudies.brown.edu/oldsite/Thesis/2003/Jessica_Galante/pages/commemerICS.html

Read the article "Which Is More Valuable: Technical or Interpersonal Skills?" as it relates to evaluating job applicants' technical versus interpersonal skills. With a partner or small group, discuss the following:

1. Do you think one skill, technical or interpersonal, is more important than the other?

2. What skills would you look for if you were hiring someone for a position?

3. How do you feel about the solutions the author of the article suggests to develop a new hire's interpersonal skills?

4. Do you foresee any problems with these solutions?

5. What solutions can you offer to improve someone's interpersonal skills for this job?

Your Turn Journal Activity

There are similarities and differences in the way we communicate with our neighbors, family, friends, and coworkers. Write about these and use examples of the types of conversations you have with each. What conclusions can you draw about how interpersonal communication varies based on particular sets of people with whom you interact? Are there times you wish communication were reversible?

Quiz

True or False

1. Interpersonal communication is a simple process. (p. 6)

True or False

2. When you debate with yourself, you are engaging in intrapersonal communication. (p. 6)

True or False

3. There is some overlap among different types of communication. (p. 7)

True or False

4. Communication models are visual, simplified representations of complex relationships in the communication process. (p. 7)

True or False

5. Shannon and Weaver view communication as a transactional process. (p. 7)

True or False

6. Four types of noise may disrupt a message. (p. 8)

True or False

7. Physical noise is also called external noise. (p. 8)

True or False

8. The physical context is everything but the tangible environment in which communication occurs. (p. 9)

True or False

9. Our notion of communication models is static. (p. 13)

True or False

10. Most employers discount the importance of interpersonal communication skills. (p.17)

True or False

Multiple Choice Questions

1. Which of the following four components are included in the linear model of communication? (p. 10)
A. sender, receiver, encoder, and decoder
B. physical noise, semantic noise, physiological noise, and psychological noise
C. sender, Context, Channel, and receiver
D. sender, receiver, message, and channel.

2. The transactional model of communication underscores the fact that giving and receiving messages is: (p. 13)
A. dynamic
B. reciprocal
C. deniable
D. retrievable

3. A unique feature of the transactional model is its recognition that messages: (p. 13)
A. have nonverbal elements
B. are interdependent
C. are intradependent
D. build upon each other

4. Which of the following is NOT a principle of interpersonal communication? (p. 21)
A. Interpersonal communication is unavoidable.
B. Interpersonal communication is irreversible.
C. Interpersonal communication involves noise.
D. Interpersonal communication involves symbol exchange.

5. Interpersonal communication has: (p. 24)
A. both content and relationship information.
B. both contextual and relationship information
C. both content and relative information.
D. both concrete and relative information.

6. Which of the following statements about interpersonal communication is a myth? (p. 22)
A. Interpersonal communication is rule-governed.
B. Interpersonal communication is always face-to-face.
C. Interpersonal communication is learned.
D. Interpersonal communication is unavoidable.

7. Every communication experience is: (p. 21)
A. unique
B. unrepeatable
C. irreversible
D. all of the above

8. When you turn away from someone, you are: (p. 21)
A. communicating
B. having some effect
C. communicating
D. not having any effect
E. both a and b

9. The golden mean is an ethical system that proposes: (p. 29)
A. we should be kind to one another.
B. we should always try to compromise.
C. we should aim for harmony and balance in our lives.
D. we should try to make many friends.

10. Nilsen argued that communication is ethical to the extent that: (p. 30)
A. it maximizes people's ability to exercise free choice.
B. it maximizes pleasure and minimizes pain.
C. it maximizes people's ability to say what they feel.
D. it maximizes rules and guidelines.

11. At the core of communication are two behaviors. They are: (p. 33)
A. Collaboration and commitment.
B. Competency and civility
C. Civility and chivalry
D. Coordination and compensation

12. Varying backgrounds can affect how a: (p. 33)
A. message is sent and received.
B. message is received but not sent.
C. message is sent but not received.
D. neither sent nor received.

13. We learn how to communicate from our: (p. 23)
A. teachers
B. parents
C. friends
D. all of the above

2.4 Pygmalion in the Classroom

http://www.wier.ca/~daniel_schugurens/assignment1/1968rosenjacob.html

Probably the most famous study of self-fulfilling prophecy was conducted by Harvard professor Robert Rosenthal and elementary school principal Leonore Jacobson. Their study examined teacher expectation and student achievement. Read the article "Rosenthal and Jacobson Publish *Pygmalion in the Classroom"* at the History of Education website, then answer the following questions:

1. What do you think about the teachers' perceptions of their students in the classroom?

2. Do you believe accurate or inaccurate perceptions can affect student performance?

3. What would happen if a teacher had a negative opinion of a student? Do you think it could actually harm a student's future success?

4. Can you think of any positive or negative messages sent to you by an influential person at a young age? Funny how these things stay with us, isn't it?

InfoTrac College Edition Activities

2.1 Attending to What Is Important

"Bet You Can't Remember How to Tie the Bows on Your Life Jackets" by Jeremy Bullmore
Marketing, 5 August 1999

Marketing and advertising experts know that we often receive many more messages than we can possibly decode. The article "Bet You Can't Remember How to Tie the Bows on Your Life Jackets" by Jeremy Bullmore uses the concept of selective perception to explain that if something is important to us or we have a need for the information, we will pay more attention to it. In particular, he discusses airplane safety videos to explore the concept of the attending and selecting stages of the perception process.

1. What do you think about his proposed study of airplane passengers?

2. For the next class period, think of some sort of message that we see or hear regularly but rarely attend to and select.

3. Share your thoughts with the class.

2.2 Cultural Perceptions and the Glass Ceiling

"Asian-Americans Face Great Wall; Perceptions, Cultural Traditions Hinder Advancement to Top Corporate Ranks" by Valerie Block
Crain's New York Business, 3 November 2003

The cultural perceptions of others can make it difficult for people outside the mainstream American culture to get ahead in the business world. This is especially true if a person's cultural heritage is perceived as being at odds with what Americans perceive as the typical business person. Read the article "Asian-Americans Face Great Wall; Perceptions, Cultural Traditions Hinder Advancement to Top Corporate Ranks" by Valerie Block and then complete the following activity:

1. With a partner, describe what you consider to be a successful business person.

2. Are any of the descriptors you use related to gender, culture, or communication style?

2.3 Sex, Gender, and Perception about Communication

"Exploring the Impact of Gender Role Self-Perception on Communication Style" *Women's Studies in Communication,* Fall 1999

Very few would argue that men and women differ in the way they interact with others, but is this difference a biological trait or perception of interaction? Read the article "Exploring the Impact of Gender Role Self-Perception on Communication Style" and then complete the following activity:

1. Go to the student center at your school and observe two women, or a group of women, interacting. What do you notice about their communication? Are you close enough to determine their topic of conversation? What is the purpose of the communication?

2. Now observe two men, or a group of men, interacting. Answer the same questions.

3. Did you perceive any differences? What were they?

2.4 Positive and Negative First Impressions

"Quality Interpersonal Communication—Perception and Reality" by Michael B. Coyle
Manage, July 1993

The article "Quality Interpersonal Communication—Perception and Reality" by Michael B. Coyle discusses perception and the self and applies this concept to communicating in an organization.

Coyle has a creative insight as he discusses self-talk and its influence on perception. In the article he states, "positive views of and feelings about one another are difficult to develop but easy to lose; on the other hand, negative views of and feelings about one another are easy to develop and hard to lose."

1. With a partner or in groups of three, discuss this insight. What is your response to Coyle's idea?

2. Together, can you recall a situation in which you had a difficult time making a positive impression?

3. How about when someone else did not make a good initial impression on you and you held on to this impression?

4. As a group, share your thoughts with the class.

2.5 The Self and the Workplace

"Quality Interpersonal Communication—Managing Self-Concept" by Michael B. Coyle
Manage, October 1993

In the workplace, how does your self-concept influence your performance and the performance of those around you? The article "Quality Interpersonal Communication—Managing Self-Concept" by Michael B. Coyle discusses the importance of self-concept in the workplace.

1. As you read the article, think back to messages sent to you by influential people in your life.

2. Identify a positive message sent to you from a "powerful other." How did it affect you?

3. Now identify a negative message sent to you from a powerful other. How did that affect you?

4. We are also powerful others for people in our lives. Consider how your past experiences with people who were powerful in your eyes could influence your interactions with people who think of you as a powerful other.

Your Turn Journal Activity

Think about a time when your self-concept was affected by your communication with another person. Did you feel particularly good or bad about yourself in response to something someone said to you? What were the circumstances of the communication? How did your dialogue influence your self-concept? Were your self-awareness and self-concept both affected? Use examples to describe and explain your experiences.

Quiz

True or False

1.When we talk about perception it's not necessary to talk about our sense of self. (p. 47)

True or False

2. The perception process occurs in four stages. (p. 48) True or False

3.The first stage is organizing because we are bombarded by stimuli. (p. 48)

True or False

4. Our cultural heritage has little to do with our present perceptions. (p. 53)

True or False

5. Low amounts of masculinity and femininity is termed undifferentiated. (p. 55)

True or False

6. Physical factors often help shape our perceptions. (p. 57)

True or False

7. Developing a relationship online shortchanges us, because we can't perceive the whole picture. (p. 58)

True or False

8. Most people's self-concept is unchanging. (p. 59)

True or False

9. George Herbert Mead believed that our understandings of ourselves and the world around us are shaped by our interactions with those around us. (p. 61)

True or False

10. We use face work to preserve our sense of self. (p. 65) True or False

3.4: Effects of Globalization

http://www.emory.edu/SOC/globalization/issues.html

Do you know what globalization is? Do you understand its effects? Check out The Globalization Website, sponsored by Emory University. Consider the six globalization issues listed.

1. In your own words, respond to at least two of the questions posed.

2. Click on the links to read the responses provided by the website. (And if you want to learn more, the links on each issue page will take you to articles for further reading.)

Summary: The Globalization Website, sponsored by Emory University, lists six issues related to globalization and its effects on women, poverty, and more.

InfoTrac College Edition Activities

3.1: Culture and Negotiation

"Next for Communicators: Global Negotiation" by William Briggs
Communication World, December 1998

Conducting business across cultures is a necessity for most successful companies. The article "Next for Communicators: Global Negotiation" discusses Hofstede's dimensions of culture applied to business negotiation. Read this article and then discuss the following:

1. Do you know of any cultural mistakes that advertisers or companies have made?

2. When you communicate cross-culturally, what do you do if someone says or does the wrong thing based on a lack of cultural knowledge?

3. If you were a businessperson, would you let such a mistake interfere with negotiation?

Summary: This article stresses the importance of cross-cultural communication and business negotiation. The article presents this topic in light of Hofstede's dimensions of culture, and also nonverbal communication and the importance of public relations.

3.2: Putting Patriotism on Ice

"Putting Patriotism on Ice: Top Figure Skating Duo Shen and Zhao Crave Gold—with Chinese Characteristics" by Hannah Beech

Time International, 4 February 2002

Do you think it's fair to compromise your cultural traditions or beliefs in order to gain the acceptance of others? Even for an Olympic gold medal? The article "Putting Patriotism on Ice: Top Figure Skating Duo Shen and Zhao Crave Gold—with Chinese Characteristics" discusses Chinese figure skaters who struggle to maintaining their cultural pride while adapting their skating performance to an "acceptable" style.

1. Have you ever judged someone or something from the perspective of your own culture?

2. What steps can you take to avoid an ethnocentric approach?

Summary: This interesting article discusses international competition and how some non-Western athletes feel pressure to adjust their cultural style in order to win higher marks with a Western-style performance.

Your Turn Journal Activity

Think about the cultural diversity of the United States to which we refer in Chapter 3 of your textbook. Choose a particular newspaper or watch a television newscast for a week. Keep a journal of the numbers of stories related to intercultural communication. How many of these stories did you perceive as positive? How many were negative? Write about your reactions to how the media contribute to images about various cultures.

Quiz

True or False

1. Some researchers have discovered over 500 different definitions for the word culture. (p. 84)
True or False

2. People who grew up in different time frames grew up in different cultural eras. (p. 86)
True or False

3. We aren't born with knowledge of cultural practices and behaviors, they must be learned. (p. 84)
True or False

4. In the United States very few people belong to co-cultures. (p. 85)
True or False

5. Those cultures that are unthreatened by change have a low degree of uncertainty avoidance. (p. 94)
True or False

6. Cultures that are low in power distance include Austria, Israel, and Denmark. (p. 94)
True or False

7. Money is important in masculine cultures while a compassion for the less fortunate characterizes feminine cultures. (p. 95)
True or False

8. Individualistic cultures tend to reject authoritarianism. (p. 95)
True or False

9. In high-context cultures, the meaning of a message is primarily drawn from the surroundings. (p. 97)
True or False

10. Native American culture is a low context culture. (p. 97)
True or False

11. The United States has fewer than 300 million citizens. (p. 87)
True or False

12. Cultures high in power distance show respect for status. (p. 97)

True or False

Multiple Choice Questions

1. Which of the following is not one of Hofstede's cultural dimensions? (p. 93)
A. uncertainty avoidance
B. technological imperative
C. individualism – collectivism
D. distribution of power

2. Today, extremely few places on earth are completely out of touch with the rest of the world. This phenomenon is referred to as: (p. 91)
A. world village
B. shrinking world
C. global village
D. global world

3. Each of us has a unique way of seeing the world through our own lens of understanding. This is known as: (p. 87)
A. rose-colored glasses
B. individualism
C. ethnocentrism
D. a world view

4. Which of the following is an example of the peace imperative discussed in your book? (p. 92)
A. The influx of immigrants from Mexico, Russia, and Vietnam has changed the workforce in the United States.
B. The global market has prompted overseas expansion of U.S. companies.
C. The Internet facilitates cross-cultural understanding of societies around the world.
D. Resolution of world conflicts, such as those in the Middle East, requires cultural understanding.

3.Equivocation is a type of ambiguity that involves choosing your words carefully to give a listener a false impression without actually lying.

X. Choices for Improving Verbal Communication.

A. Cultivate an attitude of respect for others by perspective-taking, which means acknowledging the viewpoints of those with whom you interact

B. Owning and using I – messages

C. Understanding the ladder of abstraction

D. Indexing - which means acknowledging the time frame of your judgments of others and yourself

E. Probing the middle ground

Terms for Review

Abstract
codability
code-switching
concrete
confirmation
connotative meaning
denotative meaning
disconfirmation
Ebonics
encoding
equivocation
generic *he*
grammar
I-messages
idiom
indexing
language
lexical gaps
linguistic determinism
linguistic relativity
man-linked words
muted groups
owning
perspective-taking
phatic communication
polarization
process of abstraction
referent
reification
Sapir-Whorf hypothesis
sexist-language
static evaluation
strategic ambiguity
verbal symbols

Student Activities

1. **Directions:** Read the following sentences one at a time. Before reading the next sentence, take sixty seconds to generate a list of as many substitutions as possible for the italicized word. These substitutions should represent shading, colorations, or nuances that modify the meaning of the sentence. For example, the sentence "He is *cheap*" could become "He is *thrifty*," "He is *stingy*," or "He is a *miser*." Compare your results with another student. (This exercise taken from Gamble & Gamble, 2002).

A. Della is *thin*.
B. Martin is *fat*.
C. Bernard is *smart*.
D. Louisa is *firm*.
E. Lily is *tired*.
F. Sonya is *good-looking*.
G. Kendra is *rich*.
H. Tom is *old*.
I. Javier is *cheap*
J. Simon is *frugal*.

2. **Directions**: Write your first or last name spelled backwards. Come up with a definition for the made-up word. Use it in a sentence. Ask a classmate a question using the new word. Was she or he able to understand what you were asking? Did the context help convey the meaning? Did you use more nonverbals to communicate your message?

3. **Directions:** For each of the statements below, write 2 distinct ways it might be interpreted. This exercise will provide you with concrete examples of ambiguous verbal symbols.(This exercise taken from North & Wood, 2006).

A. That is one bad woman.

Interpretation 1:_____

Interpretation 2:_____

B. Do you have any grass?

Interpretation 1:_____

Interpretation 2:_____

C. Are you straight?

    Interpretation 1:_____

    Interpretation 2:_____

D. This is very heavy.

    Interpretation 1:_____

    Interpretation 2:_____

E. You are hot.

    Interpretation 1:_____

    Interpretation 2:_____

F. I don't want you to hit on me.

    Interpretation 1:_____

    Interpretation 2:_____

4. Directions: Rewrite each sentence to eliminate any racism or sexism.

A. I don't know this doctor but I'm sure he knows what he's doing.

_____

_____

B. I called to make an appointment and a black woman answered the phone.

_____

_____

C. The Hispanic girl who cuts and colors my hair is excellent.

_____

_____

D. I missed when the minister introduced them as man and wife.

_____

_____

E. Did you call a policeman?

_____

_____

Interactive Activities

4.1: Linguistics

http://www.lsadc.org/info/ling-faqs.cfm

For more information on the study of linguistics, take a look at the website of the Linguistic Society of America. Pay close attention to the section titled Language as a Formal System. Here grammar and the concepts of semantics and pragmatics are discussed.

Talk to someone whose native language is something other than English.

Discuss with him or her some of the rules of English language, such as sounds, meaning, and structure and how these rules differ from those of his or her native language.

Summary: The Linguistic Society of America website provides background information on linguistics, or the study of speech and language.

4.2: Politically Correct Language

http://en.wikipedia.org/wiki/Political_correctness

For the definition, history, usage, and controversy of political correctness and its effects on language, check out the entry for "political correctness" at the online encyclopedia Wikipedia.

1. What are your thoughts on the controversial issue of political correctness?

2. Are we too sensitive about correctness? Explain your answer.

Summary: The entry for "political correctness" at the online encyclopedia Wikipedia provides some background on political correctness and can also be used to further explain the Sapir-Whorf hypothesis.

4.3: The Power of Words

http://dispatch.fandm.edu/read.php?id=372

Because words can be powerful, word choice often becomes an issue for journalists. Can the selection of one word over another impact the effect of a message? Take a look at the editorial "The Definition of Terror" on the use (or avoidance) of the words *terrorist* and *suicide*.

1. What other words could be defined as "powerful?"

2. Write down some of these words and compare them with those of a classmate. Are they context-appropriate? That is, in what instances would you use them for effect, and in what instances would you avoid using them?

Summary: This article in the Franklin and Marshall College *College Dispatch* discusses the media's use of the terms *terrorist* and *suicide bomber* and how each of these terms affects the impact of a message.

- Emotion is created and spreads through body.
- The mind experiences a feeling based on the change in the body.

4.4: Gender-Free Language

http://a4esl.org/q/h/dt/genderfree.html

Test your skills at replacing gender-based language with gender-neutral language by taking the Gender-Free Language Quiz. Resist the temptation to look at the answer for each exercise until you have thought of a gender-neutral substitution for the given word.

Summary: Test your skills at replacing gender-based language with gender-neutral language by taking the Gender-Free Language Quiz.

InfoTrac College Edition Activities

4.1: Moving Up and Down the Ladder of Abstraction

"The Ladder of Abstraction" by Jack Hart
Editor & Publisher, October 1994

Most effective speakers or writers will move up and down the ladder of abstraction to create impact depending on the context. The article "The Ladder of Abstraction" by Jack Hart discusses how most writers write somewhere in the middle of the ladder of abstraction.

1. Take a look at the three examples of abstract versus concrete writing.

2. Notice the difference between the article about the truck driver, the soldier, and the drug addict.

3. Where would you place each of these examples on the ladder of abstraction?

Summary: This article uses the concept of the ladder of abstraction to suggest that writers and journalists write somewhere around the middle of the abstraction ladder, rarely moving up toward deeper meaning or down toward stirring emotion.

4.2: Ebonics: Opposing Viewpoints

"Q: Would Ebonics Programs in Public Schools Be a Good Idea?" by Keith Gilyard and Nicholas Stix
Insight on the News, March 1997

In 1996 the Oakland, California, school board's decision to recognize Ebonics was quite controversial. To better understand both sides of this issue, take a look at the article "Q: Would Ebonics Programs in Public Schools Be a Good Idea?" by Keith Gilyard and Nicholas Stix.

1. What are your thoughts about the ideas raised in the article?

2. Do you think Ebonics is an acceptable form of English or a second language? Explain your answer.

3. Do you think Ebonics assists students to better understand their culture or does it provide a disservice to students? Explain your answer.

Summary: This article provides opposing viewpoints on the subject of Ebonics as it pertains to student learning and funding for bilingual programs in schools.

4.3: The Ties between Language and Culture

"Vermont Area Struggles to Keep Welsh Culture Alive" by Anne Wallace Allen
Capper's, February 2003

Take a look at the brief article "Vermont Area Struggles to Keep Welsh Culture Alive" by Anne Wallace Allen, about a fading culture and language right here in the United States. As you read the article, notice the connection between language and culture and how the fading of the language influenced the fading of the culture.

1. Think about this: If you restore the language, will you restore the culture?

2. What other cultures have become extinct? Has your own? Do you think people lose a sense of self if they don't have a strong connection to a culture?

Summary: This article discusses an example of the connection between culture and language. The author describes the passing of generations and its effects on the Welsh language and culture in Vermont.

4.4: How Words Come to Be

"How New Words Come to Be: They Travel from Abroad and Migrate from the Lab. Sometimes, Old Words Get New Meanings; Other New Ones Are Just Made Up!"
The Christian Science Monitor, July 2002

Ever wonder how new words develop? This interesting article, "How New Words Come to Be," offers a variety of answers to that very question. To get a sense of how words change from one generation to the next, complete the following exercise:

1. With a partner, make a list of "old" words that you know but hardly ever use or hear.

2. Now make a list of "new" words that you use but that might be unclear to your parents or grandparents.

Summary: This article from *The Christian Science Monitor* discusses the many ways that words are created and provides an interesting history of the Oxford English Dictionary.

4.5: Sexist Language in the Workplace

"Benefiting from Nonsexist Language in the Workplace" by Bill Daily and Miriam Finch
Business Horizons, March-April 1993

In the workplace, job titles and common business words and phrases could be considered sexist. The article "Benefiting from Nonsexist Language in the Workplace" by Bill Daily and Miriam Finch discusses the many ways in which sexist language is used at work.

1. Can you think of any job titles or duties that might be considered sexist?

2. Now can you change the words used for those titles or duties to create a gender-neutral alternative?

Summary: This article focuses on sexist language commonly used in the workplace, suggesting that we should take a second look at job and courtesy titles, as well as gender-specific pronouns. The article also discusses the benefits of promoting nonsexist language in the workplace.

10. Which of the following states that language influences our thinking, but doesn't determine it? (p. 131)
A. linguistic relativity
B. linguistic determinism
C. Sapir-Whorf hypothesis
D. social interactionism

11. The type of ambiguity that involves choosing your words carefully to give a listener a false impression without actually lying is known as: (p. 126)
A. avoidance

B. equivocation
C. egalitarianism
D. astuteness

12. When Axel first arrived in the United States from Germany, he thought he knew English fluently. However, he sometimes ran into difficulty when Americans used words or phrases that don't translate precisely. These type of words or phrases are called: (p. 127)
A. idiocentric
B. isometrics
C. idioms
D. idolatries

13. Keisha was amazed by how easily Maria and her family shifted back and forth between Spanish and English in the same conversation. This is an example of: (p. 130)
A. decoding
B. encoding
C. code-breaking
D. code-switching

14. The ease with which a language can express a thought is referred to as: (p. 132)
A. codability
B. code-breaking
C. code-ease
D. decoding

15. When you call someone or something by an extreme label, this term suggests that is how you will respond to that person or thing: (p. 139)
A. reification
B. renegotiation
C. regression
D. refraction

Essay Questions

1. Do you agree with Deborah Tannen (1995) when she argues that women prefer "rapport" talk, or talking for pleasure, while men prefer "report" talk, or talk that accomplishes a task? Why or why not? Be sure and include examples in your answer.

2. Using at least 3 different cues, explain how the phrase, "I love you," has different meanings depending on contextual cues.

3. Draw and explain the parts of The Triangle of Meaning.

4. Do you feel differently based on the label someone uses to describe you (for example, student, athlete, good-looking, stupid, weird, etc.)? Relate your answer to the power of words.

5. How has your family and/or culture affected the verbal symbols you use? Describe one or two examples.

Answers to Quiz

True or False

1. False
2. True
3. False
4. True
5. True
6. False
7. True
8. False
9. True
10. False
11. True
12. False

Multiple Choice Questions

1. A
2. B
1. D
2. C
3. C
4. A
5. C
6. B
7. C
8. A
9. B
10. C
11. D
12. A
13. A

Chapter 5: Communicating Nonverbally

Chapter Goals

- Understand nonverbal communication and its importance to human interaction.
- Identify the primary principles of nonverbal communication.
- Explain and exemplify the types of nonverbal communication
- Articulate the relationship between nonverbal communication and culture.
- Apply a variety of strategies to improve skills in nonverbal communication.

Outline

I. The Ubiquitous Nature of Nonverbal Communication

A. When we attend to nonverbal behaviors, we draw conclusions about others, and others simultaneously draw conclusions about us.

B. The influence of nonverbal behavior on our perceptions, conversations, and relationships cannot be understated.

C. Nonverbal communication can be defined as all behaviors – other than spoken words – that communicate messages and have shared meaning between people.

    1. Interaction adaptation theory suggests that individuals simultaneously adapt their communication behavior to the communication behavior of others (Burgoon, Stern, & Dillman, 1995).

II. Principles of Nonverbal Communication

A. Nonverbal communication is often ambiguous.

    1. One reason nonverbal communication is so challenging in our relationships is that our nonverbal messages often mean different things to different people, which can lead to misunderstandings.

    2. A major reason that this ambiguity exists is that many factors influence the meaning of nonverbal behaviors, including our shared fields of experience, current surroundings, culture, and so forth.

B. Nonverbal communication regulates conversation.

    1. Who talks when and to whom, referred to as turn-taking, is based primarily on nonverbal communication.

    2. We are often unconscious of our nonverbal cues.

C. Nonverbal communication is more believable than verbal communication.

    1. People believe nonverbal messages over verbal messages.

    2. Someone's nonverbal behavior can influence a conversational partner more than what is said.

D. Nonverbal communication may conflict with verbal communication.

    1. When nonverbal messages are not congruent with our verbal messages, we call this incompatibility a mixed message.

2. Adults who encounter mixed messages pay the most attention to nonverbal messages and neglect much of what is being stated.

III. Nonverbal Communication codes
    A. Visual-auditory codes
        1.kinesics
        2. physical appearance
        3. facial communication
        4.paralanguage
    B. Contact-codes
        1. touch (Haptics)
            a. 7 different functions
        2. space
            a. 4 categories
    C. Place and time codes
        1. the environment
        2. time (chronemics)
            a. 3 time systems

IV. Cultural Variations in Nonverbal Communication
    A. Body movement
        1. Greetings vary from one culture to another.
        2. Gesturing has also been studied across cultures.
    B. Facial expressions
        1. Eye contact is a much-studied facial display.
        2. Although frequent eye aversion may signal a lack of trust in people from the United States, in other countries it signals disrespect.
    C. Personal space
        1. In the United States we tend to clearly demarcate our territory.
        2. Also, interpretations of personal space vary from culture to culture.
    D. Touch
        1. Some cultures accept more same-sex touching than others.
        2. Nonverbal touching should always be understood within a cultural context.

V. Choices for Increasing Nonverbal Communication Effectiveness
    A. Recall the nonverbal-verbal relationship
        1. We need to pay attention to what is said in addition to the nonverbal behavior.
        2. We need to remain aware of this relationship to achieve meaning in our conversations.
    B. Be tentative when interpreting nonverbal behavior
        1. Because of individual differences, we can never be sure what a specific nonverbal behavior means.
        2. Be especially aware of your own biases, because they may not reflect the views of another.

C. Monitor your nonverbal behavior
    1. Becoming aware of how you say something, your proximity to the other person, the extent to which you use touch, or your use of silence is just as important as the words used.
    2. You need to look for meaning in both your behavior and the behavior of another.
D. Ask others for their impressions
    1. We need to consult others as we decide whether or not we're achieving meaning in our interpersonal relationships.

Terms for Review

bodily artifacts	mixed message	self monitor
body orientation	nonverbal communication	social distance
chronemics	paralanguage	territorial markers
citing gestures	personal distance	territoriality
delivery gestures	personal space	turn gestures
haptics	physical characteristics	turn-taking
interaction adaptation	physical environment	vocal characterizers
theory	proxemics	vocal qualities
intimate distance	public distance	vocal segregates
kinesics	seeking gestures	vocalics

Student Activities

1. The purpose of this activity is to increase awareness of how environmental features of settings include and exclude social groups.

Directions: Choose 5 places to visit: 1) a business office, such as a realty company, 2) an administrator's office on your campus, 3) a commercial building, such as a bank, 4) a waiting lounge in a hospital or doctor's office, and 5) a conference room in one of the campus buildings. (This exercise taken from North & Wood, 2006).

<u>Visit each of the 5 locations and record answers to the questions below.</u>

A. How many pictures or paintings of non-white people are present?
B. Which parts (rooms, floors) are accessible to persons who have disabilities that restrict their movement?
C. Are rooms identified with Braille and are there reading materials in Braille?
D. How many photographs or paintings of women are present?

Business office
A.
B.
C.
D.
Administrative office
A.
B.
C.
D.
Commercial building
A.
B.
C.
D.
Waiting lounge
A.
B.
C.
D.
Conference room
A.
B.
C.
D.

Discuss your observations with other students in your class. Are there consistent trends in your observations? What can you conclude about nonverbal communication of inclusion and exclusion?

2. Directions: Go to your dormitory room or your room where you are currently living. List the personal artifacts that you have put there. Do not list any that were given to you that you didn't choose. Beside each item on the list, explain its significance to you and what it communicates about your identity (This exercise taken from North & Wood, 2006).

Example: Artifact - Photograph of me and my sister in England. *This picture makes me think of my family and how I love traveling.*

A._____

_____

_____

_____

B._____

_____

_____

_____

C._____

_____

_____

_____

D._____

_____

_____

_____

E._____

_____

_____

_____

3. Directions: Invite a friend into your room or a common area where you can stand 10 – 12 feet away from him/her. Ask your friend a question or start a conversation about something familiar or a usual topic that you might discuss. Try to initiate another topic but move closer, although no more than 4 feet away. Now try a third round and only stand as close as possible to your friend.

How did your friend react? Did s/he respond in a way that was predictable or surprising? Was any one distance more or less comfortable?

Now explain to your friend that you are conducting an anecdotal study and ask your friend to help out once more. Conduct the same 3 attempts at conversation at the 3 different intervals.

Was there any difference to the outcomes? Did you feel any more or less awkward this time? Discuss your results with a classmate who tried the same activity.

4. Directions: Working with a partner, try the following. Think of a location such as the nearest restroom or a nearby building. Give your partner directions without using any nonverbal communication. Was it hard? Was it more difficult for the sender to send an accurate message, or for the receiver to interpret the message accurately? Switch roles and try again. Could you give the same directions only using nonverbal communication and no verbal communication at all?

12. We usually include place and time codes when we think about nonverbal communication. (p. 171)

True or False

Multiple Choice Questions

1. Which of the following is NOT a function of touch? (p. 168)
A. positive affect
B. submissiveness
C. accidental reasons
D. playfulness

2. Michael's research project focused on looking at distances between two people when they are discussing something upon which they don't agree. This type of communication is called: (p. 169)
A. kinesics
B. proxemics
C. chronemics
D. haptics

3. Edward Hall's four types of personal distance include each of the following EXCEPT: (p. 169)
A. intimate
B. personal
C. intermediate
D. social

4. Where you sit, sleep, dance, jog, write, sing, sew, play, or worship are all parts of your: (p. 171)
A. physical environment
B. practical environment
C. social environment
D. mental environment

5. This helps us to understand how people perceive and structure time in their dialogues and relationships with others. (p. 173)
A. kinesics
B. proxemics
C. chronemics
D. haptics

6. Which of the following is NOT one of the three time systems noted by Edward Hall? (p. 173)
A. social time
B. technical time
C. formal time
D. informal time

7. Bianca was taking a class in nonverbal communication and doing very well. Nelson asked her for advice on how he might improve his nonverbal communication effectiveness. Which statement was Bianca most likely NOT to offer as a suggestion to Nelson? (p. 180)
A. Be tentative when interpreting nonverbal behavior.
B. Monitor your nonverbal behavior.
C. Recall the nonverbal-verbal relationship.
D. Offer other people advice on their nonverbal behavior.

8. Other suggestions for improving your nonverbal communication include each of the following EXCEPT: (p. 181)
A. Increase your touching communication.
B. Ask others for their impressions of our nonverbal cues.
C. Interpret nonverbal communication within its context.
D. Avoid jumping to conclusions.

9. When Chelsea wants to speak during conversations with her friends, she notices she tends to touch the other person. This is an example of how nonverbal communication: (p. 161)
A. relaxes the other person.
B. offends the other person.
C. regulates conversation.
D. ruins conversation.

10. When nonverbal communication conflicts with verbal communication, we term this incompatibility: (p. 159)
A. turn-taking.
B. conflict.
C. inevitable.
D. a mixed message.

11. The theory that suggests individuals simultaneously adapt communication behavior to the behavior of others is known as: (p. 156)
A. individual adaptation theory.
B. interaction communication theory.
C. interaction adaptation theory.
D. simultaneous adaptation theory.

12. When Abby caught Jasper's attention he winked at her. She wasn't sure if that meant he liked her or if it meant something else. This _____ of nonverbal gestures can easily lead to misunderstandings. (p. 157)
A. practice
B. type
C. ambiguity
D. analysis

13. During his interview, Zane noticed that Mr. Wagner raised his eyebrows whenever he finished speaking and was ready for Zane to respond. In conversation, these types of nonverbal regulators are called: (p. 158)
A. queuing up
B. turn-taking
C. facial indicators
D. paralinguistics

14. Haptics and Space both fall into the nonverbal category of _____ code. (p. 160).
A. visual-auditory
B. contact
C. place and time
D. touch and tell

15. Shelby knew that Megan was probably nervous and that was why Megan was taking so long to explain things. Shelby was late for a meeting, though, and began motioning with her hand as if to pull the words out of Megan's mouth. This type of nonverbal communication is best known as a: (p. 161)
A. delivery gesture
B. citing gesture
C. seeking gesture
D. turn gesture

Essay Questions

1. Give two examples of how status is exhibited in nonverbal communication.

2. Offer at least one example of a nonverbal cue that has a variety of meanings and describe the multiple meanings that the cue evokes.

3. Discuss some of the nonverbal characteristics of paralanguage and explain how they can be used to alter meaning.

4. Discuss ways in which clothing can affect communication.

5. Define nonverbal communication and discuss why nonverbal cues can be ambiguous.

Answers to Quiz

1. True

2. True

3. True

4. False

5. True

6. False

7. True

8. True

9. True

10. True

11. True

12. False

Multiple Choice Questions

1. B
2. B
3. C
4. A
5. C

6. A
7. D
8. A
9. C
10. D
11. C
12. C
13. B
14. B
15. D

Chapter 6: Effective Listening

Chapter Goals

- Understand the complexity of the listening process
- Recognize social and personal obstacles to listening
- Identify your personal style of listening
- Describe several habits of poor listening
- Explain how culture affects listening
- Utilize a variety of techniques to enhance your listening effectiveness.

Outline

I. The Importance of Listening

    A. Our text focuses on those who can hear physiologically, but know that many individuals rely on the third most popular language in the US that uses a different communication system: American Sign Language (ASL).

    B. There is a difference between hearing and listening.

II. Hear Today: The Hearing Process

    A. Hearing occurs when a sound wave hits an eardrum.

    B. Hearing is the physical process of letting in audible stimuli without focusing on the stimuli.

III. Listen Up: The Listening Process

    A. Unlike hearing, listening is a learned communication skill.

    B. Listening is the dynamic transactional process of receiving, recalling, rating, and responding to stimuli and/or messages from another.

    C. Receiving – the verbal and nonverbal acknowledgement of communication.

    D. Recalling – understanding a message, storing it for future encounters, and remembering it later.

        1. repeat information

        2. use mnemonic devices

        3. visualize items as you listen to them

        4. chunk information

    E. Rating – evaluating or assessing a message.

    F. Responding – provide observable feedback

IV. The Barriers: Why we don't listen

    A. Noise – physical distractions

    B. Message overload – when more messages are received than can be processed.

    C. Message complexity – messages that are filled with details, unfamiliar language, and challenging arguments.

D. Lack of training – both the academic and corporate environments only offer a handful of opportunities to learn about listening.

E. Preoccupation – on occasion, everyone gets caught up in thinking about his or her own life experiences and everyday troubles at the expense of the present conversation.

    1. conversational narcissism – engaging in an extreme amount of self-focusing to the exclusion of another person.

F. Listening gap – the time difference between your mental ability to interpret words and the speed at which they arrive to your brain.

V. Poor Listening Habits

A. Selective listening – respond to some parts of a message and reject others.

B. Talkaholism – compulsively talking and hogging the conversational stage and monopolizing encounters.

C. Pseudolistening – faking attention (the classroom is a classic location for this!).

D. Gap filling – listeners who think they can correctly guess the rest of the story.

E. Defensive listening – when people view innocent comments as personal attacks or hostile criticisms

F. Ambushing – people who listen carefully to a message and then use the information later to attack the individual.

VI. Styles of Listening

A. People-centered listening style – being concerned with other people's feelings or emotions.

B. Action-centered listening style – listeners who want messages to be highly organized, concise, and error-free.

C. Content-centered listening style – focusing on the facts and details of a message.

D. Time-centered listening style – want messages to be presented succinctly and discourage wordy explanations.

E. Culture and listening process – all of our interactions are culturally-based, thus cultural differences affect the listening process (Brownell, 2002)

XI.   Choices for Effective Listening

A. Evaluate your current skills

B. Prepare to listen.

C. Provide empathic responses.

D. Use nonjudgmental feedback.

E. Practice active listening.

Terms for Review

action-centered listening style
active listening
ambushing
American Sign Language (ASL)
chunking
content-centered listening style
conversational narcissism
defensive listening
dialogue enhancers
empathy
facts
gap fillers
hearing
inferences
listening
listening gap
listening style
message overload
mindless
multitasking
nonjudgmental feedback
opinions
paraphrasing
people-centered listening style
physical distractions
pseudolisten
rating
recalling
receiving
responding
second-guess
selective listening
talkaholics
time-centered listening style
working memory theory

Student Activities

1. Directions: Read the statements that follow and decide for yourself what the answers are. Now join two or three other students and discuss each statement as a group. For each statement, arrive at a consensus. However, during the group discussion, each person should paraphrase the comments of the person who just spoke before he or she is allowed to make any new comments (this exercise borrowed from Titsworth, 2003).

A. People under nineteen should not be allowed to get married.
B. Subjective comments should be eliminated in college evaluations.
C. All students should be required to take a speech course to graduate.

After you've reached your decisions, discuss the listening behaviors in the group. Did anyone appear to be pseudolistening? Was anyone a gap filler? Was anyone particularly people-centered? How about content-centered or time-centered?

2. Directions: For an entire day keep a list of how many people you encounter who exhibit one or more of the poor listening habits discussed in this chapter. Did you run into all of them? Did some come up more than others?

3. Directions: Keep track of your own listening practices. For every hour in one day, record how much of each hour you spend listening versus hearing versus talking. What about the types of listening? Did you practice different styles in different encounters? Were you prone to using poor listening habits in certain situations? Did particular situations cause you to make more of an effort to practice good listening habits? Compare your results with another student.

4. Directions: Choose a class that usually includes a lot of lecturing by the professor. Observe your classmates listening habits. Does anyone appear to be pseudolistening? Does anyone answer before the professor finishes as in a gap filler? Do you have a classmate who seems to be listening only so s/he can correct or use the information against the professor later? Discuss your observations with another student. Would you have noticed any of these interactions before focusing on listening?

Interactive activities

6.1: Listening in the Workplace

http://techrepublic.com.com/5100-6316_11-5054191-1.html

Are managers more effective when they are also effective listeners? This website provides listening skill training to business managers so that they can improve their listening effectiveness and job success. Scroll about halfway down the page and click on the link "Next page" for a list of listening tips and habits.

1. Of the ten bad habits listed, how many are you guilty of?

2. Discuss how these habits might affect a person in the workplace. How about in an interpersonal relationship?

Summary: This site discusses the importance of listening in the workplace and offers listening skill training to business managers. The site also lists some habits of poor listening.

6.2: Emotions, Body, and the Mind

Do you ever think about the difference between a feeling and an emotion? This website describes the distinction between the two and discusses the relationship that links emotion, body, feeling and mind.

http://psy.rin.ru/eng/article/16-101.html

Read Damasio's definitions of emotion and feeling.

1. How are emotions and feelings different?

2. Using what you learned about perception in Chapter 2 in your textbook, how does perception play a role in emotion?

3. Apply the following process to an experience you have had.

   • External stimulus triggers the brain.

   • Emotion is created and spreads through body.

   • The mind experiences a feeling based on the change in the body.

Summary: This website from the Russian Information Network discusses neurobiologist Antonio Damasio and his theories of emotion and feeling. Damasio has an interesting take on the difference between emotion and feeling, and describes the process of emotion and feeling.

6.3: Empathy and Listening

"Leaders Know How to Listen" by Alexander Lucia
HR Focus, April 1997

Two concepts discussed in Chapter 5 of your text are empathy and active listening. This article, "Leaders Know How to Listen," discusses how both of these skills are necessary for effective leadership. Apply the exercises described in the article to someone you know.

1. Draw a caricature that illustrates the leadership characteristics of a good friend or significant other, especially as they relate to what you read in the article.

2. Present your drawing to your class, identifying your friend's listening and leadership abilities.

Summary: This article identifies good listening skills and empathy as the most significant characteristics of an effective leader.

6.4: Paraphrasing and Listening

"Practice Listening Skills as a Leader" by Joan Lloyd
CityBusiness (Minneapolis, MN), June 22, 2001

Want to give paraphrasing and empathic responses a try? The article "Practice Listening Skills as a Leader" will help you better understand these two concepts as they relate to effective listening.

1. Try paraphrasing with a co-worker, friend, of family member.

2. Did paraphrasing slow down your immediate response and force you to listen more closely?

3. Now try implementing an empathic response by identifying with the speaker's feelings as well as the content of his or her message.

Summary: This article encourages us to practice paraphrasing and empathy when listening, describing the benefits of each and providing examples.

6.5: Guidelines for Better Listening

"Improving Your Listening Skills" by Max Messmer
Management Accounting (USA), March 1998

We are capable of hearing 600 words per minute, yet most us speak at a rate of 100 to 150 words per minute. To find out how to fill the gap between the words a speaker says and the words we can hear, read the article "Improving Your Listening Skills" and consider its suggestions for better listening.

1. Write down the four guidelines for active listening described in the article.

2. As a student, try to listen actively when you are listening to a classroom lecture.

3. Now identify which guidelines worked best for you.

Summary: This article provides techniques for better listening, including active listening, that can be practiced by anyone wanting to improve their listening skills.

Your Turn Journal Activity

Think about how being a good listener affects your family relationships. Write about the different situations in which listening is important or when you failed to listen to a family member. Also comment on what happens when other family members don't listen to you. Are there any specific listening strategies you use with family members that may not necessarily work in other relationship types?

Quiz

True or False

1. Hearing and listening are different processes and mean different things. (p. 188)

True or False

2. People rarely take listening for granted. (p. 189)

True or False

3. When we are receiving a message, we are being mindful. (p. 190)

True or False

4. Recall is always considered long-term. (p. 191)

True or False

5. Rating means evaluating and agreeing with the message. (p. 192)

True or False

6. Opinions rarely change over time. (p. 193)

True or False

7. Messages we receive that are filled with details, unfamiliar language, and challenging arguments make listening complex but easier to understand. (p. 193)

True or False

8. Effective listeners do not become preoccupied. (p.199)

True or False

9. The listening gap is the time difference between your mental ability to interpret words and the speed with which they arrive to your brain. (p. 200)

True or False

10. Research shows that we speak an average rate of 150 to 200 words per minute, yet we can understand up to 800 words per minute (Wolvin & Coakley, 1996). (p. 200)

True or False

11. All Stuart could remember from his conversation with Jeremiah was that Jeremiah said he had been in juvenile detention. This type of listening habit is known as selective listening. (p. 200)

True or False

12. Charlie was a classic defensive listener: he perceived threats in messages where they didn't exist. (p. 202)

True or False

Multiple Choice Questions

1. Which of the following is NOT a barrier to communication? (p. 198)
A. message overload
B. noise
C. college
D. preoccupation

2. Kevin and Mike volunteered to help a neighbor move some items out of his garage. When they arrived at the specified time, the neighbor wasn't waiting in front of his garage. Mike asked Kevin what he thought might have happened, and Kevin said, "I don't know, I only remember him saying he'd pay us $50 each." What poor listening habit might have interfered with the boys getting the whole message? (p. 200)
A. defensive listening
B. selective listening
C. ambushing
D. talkaholism

3. Celia's father had a habit of correcting her grammar and asking her to get to the point when she spoke to him. What style of listening would you say best describes Celia's father? (p. 203)
A. people-centered listening style
B. action-centered listening style
C. content-centered listening style
D. time-centered listening style

4. Hans came to the United States from Germany to attend college. During a seminar one day there was a guest speaker that Hans found very interesting even though the speaker mentioned something in her presentation that confused Hans. During the question and answer period Hans was reluctant to ask the speaker to clarify herself. How did Hans' native culture affect the listening process in this case? (p. 206)
A. Hans didn't speak English very well.
B. Hans was distracted because he found the speaker attractive.

C. People from Germany often get bored and stop focusing during lectures.
D. People from Germany often do not like to ask for clarification because they see it as a sign of disrespect.

5. Which of the following is NOT suggested in your text as a suggestion for improving your listening? (p. 207)
A. evaluate your current skills
B. critique other people's conversational skills
C. prepare to listen
D. provide empathic responses

6. Which of the following is the best example of using nonjudgmental feedback (p. 209)?
A. "When you leave your clothes on the floor, it makes me feel embarrassed when people drop by our room."
B. "You are such a slob. You're not the only one who lives here, you know!"
C. "Aren't you embarrassed to have people stop by our room and see what a mess it is?"
D. "When you leave your clothes on the floor, you're being inconsiderate of me."

7. Each of the following is an element of active listening EXCEPT: (p. 210)
A. paraphrasing
B. dialogue enhancers
C. agreeing with the other person
D. silence

8. Among the reasons we listen is each of the following EXCEPT: (p. 194)
A. listening for advice
B. listening to help others
C. listening for enjoyment
D. listening to be critical

9. The four-step listening process discussed in your book does NOT include which of the following? (p. 190)
A. Reviewing
B. Receiving
C. Recalling
D. Rating

10. Which of the following would NOT be considered noise? (p.196)
A. your neighbor's stereo is too loud.
B. your roommate, Taryn, called from her skiing vacation and she couldn't get very good reception on her cell phone.

C. You skipped lunch and now all you can think about is what you're going to have for dinner.
D. None of the above.

11. Professor London admits she is fallible, so she tells her students that if they wish to challenge a grade, they should simply state the facts about why they deserve a grade change, what grade is appropriate, and then she'll consider their request. Prof. London would be considered a(n) _____ listener. (p. 204)
A. people-centered
B. action-centered
C. content-centered
D. time-centered

12. Stacey knew that due to _____ with whether or not Leslie was going to ask him out, nothing Leslie said during their review session would stick. (p. 197)
A. message complexity
B. lack of training
C. preoccupation
D. listening gap

13. Sean found it infuriating talking to Dylan because Dylan made everything about her and never remembered much of what Sean said. This is called: (p. 199)
A. ignoring someone.
B. conversational unification.
C. causal narcissism.
D. conversational narcissism.

14. Using supporting statements such as, "I hear what you're saying" or "I see" indicate that we are involved in a message. These types of phrases are called: (p. 210)
A. paraphrasing.
B. dialogue enhancers.
C. sympathizers.
D. aural supporters.

15. Placing pieces of information into manageable and retrievable sets is called: (p. 192)
A. rating.
B. coding.
C. plunking.
D. chunking.

Essay Questions

1. Explain the difference between hearing and listening. Be sure and use examples for each.

2. Discuss the four steps included in the listening process, in the order they are presented in your book. Give examples of each.

3. Discuss a time when you experienced two or more barriers to listening and how you might have overcome them.

4. Describe at least two of the poor listening habits that you have observed in people you know, according to the six behaviors discussed in your text.

5. What style of listening best describes you? Do you think you practice different styles in different situations? Why is that? If you think you could improve your listening habits, include some ways you might do that.

Answers to Quiz

True or False

1. True

2. False

3. True

4. False

5. False

6. False

7. False

8. False

9. True

10. True

11. True

12. True

Multiple Choice Questions

1. C
2. B
3. B
4. D
5. B
6. A
7. C
8. D
9. A
10. D
11. A
12. C
13. D
14. B
15. D

6. Apply the following process to an experience you have had.

   • External stimulus triggers the brain.

   • Emotion is created and spreads through body.

   • The mind experiences a feeling based on the change in the body.

   •

Summary: This website from the Russian Information Network discusses neurobiologist Antonio Damasio and his theories of emotion and feeling. Damasio has an interesting take on the difference between emotion and feeling, and describes the process of emotion and feeling.

7.3: Feeling Emotion

This site discusses the scientific link between emotion and the body, discussing the work of neurobiologist Antonio Damasio.

http://www.abc.net.au/science/news/stories/s184614.htm

1. How do you feel in an emotionally charged situation?

2. Name a positive emotional experience you've had and describe how it made you feel physically.

3. Now name a negative emotional experience you've had and how it made you feel.

4. How are these feelings similar or different?

Summary: The article "Emotion in the Body Mapped by the Mind," featured on the ABC Online website, cites a study by neurobiologist Antonio Damasio on the changes we experience in the brain and body when we recall emotional experiences.

7.4: Models of Emotion

Emotion is a subject of research for many academics, including those who study music. This website from the Ohio State University School of Music presents six models of emotions.

http://dactyl.som.ohio-state.edu/Music829D/Notes/Models.html

How do the biological and social models of emotion discussed in Chapter 4 of your textbook compare to the models diagrammed on this site? What are the similarities and differences between them?

Summary: This website from the Ohio State University School of Music diagrams and explains six different models of emotion.

7.5: Expression of Emotion

How skilled are you in reading the emotions of others? The website Espire: Your Guide to Emotions discusses emotional communication via body language.

http://maflib.mtandao-afrika.net/TQA00098/getDataS.php?pg=index1.php

1. What nonverbal emotional cues are most obvious to you when you're communicating with someone? Facial expressions, voice, or language?

2. Create a list of five or six common emotions. With a partner and using only facial expressions, attempt to display the emotions on your list and see if your partner correctly guesses the emotion.

3. Was your partner correct? What emotions were easier and more difficult to display?

Summary: The website Espire: Your Guide to Emotions thoroughly discusses the nature of emotion, types of emotion, influences on emotion, and the display of emotion in a fun and interactive format.

InfoTrac College Edition Activities

7.1: Gender, Emotion, and Stereotypes

"Speaking from the Heart: Gender and the Social Meaning of Emotion" by Kent Sandstrom
The American Journal of Sociology, May 2003

As you read in Chapter 4 of your textbook, Professor Stephanie Shields, Penn State University, argues that emotional expression defines the essence of masculinity and femininity. For more information on Stephanie Shields's work, check out the book review of *Speaking from the Heart: Gender and the Social Meaning of Emotion*. Shields uses the term "manly emotion" and "emotional double binds."

1. Do you believe that men and women are sometimes *expected* to act in ways that are consistent with emotional stereotypes?

2. Name a male emotional stereotype and think of a situation in which you think a man is expected to adhere to that stereotype.

3. Now think of a female emotional stereotype and think of a situation in which a woman is expected to adhere to that stereotype.

4. In class, discuss whether you think stereotypes are accurate and whether, socially, we are expected to follow a pattern of behavior consistent with stereotypes.

Summary: This review of the book *Speaking from the Heart: Gender and the Social Meaning of Emotion* closely examines the contents of each chapter. If you're interested in gender and emotion, you might want to read the book in its entirety.

7.2: Gender, Emotion, and Context

"Gender-Emotion Stereotypes Are Context Specific" Janice R. Kelly and Sarah L. Hutson-Comeaux
Sex Roles: A Journal of Research, January 1999

How accurate are stereotypes regarding gender and emotion? Read this article on gender-emotion stereotypes, "Gender-Emotion Stereotypes Are Context Specific," and find out if the stereotypes are correct.

1. What do you think this study's researchers mean by "interpersonal context" and "achievement context"?

2. The researchers also use the terms "overreaction" and "underreaction." Based on your experiences, do you believe men and women reinforce stereotypes, or do you feel that context is a factor for both, regardless of gender?

3. Discuss questions 1 and 2 with your classmates.

Summary: This article suggests that gender-emotion stereotypes are actually context specific.

7.3: Emotional Skills at Work

"Your Emotional Skills Can Make or Break You" by Steve Bates
Nation's Business, April 1999

Are you emotionally competent? According to this article, "Your Emotional Skills Can Make or Break You," "emotional competencies are twice as important as IQ and job-specific skills in determining the success of business people."

1. What does emotional competence mean to you?

2. Make a list of what emotions you believe are appropriate and inappropriate in the workplace.

3. Are these emotions similar or different from the emotions appropriate and inappropriate at school? In what way?

Summary: This article stresses the importance of emotional competencies in the workplace, suggests that emotional skills can be even more important than job skills, and offers strategies for the emotional development of employees.

Your Turn Journal Activity

In your journal, reflect upon the dark and bright sides of emotions and emotional communication. Which side do you experience most when you undergo emotional arousal? Does one side predominate when you talk about your emotions or when you communicate emotionally? How are the dark and light sides combined in an emotional situation? Does your answer vary depend on the type of emotion you are experiencing or communicating? Explain using examples.

Quiz

True or False

1. In the text, the term *emotion* encompasses both the internal feelings of one person *and* feelings that can be experienced only in a relationship. (p. 221)

True or False

2. Most people experience more than one emotion at a time. (p. 221)

True or False

3. Dualism refers to a way of thinking that means two things cannot coexist. (p. 223)

True or False

4. Charles Darwin believed that emotion is mainly biological. (p. 226)

True or False

5. Proponents of the social model of emotion believe emotions only surface in social   situations. (p. 228)

True or False

6. Communicating emotionally means that the emotion itself is not the content of the message but rather a property of it. (p. 229)

True or False

7. People often use a combination of cues when communicating emotion. (p. 233)

True or False

8. Emotional openness is valued in individualistic cultures, so people are more expressive of negative emotions in those cultures. (p.234)

True or False

9.According to Shields (2000), emotional expression (or lack of it) defines the essence of femininity and masculinity. (p. 236)

True or False

10. According to Hall et al (2000), men are more accurate in figuring out what others' emotional states are based on nonverbal cues. (p. 238)

True or False

11. Cultural norms used to create and react to emotional expressions are called feeling rules. (p. 239)

True or False

12. Empathy is a recommended practice for becoming an effective communicator. (p. 241)

True or False

Multiple Choice Questions

1. Which of the following contexts is not examined in relation to emotion in your text? (p. 239)
A. online communication
B. historical period
C. intimate relationships
D. others' feelings

2. Paige's colleague, Julia, got an undeserved bonus because their boss believed that Julia was responsible for a big new account brought in, when in fact the account was actually brought in by Paige. Julia accepted the bonus without mentioning Paige's hard work. When another colleague reported this to Paige during an important lunch meeting with the new clients (and Julia had embarrassed herself because she was unfamiliar with the new client's product), Paige's happiness at Julia's misfortune could best be described as: (p. 241)
A. *schadenfreude*
B. *schema*
C. shortcoming
D. *schaffoldin*

3. Competence in emotional communication begins with your ability to identify the emotion or mix of emotions you are experiencing at a particular time. This skill requires you to do all of the following EXCEPT: (p. 246)
A. recognize the emotions you're feeling
B. establish that you are stating an emotion
C. create a statement that identifies why you are experiencing the emotion
D. share the statement with a trusted friend

4. Lately, Tara had been spending hours and hours playing a computer game and Rhett had not seen her for over two weeks. The best way that Rhett believed he could express his feelings to Tara would be by owning them as in which of the following examples? (p. 251)

A. "Tara, I hate it when you play on the computer and ignore me."
B. "I want you to spend more time with me and less time on the computer playing games."
C. "I feel frustrated and lonely when you spend so much time on the computer, and I would like to spend more of our free time together."
D. "You're being selfish by spending so much of our free time alone on the computer."

5. Sally often felt herself getting irritated when she had to wait in line at a store to check out. Instead of being impatient because of what she considered other peoples' incompetence, she decided to rethink these situations and respect herself for being patient and more polite. This is an example of: (p. 252)
A. surrendering
B. reframing
C. regressing
D. suspension

6. Which of the following calls for you to suspend your own responses for a while so you can concentrate on the other person? (p. 253)
A. active listening
B. surrendering
C. empathic listening
D. suspension

7. The following pairs of words are all common dualisms in Western thought EXCEPT: (p. 225)
A. public – private
B. mind – intellect
C. right – wrong
D. good – bad

8. Indirect cues are used to communicate emotionally, often resulting in confusion. Which of the following would NOT be considered indirect? (p. 232)
A. When Savannah showed up an hour late to her cousin's birthday party, her friend Derrick said, "Nice of you to show up."
B. When Todd gave Sonya a single piece of chocolate candy for her birthday, Sonya said, "Wow, you must really love me."
C. Joey, who is a freshman, asked Lucy, who is a graduate student, if she'd like to go out some time. Lucy said, "I'm flattered, but no thank you."
D. Sherry told Lisa she had finished cleaning the kitchen, although there were still dishes in the sink. Sherry asked, "Is this where we're keeping the dishes now?"

9. Which scenario would fit someone who is from a collectivistic culture the LEAST? (p. 254)
A. Jong-wah, who is from Korea, was feeling angry that he did so poorly on the midterm for which he had studied so hard. When his friend asked him how he did, he smiled and said, "Fine, thank you."
B. Saroya, who is from India, was feeling angry because her car had been broken into and her backpack was stolen. When her friend remarked that she must be really mad, Saroya replied, "Maybe the thief needed it more than I do."
C. Akiko, who is from Japan, was very upset when she got a letter from the college saying her scholarship would soon be running out. When her advisor asked how she was feeling about this, Akiko said, "I will work harder."
D. Ren-Li, who is from China, thought she lost her favorite bracelet until a friend told her she saw another student wearing it. Ren-Li said, "I'm so mad! I'm going to make her give it back."

10. Which of the following statements is NOT true? (p. 239)
A. The feeling rules of U.S. culture have not changed much over time.
B. Emoticons are used to compensate for the lack of cues in CMC.
C. Before giving a speech, you're likely to feel more nervous around others who have to give a speech.
D. When you come home from school in a bad mood and your roommates are laughing and having fun, you might begin to feel better.

11. An attribute of emotion that refers to whether the emotion reflects a positive or negative feeling is a: (p. 222)
A. valence
B. balance
C. scale
D. range

12. This prompts us to think about things in an "either-or" fashion: (p. 223)
A. dichotomy
B. dilemma
C. dualism
D. doubt

13. Jaden's favorite show was Dancing with the Stars and watching it each week made her very happy. Her roommate, Ruby, didn't really care for the show but seeing how happy watching it made Jaden, she couldn't help but feel good even after a bad day. This is an example of (p. 229)
A. friendship
B. emotional witness

C. emotional contagion
D. emotional flipping

14. Jocelyn always seemed to be in a good mood. She always appeared so joyful that being around her made everyone feel better. This is an example of: (p. 229)
A. friendship
B. emotional witness
C. emotional contagion
D. emotional flipping

15. A message phrased to show we understand that our feelings belong to us and aren't caused by someone else is which of the following? (p.251)
A. owning
B. I-message
C. self-awareness
D. Own-awareness

Essay Questions

1. Explain what is meant by *schadenfreude* and give an example of a time when you experienced it.

2. Briefly highlight the two models of emotion and tell which model you agree with more and why.

the opposing desire of wanting to maintain our privacy.

3. There are several coping strategies to deal with the tensions involved in the self-disclosure process:

    a. cyclic alternation

    b. segmentation

    c. selection

    d. integration

        i. neutralizing

        ii. disqualifying

        iii. reframing

B. Social Penetration Theory

    1. people, like onions, have many layers (Altman & Taylor, 1973)

    2. breadth is how many topics we disclose

    3. depth is how much detail we provide

C. The Johari window

    1. open self— all the information you know about yourself and that you have shared with others

    2. hidden self— all the information you know but have chosen not to share

    3. blind self— information others know about you although you yourself are unaware of this information

    4. unknown self— information that neither you nor others are aware of about you

VII. Reasons to Self-Disclose

A. To experience catharsis and improve psychological health and control

B. To improve physical health

C. To achieve self-awareness

D. To initiate a relationship

E. To maintain existing relationships

F. To escalate a relationship

VIII. Reasons Not to Self-Disclose

A. To avoid hurt and rejection

B. To avoid conflict and protect a relationship

C. To keep your image intact and maintain individuality

D. To reduce stress

IX. Choices for Effective Disclosing
- A. Use I-statements
- B. Be honest
- C. Be consistent with your verbal and nonverbal communication
- D. Focus on your nonverbal communication
- E. Be sure your content is relevant
- F. Be sure your topic is relevant
- G. Estimate the risks and benefits
- H. Predict how your partner will respond
- I. Be sure the amount and type of disclosure are appropriate
- J. Estimate the effect of the disclosure on your relationship

Terms for Review

blind self
breadth
catharsis
cyclic alternation
depth
descriptive disclosure
dialectics
disqualifying
dyadic effect
evaluative disclosure
hidden self
history
integration
Johari Window
neutralizing
open self
private information
public information
reciprocity
reframing
segmentation
selection
self-disclosure
social penetration model
story
taboo topics
topical intimacy
unknown self

Student Activities

1. Directions:
- Fill out the form below by indicating how accurately each statement describes you.
- Ask someone who knows you well to fill out the duplicate form that follows. Write your name in the blank spaces on the second form.
- Compare the two views of you. Discuss differences with the other person and try to understand why you and the other person might perceive you differently (This exercise taken from North & Wood, 2006).

Rank each item for how true it is of you. Use the following scale:
1 = very true or always true
2 = mostly true or usually true
3 = somewhat true or true in some situations
4 = mostly untrue or usually untrue
5 = untrue or never true

1. I am an optimistic person.
2. I am personally mature.
3. I am extroverted.
4. I am thoughtful about others and their feelings.
5. I am ambitious.
6. I am generally cheerful or upbeat.
7. I am moody.
8. I am a reliable friend.

- Rank each item for how true it is of _____. Use the following scale:
  1 = very true or always true
  2 = mostly true or usually true
  3 = somewhat true or true in some situations
  4 = mostly untrue or usually untrue
  5 = untrue or never true

  1. _____ is an optimistic person.

  2. _____ is personally mature.

  3. _____ is extroverted.

  4. _____ is thoughtful about others and their feelings.

  5. _____ is ambitious.

6. _____ is cheerful or upbeat.

7. _____ is moody.

8. _____ is a reliable friend.

2. Directions: Identify a friend or romantic partner with whom you have had a long relationship. For this activity, it's important that you think about a relationship that has endured for quite a while.

Begin by recalling the early stages of this relationship. For example, think about the first 2 or 3 dates with a romantic partner or the first long talks with someone who became a close friend. Fill in the Johari Window #1 with content for each pane at the early stage of the relationship.

Next, recall a mid-point in the relationship's development. It might be when you and a romantic partner first expressed love for each other or when you took a vacation with a friend. Fill in Johari Window #2 with content for each pane at the mid-point in the relationship.

Finally, think about the relationship as it is today. Fill in Johari Window #3 with content for each pane at the current stage in the relationship. After completing the different Johari Windows, review what you've written and consider how communication both reflects and generates changes in levels of intimacy in close relationships (This exercise taken from Cole, Kobland, & Wood, 2004).

Johari Window #1
Time 1: *Early stage of Relationship*

Open area	Blind area
Hidden area	Unknown area

Johari Window #2
Time 2: *Mid-point in the Relationship*

Open area	Blind area
Hidden area	Unknown area

Johari Window #3
Time 3: *Today in the Relationship*

Open area	Blind area
Hidden area	Unknown area

Interactive Activities

8.1 Disclosing Health Information

http://www.thewellproject.org/en_US/Womens_Center/HIV_and_Disclosure.jsp

Self-disclosure is associated with intentionality, choice, intimacy, risk, and trust. Often, issues related to our health can be very difficult to disclose. Read the article "HIV and Disclosure" by Shari Margolese for helpful information about how one might proceed with the very personal decision of disclosing HIV+ status to others.

1. When and how would you disclose this type of private information to others?

2. Who do you feel should know about your health status? Who does not need to know this information?

1.2 Disclosing about a Disability

http://www2.warwick.ac.uk//services/careers/applications/disabled/dis2c/

If you believe you are qualified for a position with an employer but you have a disability, when and how do you think it would be appropriate to disclose this information? The Careers Service website of the University of Warwick provides guidelines to assist people with disabilities in disclosing information to potential employers. Take a minute to think about the following questions, then read the article "Disclosing My Disability" to see what Careers Service suggests.

1. What are the reasons why someone should disclose a disability?

2. When do you think it is unnecessary to disclose a disability?

8.3 Self-Disclosure Assessment

http://psychologytoday.tests.psychtests.com/take_test.php?idRegTest=1610

When, where, and to whom do you self-disclose? Take this on-line self-disclosure test and assess your willingness to self-disclose in various situations.

Based on the results of your test, do you feel satisfied with your disclosure in most cases?

Do you think you should be more open, or should you disclose less?

8.4 Fear of Self-Disclosure

http://www.apa.org/monitor/sep03/factor.html

Some disclosure is made purposefully for physical or mental health reasons. In such cases the patient must be willing to disclose very personal information. This online article, "Self-Disclosure a Leading Factor in Not Seeking Therapy," suggests that many avoid seeking professional because they are afraid of disclosing.

1. How do you feel about disclosing to a professional health care provider?

2. Do you believe this to be different from disclosing to a friend, or do think it's the same?

8.5 The Johari Window in a Professional Setting

http://www.businessballs.com/johariwindowmodel.htm

We can apply the Johari window model to a variety of contexts in addition to self-disclosure. Check out this business website to see how the Johari window can be used to understand organizational interaction and development.

Now that you have seen a few applications of the Johari window, think of a person you know pretty well, such as a friend, co-worker, intimate, or family member.

Create a Johari window based on your disclosure with that person, paying close attention to the size of each quadrant.

InfoTrac College Edition Activities

8.1 Expected versus Actual Responses

"Expected versus Actual Responses to Disclosure in Relationships of HIV-Positive African-American Adolescent Females" by Kathryn Greene and Sandra L. Faulkner
Communication Studies, Winter 2002

People will often choose to disclose information when they can predict the response or outcome. This research article, "Expected versus Actual Responses to Disclosure in Relationships of HIV-Positive African-American Adolescent Females," suggests that when people disclose their HIV-positive status, there is a connection between the expected and actual responses of receivers.

1. The researchers who wrote this article introduce a new model, the communication boundary management theory. When communicating with another, have you used a similar approach to that described by the model in the article?

2. Is boundary management an effective communication model as applied to disclosure?

8.2 Pruning the Grapevine

"Pruning the Grapevine" by Timothy Galpin
Training & Development, April 1995

The Johari window is used to assist theorists in a variety of disciplines. The article "Pruning the Grapevine" discusses organizational communication and the flow of messages. Take a look at how theorists apply the Johari window to disseminate information. You'll see in the article that some of the terms used are different from those in your textbook, but the theory is the same. What terms do we use instead of exposure, arena, blind spot, and façade when applying the Johari window to relationships in interpersonal communication?

8.3 The Private and Public Selves of Medical Students

"How Medical Students View Their Relationships with Patients: The Role of Private and Public Self-Consciousness" by Susana Jaimovich
The Journal of Social Psychology, **February 1999**

As you learned in Chapter 2 of your textbook, our public and private selves affect our perception and self-concept. Take a look at this interesting research article, "How Medical Students View Their Relationships with Patients," to examine medical students' private and public self-consciousness. How do you think the information in this article might affect how medical professionals interact with their patients?

8.4 The Cost of Choosing Not to Disclose
"The High Costs of Hidden Conditions"
Business & Health, January 1998

We sometime choose not to disclose information, but have you ever considered the consequences of not disclosing? For example, who has a right to know about health-related issues? Take a look at the article "The High Costs of Hidden Conditions," which identifies the potential problems of declining to disclose sensitive illnesses.

1. After reading the article, have you changed your opinion about disclosing issues of personal health? Who can possibly be affected by not disclosing?

12. A dimension of self-disclosure that indicates how many topics we disclose about within a relationship is referred to as breadth. (p. 278)

True or False

Multiple Choice Questions

1. Which of the following is NOT a coping strategy to reduce the tension of the dialectics process? (p. 276)
A. cyclic alternation
B. segmentation
C. integration
D. totalizing

2. Neutralizing, disqualifying, and refraining are all possible forms of: (p. 277)
A. integration
B. selection
C. totalizing
D. meta-communication

3. The Johari Window includes each of the following EXCEPT: (p. 280)
A. known
B. hidden
C. open
D. unknown

4. What does saying the Johari Window is a person-specific model mean? (p. 280)
A. Only certain people are able to diagram a Johari Window.
B. We need to draw a different window for each person with whom we interact.
C. The Johari Window can apply to specific people.
D. We are the only people who can interpret our diagrams.

5. What happens to our Johari Window as we choose to disclose? (p. 280)
A. Other windows disappear.
B. The open self shrinks, and the hidden self grows.
C. The open self becomes larger, and the hidden self becomes smaller.
D. The open self and the hidden self become one.

6. Kyle was flying to Lima, Peru to meet a friend. While waiting to board the plane, Kyle made several self-disclosures to a fellow passenger. This exception to the principle that self-disclosures take place in close relationships is called: (p. 273)
A. Driving the bus phenomenon
B. Catching the bus phenomenon
C. The bus rider phenomenon
D. The bus trip phenomenon

7. Sally told Beatrice her mother was in a rehab center because she was an alcoholic and needed help. Beatrice felt compelled to share something equally personal and serious with Sally. This feeling is called: (p. 275)
A. The serious effect
B. The dyadic effect
C. The caring effect
D. The guilt effect.

8. According to Derlega, Metts, Petronio, & Margulis (1993), the need for immediate reciprocity is strongest: (p. 275)
A. when people don't know each other.
B. when people don't like each other.
C. when people really like each other.
D. when people are just getting to know each other.

9. One reason psychologists are so interested in the concept of self-disclosure is probably because individuals experience catharsis. This means: (p. 282)
A. they experience a therapeutic release of tensions and negative emotion through disclosing.
B. they have a need to talk about themselves.
C. they want others to take an interest in them.
D. they gain insight.

10. Among the reasons to avoid self-disclosure are all of the following EXCEPT: (p. 288)
A. to avoid pain, rejection, or both.
B. to avoid conflict, protect a relationship, or both.
C. to initiate a relationship.
D. to reduce or forget about stress.

11. Zoe and Peter were married 4 years ago and generally got along quite well and were very happy in their relationship. They still talked about a great variety of topics except for the topic of Zoe's ex-boyfriend, Craig. Because Craig and Peter had a couple of mutual friends, his name came up once in awhile. The strategy for coping with the tension in their relationship, associated with Craig, by avoiding any discussion of him is called: (p. 277)
A. neutralizing
B. disqualifying
C. selection
D. integration

12. Jane and Kenya had been friends since 8th grade and had been through so much together and never seemed to run out of things to say to each other. But ever since Kenya announced her engagement to Paul, Jane and Kenya had an unspoken agreement that any discussion of Jane's earlier relationship with Paul was off limits. When an issue is out of bounds for discussion, it is called a(n): (p. 277)
A. selection topic
B. integration topic
C. neutralizing
D. taboo topic

13. A dimension of self-disclosure indicating how much detail we provide about a specific topic is called: (p. 279)
A. breadth
B. depth
C. penetration
D. saturation

14. Among the reasons offered in your text to self-disclose, which of the following is NOT included? (p. 282)
A. To experience catharsis.
B. To improve physical health.
C. To cheer someone up.
D. To achieve self-awareness.

15. Among the reasons offered in your text to not self-disclose, which of the following is NOT included? (p. 288)
A. To secure boundaries.
B. To reduce stress.
C. To keep your image intact.
D. To avoid hurt and rejection

Essay Questions

1. Describe an instance when someone disclosed something very personal to you and you felt you should self-disclose in return. Did you? Why or why not?

2. Discuss some of the reasons different people might be more or less likely to self-disclose a similar item such as a particular medical issue.

3. Terry wants to be a more effective communicator and has decided to work on effective self-disclosure choices. Offer Terry at least 4 choices and describe how they might be helpful.

4. Explain why engaging in self-disclosure can be a good thing. Provide at least 3 reasons along with your explanation.

5. Identify and discuss the effects of culture, gender, and individual differences on self-disclosing.

Answers to Quizzes

True or False

1. True
2. False
3. False
4. True
5. True
6. False
7. True
8. False
9. True
10. False
11. False
12. True

Multiple Choice Questions

1. D
2. A
3. A
4. B
5. C
6. C
7. B
8. D
9. A
10. C
11. B
12. D
13. B
14. C
15. A

Chapter 9: Communicating Conflict

Chapter Goals

- Understand the complexities of conflict
- Explain common myths about conflict
- Detail communication patterns in conflict
- Describe two theories of interpersonal conflict
- Identify the relationship between power and conflict
- Employ skills for communicating power and conflict that afford increased satisfaction in interpersonal interactions

Outline

I. Defining Conflict: Knowing it When You See It
    A. Interaction means that conflicts are created and sustained through verbal and nonverbal communication.
    B. Selective perception is a central dynamic in conflict interactions.
    C. Interdependence means that people involved in the conflict rely on one another, need each other, and are in a relationship with one another.
    D. Perception refers to the psychological process involved in sensing meaning.
    E. Incompatible goals are broad and cover a range of conflict types.
        1. image conflicts concern self-presentation
        2. content conflicts revolve around an issue
        3. value conflicts can be considered conflicts in which the content is specifically a question of right or wrong
        4. relational conflicts focus on issues concerning the relationship between two people
II. Myths about Conflict: What Not to Believe
    A. Conflict is always bad – one myth states that conflict is completely negative and implies that relational life would be perfection if only partners could eliminate all conflicts.
    B. Conflict is just miscommunication--a myth that says conflict results from people not clearly communicating their goals and wishes to one another.
    C. All conflicts can be resolved through good communication--a myth that tells us that if we master a certain set of skills, we can resolve all conflicts.
    D. It is always best to talk through all conflicts--a myth that represents the commonly held belief that increasing communication solves conflicts.
III. Factors Influencing Interpersonal Conflict
    A. Gender and Sex

        1. men and women are not inherently different in their orientation to conflict or in their conflict behaviors; rather they have been taught a set of responsibilities and norms that affect their conflict interactions

        2. this imbalance may cause conflict within relationships

    B. Culture

        1. differing cultural practices and norms may put us in conflict with one another

        2. culture affects our conduct of interpersonal conflict in myriad ways

IV. Communication Patterns in Conflict

    A. Symmetrical escalation exists when each partner chooses to increase the intensity of the conflict.

    B. Symmetrical withdrawal means that when conflict occurs, neither partner is willing to confront the other.

    C. Pursuit-withdrawal/Withdrawal-pursuit, unlike the previous two, are asymmetrical and mean that the behavior of one partner is complemented by the other's behavior rather than one partner mirroring the behavior of another.

    D. Symmetrical negotiation is a positive pattern where each partner mirrors the other's negotiating behaviors.

V. The Dark Side of Interpersonal Conflict

    A. Bullying is where the abuse is persistent and the person being bullied finds it very difficult to defend himself or herself.

        1. bullying often takes place in situations where there is a distinct power difference.

        2. isolating, nitpicking, excessively criticizing, humiliating, and physical abuse can all be characteristics of bullying.

    B. Violence and Aggression

        1. verbal and nonverbal acts geared to hurt or cause suffering.

        2. in communication discipline, most research on violence has focused on the family.

VI. Explaining Conflict through Theory

    A. Satir's four-part model includes the critical parts of any conflict: you, me, the context, and the subject.

    B. Cupach & Canary model conflict as a process that occurs in the following episodes: distal context, proximal context, conflict interaction, proximal outcomes, and distal outcomes.

VII. The Relationship of Conflict to Power

    A. Using Power:

        1. direct application

        2. direct and virtual use of power

        3. indirect application

        4. hidden use

    B. Sex Differences: although sex role stereotypes in the US suggest that husbands have more power in decision-making than their wives, one study suggests that sex differences do not operate stereotypically in marital decision-making.

    C. Empowerment, or helping to actualize people's power.

VIII. Choices for Conflict Management: Working it Out

A. Lighten up and reframe is a technique that includes staying in the present and acknowledging that you have heard what your relational partner just said.

B. Presume good will and express good will means that you go into each conflict interaction believing that you and your partner both want to come to a constructive resolution.

C. Ask questions after you have both had a chance to speak.

D. Listen and remember to practice all of the behaviors associated with effective listening.

E. Practice cultural sensitivity and be mindful and tune into your own culture's norms and assumptions first before evaluating others (Ting-Toomey& Oetzel, 2001).

Terms for Review

active conflict
aftermath
coercive power
computing
content conflicts
direct and virtual use of power
direct application of power
distracting
empowerment
expert of information power
hidden power
image conflict
indirect application of power
initial awareness
interaction
interdependence
interpersonal conflict
legitimate power
personal issues
persuasive power
placating
pouncing
power
prior conditions
public issues
pursuit-withdrawal
referent power
reframe
relational conflicts
relational messages
resolution
reward power
symmetrical escalation
symmetrical negotiation
symmetrical withdrawal
value conflicts
withdrawal-pursuit

9.4: Conflict in Groups

"Conflict Resolution—A Key Ingredient in Successful Teams" by Thomas K. Capozzoli
Supervision, November 1999

When you work in a group or on a team, conflict often surfaces. Read the article "Conflict Resolution—A Key Ingredient in Successful Teams" to learn more about constructive conflict and the process for resolving conflict.

1. What has been your experience with conflict when working in groups?

2. What do you like about working in groups? What don't you like?

3. If conflict has arisen in a group you've worked in, what did you do about it?

4. Did you follow any of the steps for resolving conflicts listed in the article? If not, do you think they would have helped in the situation you described in question 3?

Summary: This article suggests that if conflict in work groups is appropriately managed, it can be constructive rather than destructive. Causes of conflict and the steps of conflict resolution are also discussed.

Your Turn Journal Activity

- In your journal, note the times you engage in interpersonal conflict during a week. Record the following information about your conflicts:
- The persons involved
- The relationships between/among the persons involved
- The context surrounding the conflict
- The topic of the conflict
- A rating of how important that conflict was to you (not very important - 1 to very important - 7)
- A brief description of what was said during the conflict
- A rating of how satisfied you were with the conflict (not at all satisfied - 1 to very satisfied - 7)
- A brief explanation of how this conflict relates to the material in this chapter. If you'd like, you can use your student workbook to complete this activity.

Quiz

True or False

1. Conflict is not always bad. (p.304)

True or False

2. Sometimes people have conflict because they can't agree whose goal is most important. (p.305)

True or False

3. All conflicts can be resolved through good communication. (p. 311)

True or False

4. The best thing to do when you encounter conflict is always to talk it out. (p. 311)

True or False

5. There is little to no difference in how men and women are socialized to handle conflict. (p. 314)

True or False

6. A person whose primary orientation is toward individualism might conflict with a person whose primary orientation is toward collectivism. (p. 315)

True or False

7. When each partner mirrors the other's negotiating behaviors, it's called symmetrical negotiation. (p. 319)

True or False

8. It is usually a bad idea to ask too many questions in a conflict situation. (p.330)

True or False

9. Interpersonal conflict is easily avoidable and in fact infrequent for most people.(p. 303)

True or False

10. Value conflicts focus on issues concerning the relationship between two people. (p. 308)

True or False

11. The longer a couple is together, the more likely they are to experience serial conflict. (p. 309)

True or False

12. When the emotional aspects of a conflict are disqualified and only the rational aspects are considered, this is called computing. (p. 323)

True or False

Multiple Choice Questions

1. Rachel really likes the roommate she was assigned at school. The only problem is that her roommate likes to have other friends visit late and listen to music while Rachel prefers to study late at night. This type of conflict has to do with: (p. 304)
A. perception
B. incompatible goals
C. interdependence
D. inconsideration

2. Audra is Harry's supervisor. Several times this month, Harry has taken extra long lunch hours. Audra decides to say something about typing up a memo regarding late lunches to her assistant while Harry is filing something nearby. This use of power would best be considered: (p. 327)
A. direct and virtual use of power
B. indirect application of power
C. mishandling of power
D. hidden power

3. Satir's four-part model is made up of: (p. 321)
A. I, you, conflict, and power
B. you, me, conflict, and power
C. you, me, the context, and the subject
D. you, me, the subject, and the object

4. The first episode in The Explanatory Process Model is the distal context, which refers to: (p. 323)
A. the background
B. the time of day
C. the distance between the people involved
D. the aftermath

5. When people disqualify the *you* in conflict, they respond in an aggressive manner without acknowledging the needs of the other person in the conflict. Satir called this: (p. 321)
A. punishing
B. pounding
C. pulsing
D. pouncing

6. Evan didn't like it when his older sister referred to him as her baby brother in front of his friends because he felt it made him sound immature. This type of conflict is a(n): (p. 306)
A. image conflict
B. content conflict
C. value conflict
D. relational conflict

7. Samantha and her colleague, Gene, were working on a project together that was due the following morning. Samantha felt it was more important to get all of their facts and figures accurate before starting, while Gene was more concerned with the final product. This type of conflict can best be defined as an issue of: (p. 303)
A. perception
B. incompatible goals
C. interaction
D. stubbornness

8. When neither person wants to confront the other in a conflict, it's a pattern of conflict called: (p. 317)
A. symmetrical negotiation
B. withdrawal-pursuit
C. withdrawal-withdrawal
D. symmetrical withdrawal

9. Colin is pretty sure his girlfriend Rebecca is cheating on him. He really wants to talk about their relationship and asks her repeatedly but Rebecca keeps making excuses and avoids talking about it. This communication pattern in conflict is called: (p. 317)
A. symmetrical escalation
B. symmetrical withdrawal
C. withdrawal-pursuit
D. pursuit-withdrawal

10. The last three times Simon and Billy went out, Simon forgot his wallet and Billy   ended up paying for both of them. Rather than say anything to Simon, Billy started   avoiding him. Simon soon stopped asking Billy if he wanted to go out and the   relationship dissolved. This communication pattern is called: (p. 317)
A. symmetrical escalation
B. symmetrical withdrawal
C. symmetrical negotiation
D. pursuit-withdrawal/withdrawal-pursuit

11. A passive response, which cancels out one's own position in a conflict, is called: (p. 322)
A. placating
B. pouncing
C. computing
D. distracting

12. Disqualifying the subject of a conflict by distracting both people in the conflict with behaviors such as laughing, crying, or changing the subject, is called: (p. 323)
A. placating
B. pouncing
C. computing
D. distracting

13. When Charlotte and Trey argue, Charlotte says she left her position at an excellent law firm just so Trey could pursue his dream of being a playwright. When Charlotte does this she implicitly sends a message that states she has power to define their relationship. This type of message is called: (p. 327)
A. direct application of power
B. direct and virtual use of power
C. indirect application of power
D. relational message

14. A type of power in which one person in a relationship suppresses or avoids decisions in the interest of one of the parties is called: (p. 328)
A. direct application of power
B. indirect application of power
C. hidden power
D. suppressed power

15. Which of the following is NOT recommended as a choice for conflict management? (p. 329)
A. practice cultural sensitivity
B. give in on occasion
C. presume good will and express good will
D. listen

Essay Questions

1. How do you show and use power? Be as specific as possible. How would you like to change your use of power?

2. Identify the five suggestions for conflict management and apply them to a recent conflict you were engaged in.

3. Describe the four communication patterns in conflict

4. Describe an example(s) that proves at least two of the myths about conflict are indeed myths.

5. Describe the potential value of conflict for a relationship that you are currently a part of.

Answers to Student Activity #1

B

A

C

D

Answers to Student Activity #4

Myth

Myth

Fact

Answers to Quiz

True or False

1. True
2. True
3. False
4. False
5. False
6. True
7. True
8. False
9. False
10. False
11. True
12. True

Multiple Choice Questions

1. B
2. B
3. C
4. A
5. D
6. A
7. B
8. D
9. D

2. Directions: Identify a close friend or romantic partner. The person should be one with whom you did or do have a satisfying close relationship. Answer the questions to describe central features of a satisfying relationship in your life (This exercise adapted from North & Wood, 2006).

A.   Investments
- What have you invested?
- What has the other person invested?

B.   Commitment
- How certain are you that the two of you will remain in a close relationship?
- To what extent do the two of you talk about a shared future or future plans?

C.   Trust
- How much do you feel you can rely on your friend/partner to do what s/he says s/he will do?
- How much do you count on your friend/partner to look out for you and your welfare?

D.   Relational Dialectics
- How do you manage needs for autonomy and connection?
- How do you manage needs for novelty and predictability?
- How do you manage needs for openness and closedness?

3. Directions: Use the chart below to make a cost-benefit analysis of a relationship you are now experiencing. On the basis of this analysis, what is your prognosis for the future of the relationship? (This exercise taken from Gamble & Gamble, 2002)

COSTS	BENEFITS
1.	1.
2.	2.
3.	3.
4.	4.
5.	5.
6.	6.
7.	7.
8.	8.
9.	9.
10.	10.
11.	11.
12.	12.

4. Directions: Ask the person whom you had in mind for the above chart if he or she would be willing to fill in the same chart from his or her perspective. Engage in a productive discussion (using all the skills you've recently encountered through this class) about any differences or similarities in your perspectives.

COSTS	BENEFITS
1.	1.
2.	2.
3.	3.
4.	4.
5.	5.
6.	6.
7.	7.
8.	8.
9.	9.
10.	10.
11.	11.
12.	12.

Interactive Activities

10.1 Relationship Communication Quiz

http://www.web-research-design.net/cgi-bin/crq/crq.pl

Instructions: How effective is your communication in relationships? The way we relate to others in an intimate relationship is described by the attachment theory. For a personalized assessment of your attachment style, complete the online Attachment Style Questionnaire: Experiences in Close Relationships, Revised.

1. What do you think about your results? Do they seem to describe you accurately?

2. What do you think of the summary and graph? Did they help you understand your attachment style?

10.2 Assessing Close Relationships

http://www.thedoctorwillseeyounow.com/articles/feature/behavior/clrel_1/

Psychology professor Ann Weber, Ph.D., created this website, The Psychology of Close Relationships, as a step-by-step learning tool that may help you better understand your close relationships with others. In addition to interesting content, this site also includes two assessment tests.

To learn more about the psychology of close relationships, take this online mini-course that includes two exercises for you to complete. Keep in mind that, as the author of this site states, an assessment like this is just a summary of your knowledge and skills—it doesn't really tell us anything we didn't already know.

10.3 Knapp's Relational Stages Model

http://novaonline.nv.cc.va.us/eli/spd110td/interper/stages/models.html

This Northern Virginia Community College website explains three popular models of relational development: Knapp's Relational Stages Model, DeVito's Six-Stage Model, and Duck's Model of Relational Dissolution. It also includes a link to strategies for terminating relationships.

1. How does Knapp's model differ from DeVito's relational model?

2. It can be disheartening to analyze the stages of relationship dissolution, especially if you've gone through some bad breakups. How do you feel about the coming apart stages?

10.4 Unhealthy Relationships

http://www.charmeck.org/Departments/CMPD/Investigative+Services/Criminal+Investigations/Domestic+Violence+Unit/Unhealthy+Relationship's+Characteristics.htm

To review a list of characteristics of an unhealthy relationship, take a look at the Charlotte-Mecklenburg Police Department's website. Police officers often see the worst of relationships, so they are a good source of information for how to recognize characteristics that can create or maintain a toxic relationship. Notice the differences between the unhealthy and healthy relationship characteristics.

1. Can you identify with any of these characteristics?

2. How could you use this information to help you improve your existing relationships and avoid potentially toxic or dangerous relationships?

InfoTrac College Edition Activities

10.1 Who Are You Closer To Emotionally?

"Close Emotional Relationships with Women versus Men: A Qualitative Study of 56 Heterosexual Men Living in an Inner-City Neighborhood" by Lynne I. Wagner-Raphael, David Wyatt Seal, and Anke A. Ehrhardt
The Journal of Men's Studies, Winter 2001

This article studies close male-male relationships versus male-female relationships, self-disclosure and emotional closeness.

Given that men and women often differ in what they expect of a relationship, when it comes to emotional closeness, do you think a man would prefer communicating with a women or another man? The information in this research article, "Close Emotional Relationships with Women versus Men," might surprise you. Take a close look at the results, where each research question is answered.

1. In your same- and opposite-sex relationships, who do you feel closer to emotionally?

2. Does this situation affect your disclosure? How? What things do you talk about?

10.2 Emotions and Social Exchange

"Bringing Emotions into Social Exchange Theory" by Edward J. Lawler and Shane R. Thye
Annual Review of Sociology, Annual 1999

Emotion can be an important factor in the social exchange theory of costs and rewards. This article relates emotion and the emotional process to the theory. The article "Bringing Emotions into Social Exchange Theory" attempts to show how the consideration of emotions and the emotional process can benefit the social exchange theory.

1. As you've learned in Chapter 10 of your textbook, social exchange theory addresses the costs and rewards in a relationship. Make a list of what a particular relationship in your life costs you. Now list the rewards you gain from that relationship.

2. Apply emotion to your list of costs and rewards. How do your emotions affect the costs and rewards of your relationship?

Your Turn Journal Activity

In your journal, spend two weeks collecting metaphors you hear in daily conversation referring to relationships. You can gather metaphors from television or other popular media as well as from conversations you participate in or overhear. For instance, if you hear a friend say that they had to break up with someone because "they were stuck in a rut," that would be a metaphor. The relationship partners weren't literally stuck in a rut—that's a figurative way of describing the feeling your friend had in the relationship. At the end of the two weeks, look over your metaphors and answer the following questions: How do metaphors guide our thinking about relationships? How do metaphors influence the way we actually communicate in our relationships?

Quiz

True or False

1. Maslow's Hierarchy of Needs places our social needs at the top level. (p.338)

True or False

2. The diversity of interactions has to do with the number of different experiences people have together. (p.341)

True or False

3. Relationships as cultural performances means relationships consist of the ongoing process between partners. (p. 342)

True or False

4. Cognitive structures that contain a pattern for the key events that we expect in a relationship are known as relationship scripts. (p. 343)

True or False

5. According to Lakoff & Johnson (1980), metaphors and similes help us understand relationships by comparing them to other phenomena. (p. 344)

True or False

6. Differences between men and women have little influence on our interpersonal relationships. (p. 346)

True or False

7. In systems theory, wholeness means that you can't understand a system by simply picking it apart and understanding each of its parts in isolation from one another. (p. 352)

True or False

8. In systems theory, boundaries or openness means that human systems are closed off from one another. (p.353)

True or False

9. The dialectics of novelty and predictability has to do with how often you and your partner give each other gifts unexpectedly. (p. 356)

True or False

10. The tension between judgment and acceptance involves criticizing a friend as opposed to accepting a friend for who she is. (p. 356)

True or False

11. Rather than providing a large framework for understanding communication in close relationships, social exchange theories are more specific. (p. 358)

 True or False

12. A person's standard level for what types of costs and rewards should exist in a given relationship is called a comparison level. (p. 359)

True or False

Multiple Choice Questions

1. Emily and Stacey have been friends since elementary school and now they attend the same college. Although they don't room together, they are still friends. One day when they saw each other in the dining hall, Stacey called out to Emily by her childhood nickname. Emily was eating with some new friends including a boy who she was interested in dating and Stacey's outburst caused her great embarrassment. This illustrates the dialectical tension between: (p. 356)
A. judgment and acceptance
B. affection and instrumentality
C. internal and external dialectics
D. public and private

2. Ellen and Howard had been dating for almost a year. Howard still found Ellen attractive but now that he was at a different school he was making many new friends and Ellen always seemed to be calling with some crisis or another that to Howard were very minor issues. He felt as though returning her calls was a burden and an obligation. Ellen felt Howard was no longer being supportive or interested in her affairs while Howard no longer felt he gained anything by dating Ellen long distance. Their situation is best illustrated by what kind of theory? (p. 358)
A. systems theory
B. dialectics theory
C. social exchange theory
D. management of meaning theory

3. Howard keeps finding excuses not to visit Ellen and keeps telling his roommate he's not in when she calls. This is an example of which stage of coming apart according to Knapp's model of relationship development? (p. 361).
A. circumscribing
B. stagnating
C. avoiding
D. terminating

4. When Ren Li and Jon started dating, Jon was pleased to learn Ren Li also enjoyed cooking and suggested they cook dinner together. Jon's suggestion of cooking together illustrates his wanting to enter which stage of coming together in Knapp's model? (p.361)
A. bonding
B. intensifying
C. integrating
D. initiating

5. The final stage in the coming together part of Knapp's model is: (p. 361)
A. bonding
B. intensifying
C. integrating
D. initiating

6. The first stage in the coming apart section of the model is: (p. 361)
A. differentiating
B. circumscribing
C. stagnating
D. avoiding

7. If a relationship stagnates for too long, the partners may decide that the relationship is unpleasant and as a result, they move to: (p. 365)
A. differentiating
B. circumscribing
C. stagnating
D. avoiding

8. The ability to achieve the same goals (or ends) by a variety of means is called: (p. 355)
A. compatibility
B. machiavelliness
C. equifinality
D. mutual equality

9. Sometimes relationships need adjustment to accommodate changing needs of the parties. This type of resetting the rules of a relationship is called: (p. 354)
A. feedback
B. calibrating
C. recalibrating
D. equifinality

10. Perry wanted to ask Kayla on a date. Perry had a class with Michelle who he knew was a good friend of Kayla's, so he made a point of leaving class at the same time in order to talk to Michelle and get information about Kayla. This skill for beginning a relationship is called: (p. 368)
A. approaching
B. offering
C. networking
D. affinity seeking

11. Behaving in a way that keeps an initial conversation going, such as asking questions is referred to as: (p. 369)
A. facilitating
B. sustaining
C. including
D. confirming

12. Dynamism, optimism, openness, and supportiveness are all types of: (p. 369)
A. affinity-seeking strategies
B. bonding strategies
C. maintenance strategies
D. conflict-prevention strategies

13. Making descriptive comments rather than evaluative comments are excellent examples of this type of communication climate: (p. 370)
A. selective
B. subordinate
C. supportive
D. colorful

14. Although Kate apologized, she offered no _____ or an explanation for her transgression. (p. 373)

A. account
B. elaboration
C. remorse
D. satisfaction

15. _____ are those things in relational life that we judge as negative, while_____ are those parts of being in a relationship that we find pleasurable. (p. 358)

A. Rewards, costs
B. Costs, parties
C. Parties, rewards
D. Costs, rewards

Essay Questions

(some questions taken from Cole, Kobland, & Wood, 2004)

1. Think of a time when you had to negotiate intimacy (kissing, hugging, safe sex, etc.). What relationship dialectics were present? How did you and your partner negotiate the tensions?

2. How do you think communication in a long-distance relationship might differ from a romantic relationship in which you and a partner are geographically together? Be specific.

3. Describe a friendship you have with a member of the other sex. Analyze the extent to which it conforms to the gender patterns described in your text.

5. Describe a friendship you have with a member of your sex. Analyze the extent to which it conforms to the gender patterns described in your text.

6. Discuss and provide examples of the three suggestions in your text of communication skills for repairing relationships.

Answers to Quiz

True or False

1. False
2. True
3. True
4. True
5. True
6. False
7. True
8. False
9. False
10. True
11. True
12. True

Multiple Choice Questions

1. D
2. C
3. C
4. B
5. A
6. A
7. D
8. C
9. C
10. C
11. B
12. A
13. C
14. A
15. D

Chapter 11: Technology and Interpersonal Communication

Chapter Goals

- Identify and explain characteristics of technology.
- Understand issues related to the presentation of self online.
- Articulate the dark and bright sides of CMC.
- Discuss the pervasiveness and importance of social networking.
- Explain how relationships function online.
- Utilize skills that help improve electronic discussions and relationships.

Outline

I. Society and Technology
- A. Convergence is the integration of various technologies.
- B. As a society, we have grown accustomed to convergence.
- C. This chapter examines the role that technology plays in our interpersonal communication.
- D. Specifically, the focus is on computer-mediated communication (CMC).
- E. A valuable theoretical framework to consider throughout this chapter is technological determinism.

II. Characteristics of Communication technology
- A. Technology affects our conversations and relationships with others.
- B. Because technology is everywhere, we rely on it as a matter of course.
- C. Technology is paradoxical, meaning that it is conflicting, inconsistent, and ironic.
- D. Saying that technology is powerful means that it influences people, events, and entire cultures.

III. The Accessibility of Technology
- B. Accessibility helps eliminate the technological gap that exists between people and between cultural communities, sometimes called the digital divide.
- C. The digital divide is evident with nearly all communication technology.
- D. Accessibility and interpersonal communication's relationship
    - 1. If everyone does not have access to all technology, language barriers may exist.
    - 2. Accessibility to communication technology has many positive benefits.

IV. The Internet: Connecting Now
- A. Background of the Internet
    - 1. The terms Internet and World Wide Web ("the web") are not synonymous.

a. the Internet connects computers together

b. the web is just one of the ways information is shared over the Internet

2. Scholars now refer to the web as it first appeared in the 1970s as web 1.0.

3. The label web 2.0 has been used to describe the web in the past several years as it has expanded.

B. The dark side of the Internet: proceed with caution.

   1. little accountability

   2. fostering hate

   3. flaming

   4. sacrifice of privacy

C. The bright side of the Internet: new opportunities

   1. With the Internet, you can widen your social network.

   2. With the Internet, you have enhanced educational accessibility.

V. The Presentation of Self Online

  B. Assumptions of online presentations of the self

    1. Assumption 1: the computer screen can deceive

    2. Assumption 2: online discussions often prompt introspection

    3. Assumption 3: online discussions promote self-orientation

    4. Assumption 4: self-disclosure occurs online

  B. Identity markers on the Internet

    1. screen names

    2. personal home pages

VI. Communication Technology and Relational Maintenance

  A. The electronic and face-to-face relationship

    1. traditional dating tends to be random (Silverstein & Lasky2004)

    2. online relationships typically have a highly accelerated development

  B. The "language" of online relationships

    1. abbreviated language

    2. graphic accents

    3. blogging

  C. Social networking: Beyond the keyboard

    1. linking individuals and communities of people who share common interests, activities, and ideas

    2. first social network appeared in 1997

    3. between 1997 – 2003, 13 social network sites appeared

    4. Facebook and MySpace have captured a niche that began in the college community

      a. some estimates say there are over 115 million users of MySpace and it grows approximately 50% per year

      b. Facebook, founded by a Harvard university student was originally available only to college students but now is open to anyone over the age of 13 and has approximately 72 million users.

VII. Choices for Improving Online Communication
  A. Sender skills for electronic messages
        1. be succinct when necessary
        2. write literally
        3. stay polite
        4. take a deep breath
  B. Receiver skills for electronic messages
        1. check in with the sender
        2. show empathy when possible
        3. listen beyond the words
  C. Sender and receiver skills for electronic messages
        1. take responsibility for your own words
        2. build your dialogue
        3. recall the challenge of online communication

Terms for Review

abbreviated language
articon
blog
browser
chat rooms
computer-mediated communication (CMC)
convergence
cookies
electronic trail balloon
flaming
global village
hate speech
homepage
hyperdating
hyperlink
identity marker
Internet
personal home page
postcyberdisclosure panic (PCDP)
screen names
search engine
spam
uniform resource locator
world wide web

Student Activities

1. Directions: Read through the personal profiles of an online dating site such as; Match.com, or Yahoo personals, to get a sense of what people look for in a partner online. This time, unlike a similar activity in the last chapter, write a personal ad based on the person you'd like to be ten years from now. How is your self presentation different here from what it is right now? If you wrote a profile of yourself as you are today, what would you include?

2. Directions: Print out a page from a recent instant message exchange or a chat room you've visited. What abbreviated language is used? Are there any codes or jargon used that might be unfamiliar to someone who is not familiar with computer-mediated communication? Translate the page into Standard English. What are the positives and negative results from using a specialized language? What happens if you don't know what an abbreviation stands for? How important is it to the rest of the text?

3. Directions: Compare the help wanted section of a newspaper in hard copy to the want ads through a job site such as monster.com. Are there any differences in the job descriptions? What about the length of the ads? Do you get a different impression from the different types of ads? Are there any differences in how you are instructed to respond to the ads? Do any of the ads say they will only accept online applications? Are there any that say no online applications accepted?

Interactive Activities

11.1 What Digital Divide?

http://www.news.com/2010-1071-858537.html

Will bridging the digital gap in the United States help solve some of our economic and social problems? Take a look at this article, "What Digital Divide?" to better understand the implications of the digital divide and the growing usage of the Internet in the U.S.

1. What do you think? Is the digital divide the crisis of our century? What are some potential problems with technological inequality?

2. What do you think of the terms "classic apartheid" and "technological segregation" to describe the digital divide?

11.2 Safe Online Relationships

http://depression.about.com/od/onlinesupport/tp/onlinesafety.htm

Meeting new people online can be exciting, but remember that it's important to maintain your safety and security online. For some safety tips and warnings of potential dangers, take a look at the site "Keeping Online Relationships Safe."

1. List the advantages, disadvantages, and safety considerations of communicating and developing relationships face to face versus online.

2. Which do you prefer, face to face or online? Or do you like a combination of both? Explain your answer.

11.3 Netiquette Quiz

http://www.albion.com/netiquette/

Just as in face-to-face communication, it is important to follow the rules of common courtesy in cyberspace. Netiquette is the term used to explain the rules of common courtesy to follow when you communicate online. Click on some of the links at the Netiquette site to learn about the rules of conduct, then take the Netiquette Quiz.

1. How did you do? Did taking it help you realize what sort of impression you make as you send online messages?

InfoTrac College Edition Activities

11.1 Self-Disclosure Online

"Relationship Formation on the Internet: What's the Big Attraction?" by Katelyn Y. A. McKenna, Amie S. Green, and Marci E. J. Gleason
Journal of Social Issues, Spring 2002

This research article discusses self-disclosure on the Internet and how some people fared moving from online to face-to-face relationships. Are you more comfortable discussing your true self face to face or online? This article, "Relationship Formation on the Internet: What's the Big Attraction?" discusses self-disclosure online as it relates to relational formation and success.

1. Are you surprised at the success rate of some of the online relationships discussed in the article as they moved from online to face-to-face meetings? Explain your answer.

2. Some people believe they can better express themselves online. What do you prefer? Why?

11.2 Can You See the Real Me—Online?

"Can You See the Real Me? Activation and Expression of the 'True Self' on the Internet" by John A. Bargh, Katelyn Y.A. McKenna and Grainne M. Fitzsimons.
Journal of Social Issues, Spring 2002

In this article, the true versus actual self is examined as it relates to disclosure in online relationships. Do you let others discover the real you when you are online? The article "Can You See the Real Me?" examines variations of the self and applies them to online disclosure.

1. Are you more comfortable self-disclosing information about yourself online than you are disclosing face to face? Why or why not?

2. Is the actual self or the ideal self always the true self? Explain your answer.

11.3 Finding Love Online the Safe Way

"Finding Love Online—How to Be Safe and Secure; Over 4 Million Matchmaker.com Members Have Safely Developed Relationships Online"
PR Newswire, April 4, 2000

This article reminds us that we are responsible for our own safety online in that we can control who we talk to, what personal information we give out, and if, when, and where we decide to meet a new online friend. Online dating services provide a popular way to meet others. The article "Finding Love Online—How to Be Safe and Secure" states that these services are a safe way to meet people if you play it smart. Take a look at these safety tips for online and offline dating. If you feel comfortable talking about your online dating experiences with your classmates, have a class discussion about cyberdating.

1. Have you or anyone you know participated in an online dating program?

2. What were the results? Do you think it is a viable option for some people?

3. What are some advantages and disadvantages of online dating?

11.4 Reducing Uncertainty Online

"Interrogative Strategies and Information Exchange in Computer-Mediated Communication" by Laurie Pratt, Richard L. Wiseman, Michael J. Cod, and Pamela F. Wendt
Communication Quarterly, Winter 1999

This article discusses forming online relationships by asking questions that can help us reduce our uncertainty of others. When we're getting to know someone, we usually ask that person a lot of questions. Is getting to know someone online by asking questions different from doing the same thing face to face? The article "Interrogative Strategies and Information Exchange in Computer-Mediated Communication" takes a look at an interrogative approach to asking questions that can help us reduce our uncertainty of others.

1. What is the uncertainty reduction theory in interpersonal communication?

2. How can it this theory be applied when communicating online?

3. Is getting to know someone online by asking questions different from doing the same thing face to face? Why or why not?

Your Turn Journal Activity

Identity markers are prevalent on the Internet. Examine different types of identity markers by surfing some chat rooms. Go to chat rooms on topics that interest you and be particularly careful of chat rooms that may be potentially offensive. What conclusions you can draw from the identity markers you reviewed? What consistencies exist across different types of chat rooms? What differences did you encounter? Explain with examples.

Quiz

True or False

1. According to McLuhan (1988), technology is irreversible, inevitable, and inescapable. (p.382)

True or False

2. McLuhan (1964) coined the term global village to describe how technology ties the world into one political, economical, social, and cultural system. (p.384)

True or False

3. Accessibility refers to how quickly you can log onto your home computer. (p. 385)

True or False

4. The digital divide is only a useful and practical term in reference to telephones. (p. 387)

True or False

5. The Internet is actually an extended network of smaller networks interconnected with each other. (p. 388)

True or False

6. A lot of stranger danger lurks on the Internet. (p. 389)

True or False

7. Although hate speech is protected by First Amendment Rights, such extremist communication has the potential to negatively affect another's communication. (p. 391)

True or False

8. Flaming is like electronic road rage. (p.392)

True or False

9. There is no research that indicates entire communities are built and maintained online. (p. 395)

True or False

10. It is difficult for strangers to truly become linked through technology alone. (p. 395)

True or False

11. Communication between and among individuals is forever changed because of technology. (p. 403)

True or False

12. Hyperdating is hurrying through a date so you can rush home and check you email or Facebook. (p. 404)

True or False

Multiple Choice Questions

1. Which of the following is NOT an assumption of online presentation of self? (p. 397)
A. The computer screen can deceive.
B. Online discussions often prompt introspection.
C. Online discussions promote collectivism.
D. Self-disclosure occurs online.

2. An identity marker is best defined as: (p. 401)
A. a password that gains you access to the Internet.
B. a personal profile on a dating site.
C. your feelings toward CMC.
D. an electronic extension of who someone is.

3. A blog can best be defined as: (p. 406)
A. a website that blocks access to another website.
B. a running commentary – a journal of sorts - that usually includes personal thoughts and feelings about a particular topic or individual.
C. writer's block while writing via email.
D. a private journal entry that is saved and added to online about one's dreams.

4. Which of these is NOT a suggestion for both sender and receiver skills? (p. 414)
A. Take responsibility for your own words.
B. Build your own dialogue.
C. Use a clever screen name.
D. Recall the challenge of online communication.

5. Which of the following is NOT included as a sender skill for e-messages? (p. 410)
A. Use humor.
B. Be succinct when necessary.
C. Be polite.
D. Take a deep breath.

6. When Lee first met Bethany online and asked her what she does for fun, Bethany responded, "If U mean what do I do in my spare time, I like mountain biking, tennis, and traveling. What did U mean?" What Bethany offered was a(n): (p. 412)
A. electronic trial balloon.
B. blow off.
C. airborne response.
D. cyberspace response.

7. The rules of common courtesy for online communication are called: (p. 415)
A. etiquette
B. netiquette
C. CCOC
D. cybermanners

8. According to Silverstein and Lasky (2004), there are a number of advantages of meeting someone online that include each of the following except: (p. 404)
A. many people online are available and seeking companionship.
B. you know something about how another thinks or writes.
C. it's easy to pretend to be someone you're not.
D. you have the chance to exchange e-mail and talk on the phone without ever revealing your identity.

9. An articon is: (p. 405)
A. an online message in pictures.
B. a picture that consists only of keyboard characters.
C. a picture that is downloaded from another website.
D. a picture used in an electronic message, either downloaded from a website or compiled of keyboard characters.

10. It makes sense to use abbreviated language online because: (p. 405)
A. college students are the main users of the Internet and are often impatient.
B. it is efficient and people often communicate on the go.
C. most people are bored by too much text.
D. it's harder for someone else to interpret your messages.

11. When we say that technology is powerful, we mean that: (p. 384)
A. a lot of work goes into creating it.
B. it influences people, events, and entire cultures.
C. hate speech is hurtful even when anonymous.
D. the anonymity factor is strong.

12. All of these are given as examples of the dark side of the Internet except: (p. 3
A. little accountability
B. fostering hate speech
C. sacrifice of privacy
D. inattention to grammar and syntax

13. Anna was reading comments people made on a website about the impact of r footprint on
the earth. She was appalled by the first two comments that were malicious and sulting to
anyone who cared about environmental issues. This is an example of: (p. 392
A. hate speech
B. little accountability
C. ignorance
D. flaming

14. According to the text, technology is paradoxical. This means that: (p.)
A. we cannot email and talk simultaneously.
B. you should only use one piece of technology at a time to be efficient.
C. messages cannot be sent simultaneously.
D. it is conflicting, inconsistent, and ironic.

15. Although she is sometimes resistant to new technology, Debbie kn that she bette ep
up because technology is irreversible, inevitable, and inescapable. Thi st illustrates at
theory? (p, 382)
A. technological determinism
B. technophobia
C. technical literacy
D. technocracy

Essay Questions

1. In your own words, explain what accessibility and computer technology have to do with interpersonal communication.

2. How has technology changed in your lifetime? Be sure to use examples.

3. Explain what is meant by the dark side of Internet usage. Be sure to use examples.

4. Using examples, discuss the bright side of Internet usage.